The
Fire of His
Genius

*Robert Fulton
and the
American Dream*

Kirkpatrick Sale

A Touchstone Book
Published by Simon & Schuster
New York   London   Toronto   Sydney   Singapore

TOUCHSTONE
Rockefeller Center
1230 Avenue of the Americas
New York, NY 10020

First Touchstone Edition 2002

TOUCHSTONE and colophon are registered trademarks
of Simon & Schuster, Inc.

For information about special discounts for bulk purchases,
please contact Simon & Schuster Special Sales:
1-800-456-6798 or business@simonandschuster.com

Designed by Deirdre C. Amthor

Manufactured in the United States of America

10   9   8   7   6   5   4   3   2   1

Library of Congress Cataloging-in-Publication Data
Sale, Kirkpatrick.
    The fire of his genius : Robert Fulton and the
American dream / Kirkpatrick Sale.
        p.   cm.
    Includes bibliographical references and index.
    1. Fulton, Robert, 1765–1815.   2. Marine
engineers–United States–Biography.
3. Inventors–United States–Biography.
4. Steamboats–History.   I. Title.
VM140.F9 S25 2001
620'.0092–dc21
[B]   2001023064

ISBN 978-0-7432-2321-8

for Delilah,
my American dream

Contents

The
Fire of His
Genius

The Americans are a very old and a very enlightened people, who have fallen on a new and unbounded country, where they may extend themselves at pleasure, and which they may fertilize without difficulty. This state of things is without parallel in the history of the world.

−Alexis de Tocqueville

This great pressure of a people always moving to new frontiers, in search of new lands, new power, the full freedom of a virgin world, has ruled our course and formed our policies like a Fate.

−Woodrow Wilson

Introduction

ALTHOUGH THE IDEA of a boat propelled by steam was suggested in Europe as early as the seventeenth century, and experimental steamboats had been tried at various times in Britain, France, Italy, and Germany in the eighteenth century, it was almost inevitable that the first successful and protracted steamboat operation should take place in America. Not that the United States in the early nineteenth century was particularly well endowed with workshops of mechanical sophistication or trained artisans to run them, certainly by comparison with Britain. But unlike Europe, it had the greatest need for, and clearest benefits from, a system of transportation that would take advantage of the numerous long rivers of the continent and overcome the difficulties of too few roads, too many mountains, and great distances to travel—and though necessity is not always the mother of invention, it is without doubt a forceful midwife. America was special, too, in having a long tradition, also stemming from necessity, of practical problem-solving and technical ingenuity, substituting local and native methods and materials for foreign ones unavailable or prohibitive.

That is why steamboat experiments in Europe, even when they showed considerable promise (as, for example, a steam-powered tugboat that pulled two barges on a Scottish canal in 1803), were never capitalized on, never developed into full-fledged activities. And why, for more than twenty years, a good many American inventors and entrepreneurs worked steadily to surmount the considerable obstacles posed by putting a large and heavy steam engine onto a floating wooden frame and figuring out some method of propulsion to allow it to defy the winds and tides. And why eventually, in the summer of 1807, one quintessential American finally assembled a machine that solved these problems and began the first successful commercial steamboat operation in history, establishing a system of transportation that permitted humankind to surmount forces of nature that had impeded it since the dawn of time.

Fittingly, the steamboat became the emblematic image of the American industrial culture that it was launching, as the steam factory was of Britain's. Not only did it show off the characteristics of what was even then the American stereotype—large, noisy, showy, fast, brash, exciting, powerful, and audacious—and with an impact that made it an icon of American society soon recognizable anywhere in the world. More than that: in its creation as in its operation, first on the Hudson and then throughout most American waterways, it revealed in a remarkable way the American dream itself, as that dream had taken shape in the early settlement and colonization of the vast new continent and as it had burst forth, just eighteen years before, with a new and energetic republic proclaiming its unique status and mission to the world.

Much went into that dream, to be sure, but its basic tenets included these: the pursuit of happiness through material betterment, Yankee know-how in service to technological improvement, a belief in human perfectibility and individual achievement, a national destiny of expansion and conquest, and a government formed to advance industry and promote prosperity. These were the principles embodied in the steamboat from the start, inherent as it were in its very purpose, and they stood behind its improvement and expansion as the dominant mode of transportation in America for more than half a century, the technology that above all produced the thriving and expansive commerce of the Eastern seaboard and the swift and thorough development of the continental interior. And they were, perhaps necessarily, the principles that guided the man responsible for the success of the steamboat, whose life story was in its way the prototypical carrying out of the American rags-to-riches, by-his-bootstraps success story at the heart of that dream.

But there is another, darker side to the American dream, a tragic defect that seems to be woven into its design, that this man's life also reveals, suggested in a eulogy by one of his friends when he came so suddenly to his end: "Like the self-burning tree of Gambia, he was destroyed by the fire of his own genius and the never-ceasing activity of a vigorous mind." Genius there certainly was, of a singular kind, but it is the self-destruction that is so striking and poignant here, because it, too, seems all too often to characterize the national dream, the almost inescapable tragedy that befalls those whose devotion to material improvement and individual empowerment is so all-encompassing that even when they achieve the success to which they have devoted their lives, they find themselves, and often those around them, consumed in the task. It is as if a kind of larger retributive force exists to assess the costs that those lives have exacted from the social and natural environments and to pass a judgment that the attainment of self-aggrandizement by exploitation and consumption comes at a considerable price and cannot be sustained.

The story that follows, then, is one act in the drama of the

Introduction

American dream in all its complexity, but one that helps us see clearly the ideas and ideals, the fates and forces, that have shaped this country from the beginning. Steam technology, of course, is largely gone, supplanted by gasoline, and electricity, and the silicon chip. The American dream, however, is still very much alive. It guides the nation still.

1.

The *North River*

Monday, August 17, 1807, was another hot summer day in New York City, and most of the women of fashion on the pier, arms linked to laced and ruffled gentlemen, had their little pastel parasols up against the sun. It was not their custom to parade out in midday on a Monday, certainly not two miles uptown from the stylish promenades of Broadway, but they were here on the Hudson shore just by the little village of Greenwich, almost within the shadow of the imposing stone walls of the new state prison, because so much excitement had been stirred up in the city lately by the prospect of Mr. Fulton's strange and improbable boat today making its planned maiden voyage to Albany.

Interest was particularly high since the thing had successfully and dramatically puffed and roared its way here around the tip of Manhattan the day before, in clouds of smoke and spangles of sparks, its bizarre paddles churning at the sides, on view for the crowds that typically filled the tree-lined walks of the Battery park on a Sunday. Higher still because it was widely held that the whole outlandish contraption was likely to explode in a exhibition that would rival the fireworks of the annual Evacuation Day proceedings–the grandest of any, since it celebrated the British departure from the city, in a calendar full of pyrotechnics.

No doubt some in that crowd had also been present just a few weeks earlier, on July 20, when the energetic–and most inventive–Mr. Fulton had put on something of a show of a different kind for the Battery audience, at least for those willing to stay past that afternoon's dinner hour. On that day he had promised a demonstration of a new device he called a "torpedo"–the name taken from the torpedo fish, or electric ray–that, he said, by moving silently along the water's surface would evade detection and then be carried by the tide to hit and explode into the side of any enemy ship, thereby making New York's harbor invincible and rendering naval warfare virtually obsolete. He had not, in truth, had very much success with this invention in Europe, where he had spent years trying to convince first the French and then the British of its utility, but he had recently managed to persuade the similarly inventive Thomas Jefferson, then in the fullness of his second term, to sponsor this experiment in New York harbor and to dispatch some senior naval advisors up to observe it.

Somewhere Fulton had dug up a decrepit old 200-ton brig and caused it to be towed to a point between Governors and Ellis islands, in full view of a shoreline crowd of several thousand. The turnout was so sizable because, as was explained by a young writer named Washington Irving, describing the *"blow up"* in the occasional magazine *Salmagundi* he had started in January of that year, "it was the first *naval* action ever exhibited in our port; and the good people all crowded to see the British navy blown up in effigy."

In the event, however, they were somewhat disappointed. The first two bombs just floated there, harmless, and another pair exploded, but a hundred yards from the ship–as Irving noted, "the brig most obstinately refused to be decomposed."

Long minutes passed as the afternoon waned, and "the dinners grew cold, and the puddings were overboiled, throughout the renowned city of Gotham," where, as throughout the new nation, the main meal of the day was generally eaten around two or three P.M. "All returned home, after having threatened to pull down the flag-staff by way of taking satisfaction for their disappointment."

Not quite all. Fulton and his crew remained, along with some of the more rakish elements who wanted the last laugh, and a third attempt was made, this time with mines directed close enough so that the brig became an easy, not to say charitable, target. At last, on toward seven o'clock, the recalcitrant new invention worked, the ship exploded in a satisfying shower of sparks and flames, and Fulton had his triumph, belated though it may have been. "It was rent in two and went to the bottom in 20 seconds," the inventor reported proudly afterward, thus proving "the practicability of destroying vessels by this means."

Of course, it seemed to have some limitations militarily, as was pointed out by one of Irving's friends, a certain Ichabod Fungus, who had stayed for the whole show: "Observe, sir, all that's necessary is that the ships must come to anchor in a convenient place–watch must be asleep, or so complacent as not to disturb the boats paddling about them–fair wind and tide–no moonlight–machines well-directed–mustn't *flash in the pan*–bang's the word, and the vessel's blown up in a moment." It did seem to demand, he felt, some measure of cooperation from the enemy ship in order to work.

Fulton was not dismayed. His torpedo project had been dear to his heart for years, and he would continue to press the American government for support, certain that with its success the world would gain the complete freedom of the seas and the benefits of untrammeled commerce. As for New Yorkers, though, the demonstration simply served to suggest that the new breed of inventors springing up around town–"surely never was a town more subject to mid-summer fancies and dog-day whims," Irving reported, than "this most excellent of cities"–was not quite as ingenious as it claimed to be. And for some to suggest in fact that Mr. Fulton's other project, his infernal steam-powered machine to ply the Hudson, was likely to prove as ridiculous a failure, and most probably end in the same sort of conflagration.

<hr/>

New York City in the year 1807 was a place of some 83,000 people, 1,776 of them slaves, clustered into less than a square mile at the foot of Manhattan Island. Shipping, and the commerce it transmitted, was the city's life–for, as James Fenimore Cooper was to attest a few years later, "Nature herself intended the isle of Manhattan for the site of one of the greatest commercial towns of the world," giving it "a vast harbour, an unusually extensive natural basin, with two outlets to the sea, and a river that, in itself, might contain all the shipping of the earth." Which is why even then New York was surpassing the long-established ports of Philadelphia and Boston to become the most important entrepôt of the new nation, with exports of $16.4 million, more than five times what they had been just four years earlier.

The wharves themselves (here called "slips"), which stuck out into the harbor like little beckoning fingers all around the tip of the island–for two miles along the East River, a mile along the Hudson–were centers of hivelike intensity throughout the day, every day but Sunday. "All was noise and bustle," wrote an English visitor that year. "Everything was in motion; all was life, bustle and activity. The people were scampering in all directions to trade with each other." Bales and barrels, hogsheads and chests, boxes and cases and amorphous packages were piled everywhere on the docks. The sound of axes and hammers, the ringing of blacksmith anvils, the cries of sailors and stevedores, merchants and hawkers, were in the air. "Every thought, word, look, and action of the multitude seemed to be absorbed by commerce; the welkin rang with its busy hum, and all were eager in the pursuit of its riches."

Commerce there was in Baltimore and Boston, in Charleston and Philadelphia, but nowhere was it so much the culture, the oxygen, of the city as it was in New York. Nowhere else was it the prevailing talk of the pubs and taverns (about 1,400 of them in 1807, of which 160 were licensed for "strong drink"), the street corners and promenades, the parties and balls, and nowhere else was there the tumultuous three-story brick building at the corner of Wall Street and Water that housed the Tontine Coffee House, America's stock exchange, where from late morning to dinnertime every weekday, inside the noisy rooms gray with cigar smoke and outside on the capacious railed porch, deals of every kind could be made. Only in New York, "the great mart of the western hemisphere" as young Cooper saw it, a place where "exchanges can be regulated, loans effected, cargoes vended in gross, and all other things connected with trade, transacted on a scale commensurate to the magnitude of the interests involved in its pursuits."

On any given day the city would be surrounded with masts, a bare forest of spikes poking up from the slips, as tall as the roofs of the downtown buildings, and the harbor would be full of schooners and sloops and brigs, sails billowing, freighted down and riding low in the water, back and forth past the harbormaster's offices on Staten Island. Some made good speed—the faster ships could sail in seven or eight weeks from New York to London, and about fifty hours from New York to Albany if the winds were strong and the weather fair–but imagine what realms of commerce might be opened if those times could be cut by a half, or more, and with a vessel that would move at a steady pace without regard to the variable elements.

Imagine what might be opened if the powerful engine recently perfected by Mr. Watt, in England, could finally be installed on the right kind of boat, with the right kind of propulsion, with the right kind of technologist to oversee it.

❦

It is hard to know where the memorably derisive phrase "Fulton's Folly" originated, but the primary biographers agree that it was in the air in the weeks before the initial launch. Clearly some such sentiment was prevalent in the town, as even Fulton knew, for in a later account he said:

> *As I had occasion to pass daily to and from the building-yard, while my boat was in progress, I have often loitered unknown near the idle groups of strangers, gathering in little circles, and heard various inquiries as to the object of this new vehicle. The language was uniformly that of scorn, or sneer, or ridicule. The loud laugh often rose at my expense; the dry jest; the wise calculation of losses and expenditures; the dull, but endless, repetition of the Fulton folly. Never did a single encouraging remark, a bright hope, or a warm wish, cross my path.*

Certainly the appearance of the boat, riding there in the Hudson off Greenwich village, gave no reason for optimism. It was awkwardly long and thin–142 feet by 14 feet, capable of fitting very neatly into one of the narrower streets of lower Manhattan from corner to corner and curb to curb–and looked more like a scow than the stately sailboats that filled the harbor.[1] It was flat-bottomed and square-sided, straight across at the stern and gently rounded at the bow, with a deck only a few feet from the water's surface. In the middle–nakedly open on this first, experimental craft, but with many parts later decked over–were a large copper boiler with a fifteen-foot smokestack, a large upright cylinder that was the steam engine itself, and an assemblage of levers and rods and cogs and wheels whose purpose seemed entirely unfathomable. On each side, about three-quarters of the way along the craft, were two fifteen-foot circular wooden paddlewheels, unhoused and liable to splash any passengers nearby, and at each end were large oak masts rigged for sails, as if the inventor was not quite sure his elaborate steam gadgetry would work and had decided to hedge his bets. "She was a queer-looking craft," one eyewitness wrote, in something of an understatement, "and like everything new excited much attention, and not a little ridicule."

And, to be sure, some fear. It is doubtful that any in the fashionable crowd of several hundred gathered to see the launch would have known much about the previous experiments in steam propulsion that had taken place on both sides of the Atlantic for better than thirty years, or would have known that, though all of the boats had eventually failed in one way or another, none of them had been destroyed by explosion. It was enough to watch the black smoke belching steadily from the smokestack when Fulton fired up the boiler about midday, and see the splash of sparks carried in the breeze whenever the fire was stoked, to believe that the whole affair might well burst into flames at any minute.

Of course, the very idea of an engine run by steam was an extraordinary one–and reasonably frightening–at this point, for that upheaval known as the Industrial Revolution, with its everyday intrusion of steam power, had yet to descend upon America. A half-dozen steam engines did exist in the new land, some based on James Watt's ingenious machines in Britain, others fashioned to homespun designs with more or less success, and one had been used to raise water in lower Manhattan itself for some years; but to most people the device was both foreign and mysterious, and, as Fulton himself put it, "how true it was that fear frequently arose from ignorance." Americans still did not appreciate the potential of harnessing a source of power essentially independent of the forces of nature–technology free of the limits of geography or season or weather, of sun or wind or water, of either human or animal labor–and it would not be until the implications of this actual boat-with-steam-engine were made manifest over the next few years that steam would begin to transform the American economy, and the steamboat usher in the American Industrial Revolution. And so this peculiar floating implementarium tended to cause more consternation than appreciation, and it is not hard to see how one among these early onlookers could describe it as "a monster moving on the waters defying the winds and tide, and breathing flames and smoke."

Even some among the select crowd that Robert Fulton had invited along for the maiden voyage were apparently fearful, as much as they had mustered the nerve to be there, and Fulton felt their anxiety as he moved among them. A striking presence, agile and healthy at forty-one, he was six feet tall (four inches above the average stature of the time), with a handsome face marked by a prominent though shapely nose, piercing dark eyes under heavy brows, and sideburns full to his earlobes in the fashion of the day; he was probably wearing an open dark cutaway coat and trousers, with a loosely tied white cravat, his normal costume. He was mainly preoccupied with directing his small crew–Davis Hunt, the captain; Andrew Brinck, his assistant; George Jackson and Charles Dyck, the engineers; and presumably a steward or two to serve the wine and brandy he had put aboard[2]–but he was attentive to the three dozen guests gathered toward the stern, and their mood.

Many of the passengers were relatives and friends of his

partner in the steamboat venture, the rich and well-connected Robert R. Livingston, nineteen years Fulton's senior and former chancellor of the New York State equity court (and called "Chancellor" to distinguish him from the rest of the numerous Livingston clan), recently returned from his stint as special minister to France, where he had helped negotiate the amazing windfall treaty that had more than doubled the size of the United States, the Louisiana Purchase. Chancellor Livingston had invited a good many of his family, some quite giddy at the opportunity ("Cousin Chancellor has a wonderful new boat," one cousin had gushed, that "will be something to remember all our lives"), and others convinced the scheme was daffy ("Bob has had many a bee in his bonnet before now," the Chancellor's brother John is reported to have said, "but this steam folly will prove the worst yet").[3]

We know particularly about Fulton's assessment of the assemblage because he later noted, with some asperity, that, "in the moments before the word was to be given for the boat to move," his friends on deck showed "anxiety mixed with fear" and were "silent, sad, and weary." He had endured a good deal of doubt and discouragement in the weeks beforehand, but to find it here, now, and among those he honored with his maiden trip must have been a dispiriting blow. As confident as he had been after the boat's two-mile test run a week earlier–"she will, when in complete order," he had written the Chancellor, "run up to my full calculations"–he now seemed somewhat flustered and irresolute.

"I read in their looks nothing but disaster," he later admitted, "and almost repented of my efforts."

A great deal, of course, was at stake. Robert Fulton had been dreaming of just such a venture for much of the last dozen years–his first certain word on the subject had been on November 4, 1794, a letter to Boulton, Watt & Co.–and had spent the last five years in a formal partnership with Livingston that promised that "a passage boat moved by the power of a Steam Engine shall be constructed at New York, for the purpose of navigating between New York and Albany," on the strength of which they had won a fourteen-year monopoly on New York waters from the legislature in Albany. He had also spent upward of $20,000 on the craft–a goodly sum at a time when an ample building lot on Wall Street might go for $8,000–of which he had personally put up half; and in the past few weeks he had had to importune a number of his friends for an extra $1,000 to take care of last-minute expenses. Besides, he could not really point to much success in his career, despite a decade of drawing up schemes and tinkering with inventions, and the ignominious fate of his recent torpedo project, despite his optimistic account of it, suggested that he was unlikely to get a favorable reception for any of the proposals he had put to various government offices if this one was to fail.

Even more than his reputation and his solvency rested on the success of the steamboat, however. As Fulton well knew, if the vessel was proved here, it would serve most importantly as a swift and reliable means of navigating the Mississippi and its labyrinth of tributaries, and thus of conquering the western lands so recently acquired. In an interview with the *American Citizen* published the day of the launch, in fact, he asserted that his "ingenious Steam Boat, invented with a view to the navigation of the Mississippi from New Orleans upward . . . will certainly be a very valuable acquisition to the commerce of Western States." Or, as he had written the Chancellor after his initial test of the boat, "Everything is completely proved for the Mississippi, and the object is immense."

Immense, indeed. For, as Fulton could not have fully realized, the steamboat would be the single most important instrument in the transformation of America in the first half of the nineteenth century: it promoted the penetration and settle-

ment of the American interior by a mass immigration of whites
that increased the population by more than twenty times and
established a political power to rival the original colonies; it
thus abetted the destruction of the remaining Indian nations
and their cultures, along with most of the wild nature and native species they depended on; it provided the transportation
system that shifted economic power from the Eastern seaboard to two new dynamic economic systems, one industrial
and agricultural in the northern part of the Mississippi Valley,
the other plantation- and slavery-based in the southern; and it
was the basis of the transatlantic steamship trade that begot a
new maritime industry with the United States at its heart. It
is not too much to say that, more than any technological
achievement between the cotton gin in 1793 and the Colt
firearms system in 1853—and not forgetting the railroad, economically important only after the 1850s—it was the steamboat
that was responsible for the shape of America's destiny.

A great deal at stake.

The highest point in the village of Greenwich was
Richmond Hill, and from the handsome mansion at its
crest one could easily look down, not more than a few
blocks to the west, on the crowd gathered at the dock
near Bank Street where Fulton readied his steamboat for
the voyage. One of its earlier residents, Abigail Adams,
who lived there with her husband in 1789 when he was
serving in New York as General Washington's vice
president, said of that view: "In front of the house, the
noble Hudson rolls his majestic waves, bearing upon his
bosom innumerable small vessels," beyond which "rises
to our view the fertile country of the Jerseys, covered with
a golden harvest." It is doubtful, however, that anyone in
the mansion took advantage of its convenient situation

this summer day, for the place had gone largely unoccupied for the past three years in spite of its splendid furnishings and elegant appointments, and the owner himself was languishing in jail in Richmond, Virginia, on trial for treason.

Aaron Burr had been the proud owner of Richmond Hill from some time in the early 1790s, when he was a U.S. senator from New York, and he maintained it even after he became vice president in 1801, although most of the business of state had by then moved to the wetlands along the Potomac donated by Maryland and Virginia for the nation's capital. He left it, in some haste, at the end of July 1804, when he was indicted in both New York and New Jersey for the killing of his archrival Alexander Hamilton in a duel across the river in Weehawken.

Burr stayed on the move and out of sight for the next three years, until a harebrained scheme hatched with delusionary and untrustworthy men got him into trouble with the law. It seems that in his travels down the Ohio and Mississippi rivers he contrived a scheme to assemble a small army with the aim of conquering Texas, then owned by Mexico, and setting up an independent nation under his control. The idea of seizing land to the west was highly popular at the time—the Louisiana Purchase whetted, rather than sated, the American craze for land speculation—but since this was properly the business not of private citizens but of the federal government, the shenanigans of the ambitious Mr. Burr were regarded as treason and he was arrested in March 1807 and shipped up to Virginia to stand trial before the Honorable John Marshall, the federal circuit judge for Virginia as well as the nation's chief justice.

Burr immediately became the center of a nineteenth-century media circus: journalists descended on Richmond from all over the country, as did crowds of supporters and detractors and the merely curious, swelling the little capital to twice its size, and in the sweltering summer months, too. One visitor was the intrepid Washington Irving, who wrested an interview with Burr in May and described him as one who "retains his serenity and self-possession unshaken," although two months later, after the rigors of the trial, he was "in lower spirits than formerly . . . and I bid him goodbye with a heavy heart." There was, however, no need to worry: the evidence against Burr was skimpy at best, and later that summer he would be found innocent of treason and cleared of "high misdemeanors" in the fall.

Burr returned surreptitiously to New York, but by then he had sold Richmond Hill to the wealthy John Jacob Astor and was obliged to stay with various friends until the spring of 1808, when he went off into exile in Europe. Astor waited a few years for the city's growth to push up property prices, and in 1820 he had the elegant mansion rolled off the hill and down to Charlton Street, whereupon he leveled the property, cut streets through it, and sold off the lots at top market prices.

Burr's deranged military adventure exposed one fact understood by at least some of the leaders of the day, including President Jefferson, who strenuously tried to have Burr put behind bars for it. It was that a great many people in the territories beyond the original colonies, where maybe 400,000 people of European origin were spread from the Appalachians to the Mississippi, felt little loyalty and much resentment toward the official government and were liable at any time to grab the plentiful lands there for themselves and govern them any way they pleased. It was the task of the government in Washington to try to impose its will and its institutions on those territories as quickly and thoroughly as possible, to push back Spanish, British, and Indian interference, and to fill them up with a large, stable, prosperous, and therefore loyal American populace.

Few could have realized it—not even Jefferson, whose prime concern this was, and who knew from personal contact of Fulton's plans—but the principal instrument by which this task would eventually be achieved was just then ready to embark beneath the prospect of the elegant mansion on Richmond Hill.

Steeling himself, Fulton gave the signal at about one o'clock for the boat to be cast off. It moved slowly from the pier, guided by the captain at the tiller in the stern. Suddenly it was without power, "then stopped, and became immovable," as Fulton's account put it.

One may well imagine the increased despondency that descended on the refined crowd of passengers, then rocking aimlessly on the Hudson's gray waters. "To the silence of the preceding moment," the inventor said, "now succeeded murmurs of discontent, and agitations, and whispers and shrugs. I could hear distinctly repeated, 'I told you it would be so—it is a foolish scheme—I wish we were all out of it.' " It would be surprising if there were not jeers and catcalls from the bystanders on the shore as well, but Fulton did not record them.

Though it would be correct to say that Fulton's career to date was checkered at best, it was marked by nothing so much as a dogged determination: he would work on a project until he was satisfied he had it right in every detail, and then would advance it to anyone he could find, friend or foe, trustworthy or not, who might help him see it through. He had done endless pages of calculations to determine exactly the right shape and displacement a boat should have to use steam power efficiently; he had built scale models and even one half-size version that he had tested on the Seine four years earlier; he had overseen every step of the building of this craft now powerless, including instructions to James Watt's firm in England as to how the engine was to be set up, repeatedly testing its parts both large and small; and he had put it through a test run a week before, during which the engine worked so well that he could boast of beating all the sloops on the river with him.

What's more, Fulton had studied the experiments in steamboating by others over the previous thirty years–when he was in Philadelphia in 1787, he may even have seen one of the earliest boats, built by an unstable genius named John Fitch, that ran on the Delaware at two and a half miles an hour against the current–and he knew that a score of boats of various designs and capacities had been built so far ("Hundreds have tried it and failed," he scoffed). He had examined the twelve patents that had been granted by the United States since 1790, plus designs patented or published in Europe while he was there. He had decided at this point what worked and what did not: whatever his passengers were now thinking, he wasn't starting from scratch, he was following in well-trod footsteps and well-furrowed wakes.

He would not surrender now.

"I elevated myself upon a platform, and addressed the assembly. I stated, that I knew not what was the matter; but if they would be quiet, and indulge me for half an hour, I would either go on, or abandon the voyage for that time." For that time: the worst he would admit to was postponement, not discontinuance.

The passengers agreed to the respite–they had little choice–and Fulton went below and began an examination of the machinery. Eventually he found "that the cause was a slight maladjustment of some of the work"–he was never more specific than that–and in a short time it was fixed. "The boat was again put in motion. She continued to move on." How he must have enjoyed that moment: "All were still incredulous. None seemed willing to trust the evidence of their own senses."

Although New York was a city then with eight daily newspapers, there was no coverage of this event other than the brief notice in the morning's *American Citizen,* along with Fulton's self-serving remarks, that the boat "sails today from the North River, near State's Prison, to Albany." Hence we do not know the reaction of the crowd left on the shore when the strange craft chugged off successfully, a broad white wake and thick black smoke behind, or even the response of those on board; later on its journey, though, several accounts mention that people spontaneously rushed to the river's edge with shouts of "Huzzah, huzzah," and the New York dandies on the dock, as well as the now placated friends around him, must have offered Fulton the same: "When the shouts of spectators began to rend the air," a friend of Fulton's remembers him recalling later, "then he felt as if he should have fainted away, his feelings so overpowered him, and such, he added, was his state of excitement during the whole voyage."

"North River" was a common alternative name for the lower Hudson in the early nineteenth century, a bit of nomenclature dating from the Dutch occupation in the seventeenth century, when the Delaware, on the southern border of their territory, was called the South River and the Hudson, on the northern, was called the North. Fulton in his correspondence refers to the river alternately as the Hudson and the North River, but when it came to naming his craft he chose the latter, advertising it two weeks later as the "North River Steam Boat," and then registering it as the "North River Steamboat of Clermont," and always referring to it as the *North River Steamboat* or simply the *North River.*

And *Clermont,* as the boat is known in the textbooks? This was the name of the enormous tract of land owned by Chancellor Livingston and his family about ninety miles up the Hudson, stretching for twelve miles along the river and twenty-four miles to the Massachusetts line, from whose mansion the patriarch oversaw several branches of his large and prosperous family, a small army of sharecroppers, and several dozen slaves. It was only politic for Fulton to enroll the steamboat as being based at the Chancellor's home, although it never berthed there for long, but its port of origin had nothing at all to do with its name (no boat is called by the name of its registered port) and the idea that Fulton's steamboat was called the *Clermont* is completely without foundation. The error originated with Fulton's first biography, published by his friend Cadwallader Colden in 1817, which says flatly that the steamboat "was called the Clermont," although in his list of Fulton's boats Colden hedges with "North River, or Clermont" and in a subsequent book never used that name again. How he contrived such a mistake is a mystery, for it is clear that Fulton never referred to his boat as the *Clermont* in all his writings and most improbable that he ever did so in speech.[4]

In any case, on the sternboard of the vessel itself there was no name, now or later, and as it moved out smoothly into the Hudson at a steady four miles an hour, the crews on the boats it passed so brusquely would have thought of it simply as "the steamboat," for there was nothing else like it on the water. "I overtook many sloops and schooners, beating to the windward," Fulton boasted, "and parted with them as if they had been at anchor." Soon, at a little past two o'clock, the tide turned in the craft's favor, and when it reached the vicinity of Spuyten Duyvil, the stream dividing Manhattan from the lands once owned by the Broncks, it picked up to five miles an hour despite the slight breeze against it. All Fulton had to say was, "We left the fair city of New York."

The fateful journey was begun. If the machinery did not fail and the boat could stay at that same rough speed, it should be able to put into Clermont in twenty-four hours and set off the next day to make Albany by late afternoon. In two days, weather and fate permitting, Robert Fulton could prove the technology by which America would embark on its course of industrial might and economic dominance.

2.

Precursors

In 1796, as he began his career as an inventor, then styling himself a "civil engineer," Robert Fulton set out his idea of what was involved in the creative process of mechanical innovation:

"As the component parts of all new machines may be said to be old[,] it is a nice discriminating judgment, which discovers that a particular arrangement will produce a new and desired effect. . . . Therefore, the mechanic should sit down among levers, screws, wedges, wheels etc. like a poet among the letters of the alphabet, considering them as the exhibition of his thoughts; in which a new arrangement transmits a new idea to the world."

By the time he came to start building his steamboat in New York in 1806, Fulton had a full complement of levers, screws, wedges, and wheels to sit among, not to mention articles, treatises, diaries, calculations, and models—and even a dozen patents. Steam navigation had by then preoccupied the inventive on both sides of the Atlantic for more than thirty years, and in America there had already been some fifteen full-scale experiments of various ingeniousness and accomplishment. Fulton brought the merits of perseverance and self-confidence to his "new arrangement," plus a mechanic's mind and an artist's eye, and the considerable support of one of the richest men in America, but there is no disputing that around him was a good deal of steamboat knowledge and experience on which to draw.

We may dispense with the merry myth that Fulton invented the steamboat—even his later claims to have done so sound as if they rang hollow in his own ears—and acknowledge that there were other boats before more sophisticated than his first elongated firemill on the Hudson, others had gone farther than the three hundred–plus miles Fulton would achieve on his maiden voyage, and some were faster, too. None, however, was successful in the ways that Fulton's was. For one thing, he designed and built his craft on sound engineering principles and scientific techniques that he understood after persistent experimentation, and so he knew how to put it together, test it, duplicate it, improve it when necessary, and set out for others the crucial elements of his creation. For another, he was able to establish a working operation, with paying customers, that would ply a waterway on a regular basis and sustain a commercial enterprise, something no earlier inventor had done. And finally, by producing his accomplishment under the eyes of America's commercial and maritime capital, he was immediately acknowledged and given credit, and his fame immediately established for a nation that then was short on heroes—and was eager to accept any novelty as an invention, and as evidence of American genius. It little mattered that no rightful claim to invention existed. What mattered was that to a nation that needed it, and could exploit it better than any other in the world, the steamboat was given, and Robert Fulton was the giver.

❧

In fact, it was twenty-four years earlier, at Lyons, Beaujolais country, on the River Saône just before it reaches the Rhône, that the first boat is known to have moved against a current under its own manufactured power. The Marquis Claude-François-Dorothée Jouffroy d'Abbans, a nobleman who for reasons unknown had been preoccupied with the idea of steam power since his release from prison in 1775, had mounted a two-cylinder Newcomen engine and a bunch of pulleys and rods on a long thin boat, and on the afternoon of June 15, 1783, with the wharfside full of spectators, he signaled for the fire to be lit. Sparks flew; the heavy pistons began to move; smoke belched; the wooden fan at the stern pushed at the water. Perceptibly the boat edged forward, to the cheers of the unbelieving crowd, steadily but at a pace said to be no faster than a walk, and for a full fifteen minutes chugged its way upriver. Then, the floorboards apparently giving way from the steady pounding of the cylinders, the hull suddenly split and the river poured through, while the boiler burst its seams and clouds of steam rose from the boat.

Somehow Jouffroy maneuvered the crippled hulk to shore, leapt out jubilantly, and was returned to Lyons to bask in the admiration of the dockside throng. The boat itself was now useless, but Jouffroy confidently sent the government in Paris a statement signed by local dignitaries testifying to its brief achievement, expecting in return a fifteen-year steamboat monopoly for French waters. Government ministers turned to the savants of the Academy of Sciences to verify the feat, but they, undoubtedly giving little credence to the tale of an unknown provincial and his credulous companions, declined to do so.

Jouffroy was crushed. He had no money, no backing: his local patrons would not continue to support him without a government monopoly. In desperation he sent his plans and drawings to the Périer brothers in Paris, well-known engineers then working with pumps to supply the city with water, in hopes of enlisting their collaboration. It was not forthcoming:

the only response was a haughty rejection from the brothers, who nonetheless kept the plans–and almost assuredly showed them twenty years later to a client for whom they did agree to work, a Mr. Robert Fulton.

The French Revolution forced Jouffroy into exile. When he returned, the Bourbons safely restored, he raised enough money to try steamboating one more time. But like his sovereigns, he had learned nothing and forgotten nothing in the interim, and his second boat, launched in 1816, was a failure.

It would have been poor comfort to him, especially since his achievement was known to only a handful of Frenchmen and ignored by the rest of the world, then as now, and indeed he probably never realized it, but Jouffroy may truly be said to be the first to have built a steamboat that, however fleetingly, worked.

Europe toyed with steamboating–other Frenchmen, a few Englishmen, a pair of Scots, an Italian–but it was fated to be in America that the process of tinker and tryout came to fulfillment, for there the technology fit best both the land and the people. The land, because its long north-south rivers provided a natural pathway for the exchange of goods–cotton and cattle up, for example, grain and manufactures down–if only the problem of moving upstream could be solved; the people, because they had learned in two centuries how to apply their energies, even with limited training and skills, to solving problems in the way of their material improvement.

The trajectory that ended with Fulton's launch of the *North River* in August 1807 in some sense began in August 1787–oddly enough, the exact date is unrecorded–when an unstable and unschooled hulk of a man named John Fitch succeeded in moving a boat with a steam engine of his own design a little way up the Delaware just off Philadelphia. The craft, propelled by a series of flat oblong paddles moving on both sides of the hull, was effectively useless, since it could go no more than three miles an hour and would prove no competition to either sails on the river or hooves beside it, and would be utterly worthless against the currents of the Mississippi. But it made several demonstration runs that fall and impressed a number of the distinguished delegates who were gathered in Philadelphia to put together a constitution for a new federal republic and must have been amazed to see a boat traveling under its own power, however slowly. And it so energized Fitch, and encouraged his backers, that he was able to put another boat in the water the following spring, which also ran a little, and slowly, and after that another the next spring, which ran a little less, and no faster . . . and after that, seeming to thrive on failed calculations and fruitless trials, still another boat (or rather, the old boat with new machinery) the next spring, which ran—which ran with astonishing success, without a breakdown, on its second test, April 16, 1790, and prompted its inventor to boast afterward, "We reigned Lord High Admirals of the Delaware, and no boat on the river could hold way with us."

Very quickly the subscribers to Fitch's project took steps to make it commercial, installing a small cabin aft for passengers. Long-distance trials proved the steamboat capable of going on the run to Trenton at an estimated six miles an hour against the current, and on June 14 this announcement appeared in the *Federal Gazette:* "THE STEAMBOAT is now ready to take passengers and is intended to set off from Arch Street Ferry, in Philadelphia, every Monday, Wednesday, and Friday for Burlington, Bristol, Bordentown, and Trenton, to return on Tuesdays, Thursdays, and Saturdays." The first regular steamboat line was launched, and for the whole summer it plied between Philadelphia and Trenton, rolling up some two thousand miles at least, with no more than half a dozen accidents, none serious.

And that should be an end to who invented what, and when.

Except that the irascible Mr. Fitch somehow could not even make a success of success. Nobody, it seemed, much wanted to ride on his boat. Passengers were just as happy to take stagecoaches, which were faster along the broad and open pathways by the sides of the river, or the sailing packets they had long been used to; the boat was not constructed for freight and could not take on much additional weight over the heavy machinery and its brick foundation. Fitch decided that there was a conspiracy against him, led by sailing interests whose profits were threatened and fueled by jealous inventors, though he also acknowledged that his "despicable appearance" and fancy for rum might have kept patronage low. In any case, there were many times when the passenger fees did not bring in half the $4 it cost the company for a one-way trip, and when the books were totaled after the boat was put up for the winter, they showed a considerable loss. Plans to build a second boat were abandoned, and company subscribers concluded that, at a minimum, they wanted nothing more to do with Fitch: an invention that doesn't make money, well, that's not an invention at all.

The poor man never built another boat, though he tried hard to attract more supporters over the years.[1] As an inventor he brought inspiration and perseverance to his tasks, and an acerbic egotism that sustained him as it irritated others, but his approach was always makeshift tinkering, trial and error without theory, without basic principles, without science, and he was not the sort to inspire the hefty sums that he needed for that kind of prolonged experimentation. (Nor was he, it must be added, shrewd enough to realize that for commercial success, he should have picked a river like the Hudson, whose steep and hilly shores made stagecoach travel difficult and slow, and whose winds and currents made sailboat journeys hazardous and erratic.) He wandered about, penniless and drunken, took his dream to France and then England with continued futility, and finally returned home, drifted west, and in Kentucky one night in 1797 took a handful of opium pills with a bottle of whiskey and laid his anguish to rest.

⚜

"A thousand special causes," Tocqueville was to write—among them two centuries of seat-of-the-pants survival, a primarily material value system, and a land both vast and rich—"have singularly concurred to fix the mind of the American on purely practical objects: his passions, his wants, his education, and everything about him, seem to unite in drawing the native of the United States earthward." That this should be true of the average citizen seems obvious enough, given the hard business of making a living and keeping a home, but what is remarkable is that this strain of the "purely practical" ran through American society right up to so many citizens of high stature and political eminence.

The capacity and fascination for invention are found in almost all the leading figures of this age of the early republic: in a philosopher and agitator like Thomas Paine, who patented a prefabricated cast-iron bridge and claimed to have made a smokeless candle; a painter like Charles Willson Peale, who constructed models with which he could reconstruct famous naval battles, complete with armaments that fired; a politician and realtor like David Rittenhouse, who was an accomplished astronomer and created an orrery showing the movements of the solar system, powered by clockwork machinery; a lawyer and politician like Aaron Burr, who tried his hand at making guns (he was, as Hamilton should have known, a crack shot) and at one point drew up plans for a steamboat.

Thomas Jefferson was perhaps the paradigm of the

figure as inventive as eminent, though it might be added that in an un-American way he made money from neither crafts nor politics and died considerably in debt. Among the devices he not only dreamed up but had built for him were a copying machine (two pens connected by a horizontal arm so that they moved in tandem), a revolving music stand, a two-story clock, a mechanical drill, and a field plow that looked better than it worked. He was also a surveyor, an architect, and an inveterate experimenter and note-taker, measuring daily temperatures, climate changes, plant growths, and almost anything else connected to botany, agriculture, horticulture, and silviculture that fell under his scientific eye.

Benjamin Franklin was even more of an inventor and was enough of a scientist to have thought up and then proved a theory about the nature of electricity that was a landmark in eighteenth-century thought. With a mind nearly as fertile as Leonardo's and access to mechanics and craftsmen far more numerous and accomplished, he spun out a series of devices over a career of more than forty years that included the lightning rod (a by-product of his experiments with electricity), the Franklin stove, bifocal lenses, a chair that becomes a stepladder, a printing press, an electric generator, and a chair with a writing surface built into its arm of the kind now familiar on college campuses.

Franklin was also instrumental in creating an American Philosophical Society in Philadelphia to encourage and propagate all manner of artistic and scientific ideas, and it was to one meeting of that group in December 1785 that a paper of his was read concerning the propulsion of boats. Paddlewheels, he concluded, were a futile waste of energy, but with a "fire engine" connected to pipes, it should be possible to draw enough water in at the bow and force it out at the stern–hydraulic jet propulsion–to make a boat travel at a useful pace. It was that learned opinion that caused John Fitch for several years to dream of boats with pump propulsion before finally turning to paddles at the sides.

~~~

In the seventeen years after John Fitch's unsuccessful venture with a successful steamboat, as many as a dozen such vessels were tried out in American waters, with differing levels of accomplishment–a testimony, if nothing else, to the bubbling spirit of hope and determination inherent in the American dream. Some of these even proved to be operable (at least six, by my count[2]), but most of them were slow and inefficient, all were plagued by problems, and none was deemed satisfactory enough to be put into commercial use. And in a nation whose collective mind, as Tocqueville saw it, was "swayed by no impulse but the pursuit of wealth," the only conceivable purpose of taking the trouble to make an operable steamboat was a commercial one.

Which brings us to the tall, substantial, and decidedly patrician figure of Robert R. Livingston, the Chancellor. A man of considerable wealth and patron of the Clermont estate, he was a powerful figure of public life who also saw himself as a philosopher, a man of learning and letters who also was proud to be a patron of mechanical developments (and in 1794 became the first president of the New York Society for the Promotion of Arts, Agriculture, and Manufactures). Better than most, he understood the priorities of the new nation he had been instrumental in creating, as a member of the Continental Congress and a drafter of the Declaration of Independence, and hence he knew that the need for men of his stature to improve the conditions of the American people was not inconsistent with the need to improve the condition of one's own circumstances; as pleased as he was with his patent on a machine "For Manufacturing Paper out of River Weeds," he was not unmindful of its use in exploiting the marsh vegetation that grew in profusion along much of his plantation on the Hudson, as well as on some of his other extensive holdings on the Esopus, Delaware, Schoharie, and Catskill rivers. And when he first became acquainted with the potential of the steamboat, he immediately thought of it in financial terms.

That acquaintance was made apparent during a ride on a boat that a New Hampshire artisan, Samuel Morey, built in New York City around 1796, traveling from lower Manhattan to Greenwich village and back at what Morey estimated to be "about 5 miles an hour." The Chancellor was sufficiently impressed that he proposed going into business with him for a Hudson River operation, Morey later said, offering $7,000 for the partnership, but Morey, luckily for the eventual Robert Fulton, "did not deem that sufficient and no bargain was made."[3] Having sensed the potential, however, Livingston would not be stopped: he spent the next year trying to devise a workable craft himself, first contriving a boat using horses on deck to turn a wheel mounted horizontally beneath the keel and, when that didn't work, opting for a steam engine with a horizontal wheel.

At some point in his labors Livingston had the good sense to approach his wife's brother, John Stevens, wealthy scion of a well-bred family in New Jersey, who had been dabbling in steamboats for more than a decade by then and in 1791 had even been granted a patent (ambiguous because essentially unenforceable in those days) for a boat that would use steam for jet propulsion, much as Franklin had suggested. Together they agreed on a partnership—Stevens, with some trepidation, agreed to go along with Livingston's designs—and then found a young New Jersey craftsman named Nicholas Roosevelt, who had established a machine shop near Newark on the Passaic River. In December 1797, the Chancellor approached Roosevelt and showed him designs for his steamboat based on "perfectly new principles which both in the model and one on

31

a large scale have exceeded my expectations," probably a bit of an exaggeration. Roosevelt, a skilled mechanic who had for several years supervised a steam engine draining a copper mine in New Jersey and who would go on to build Philadelphia's first steam-powered waterworks, realized that those designs left much to be desired–the horizontal wheel in particular he felt was unworkable–but, perpetually in financial trouble, he agreed to take on the job and join the partnership with the two wealthy patricians.

Having begun the boat, Livingston then set to work to get the monopoly that would make it financially worthwhile. An important maneuverer in the state's back rooms of power, he let it be known that he wished the New York State legislature to grant him the monopoly over steamboat transportation in New York waters that had previously been granted to (and, unwisely, never used by) John Fitch, who was now presumed to be either dead or vanished. The idea was greeted with some jocularity by the legislators–"The navigation by steam," one member said, "was thought to be much on a footing as to practicability as the navigation by reindeer in the Chancellor's park"–but on March 27, 1798, Livingston was granted the monopoly for the next twenty years, the only stipulation being that he should produce a boat of 20-ton capacity and four-mile-an-hour velocity within a year.

This he eagerly proceeded to do, bombarding Roosevelt with instructions almost weekly–thirty letters between January and September survive–and even deigning to show up at the Passaic workshop from time to time when he felt his white-laced hand was needed. Roosevelt and his craftsmen did their best to follow the instructions when they were not patently unworkable, and by late summer they had a vessel nearly ready for launching. It was then that Roosevelt suggested that "2 wheels of wood over the sides" would be a more efficient method of propulsion than the horizontal wheel, and on this basis he later tried to claim that it was really he who had invented the crucial part of what made Fulton's steamboat successful. Livingston, however, was not the sort to brook suggestions about wheels from pipefitting inferiors: "They are out of the question," he replied.

The Chancellor's boat was put in the water on October 21, 1798, with the patron absent on other, more pressing business, and it managed to move at a speed that Roosevelt calculated as "3 miles in still water" at best and a Spanish government official on board for the occasion more charitably as six miles an hour with the wind and tide behind it. That sluggishness might have been overcome with more experiments, but the fact that the heavy engine vibrated so severely that it opened up seams in the boilerwork argued strongly that there were fundamental problems no amount of additional jiggering would be likely to solve. And that, eventually, was what the partnership concluded, discarding this vessel and then failing ever to agree about putting another boat of anyone's design into the water.

⚜

Chancellor Livingston did not give up his belief in the importance of steam navigation, or his monopoly of its use on New York waters, which he merely renewed periodically despite his failure to come up with a vessel to carry it out. But he was diverted from any further concentration on the project by the necessity of responding, at the age of fifty-five, to his country's call to serve as the United States minister plenipotentiary to the government of revolutionary France.

Livingston's principal task was to negotiate with the French for the right to establish open transportation for the growing body of American exports through New Orleans to the seas, and to explore whether the French might be interested in selling off any part of that entrepôt.

Spanish authorities actually ran New Orleans at the time, but in diplomatic circles it was known that Napoleon had forced Spain to cede its territory to France in a secret treaty in 1800, in return for the Italian duchy of Tuscany. Napoleon was the man to deal with.

Jefferson chose a man of Livingston's stature for this task—a man who had also been secretary of foreign affairs under the Articles of Confederation—because he well knew how vital it was to secure open commerce down the Mississsippi even before Aaron Burr made it glaringly clear that this was an urgent passion among many who had settled there. The problem was that every year thousands of Americans were moving out there, so distant from the original colonies that it took weeks to reach the farther settlements by coach, yet they all were sure to claim an equal voice in national affairs, demand statehood for their territories, and try to impose their will upon the more mature and cultured populations of the coast—sure recipes for dissension and discord if not outright rebellion. Without the unifying forces of church or king or army—or history—familiar to European nations, what was there to unite the sectional templates already drifting apart along political, economic, and even cultural fault lines, what could keep the new settlements from causing that tectonic shift from which the nation might not recover?

The answer, inevitably, was commerce. It was commerce, at bottom, that had led the people of Europe to conquer and settle North America, it was commerce that had driven the British colonies to expansion and eventually rebellion, it was commerce that now permitted Yankee shipmaster and Georgia slave master, Quaker shopkeeper and frontier innkeeper, to join hands in common cause despite their rankling disagreements. In Europe money was spent on war, on armies and navies, on bureaucracy and government, very little of which burdened Americans; their money was spent on making money.

Therefore it would be commerce, Jefferson decided, that would keep this expanding and diversifying nation together. It would be "roads, rivers, canals, and such other objects of public improvement" for trade and industry, as he put it in his annual message to Congress in 1806, by which "new channels of communication will be opened between the States, the lines of separation will disappear, their interests will be identified, and their union cemented by new and indissoluble ties." One of those rivers must be, of course, the Mississippi, and its outlet at New Orleans must be secured for America.

That was Livingston's mission.

In the same month that Napoleon decided to make Livingston's mission a success—April 1803—the distinguished architect and designer Benjamin Latrobe, then thirty-eight years old and a resident of Philadelphia, delivered a paper to the American Philosophical Society, apparently still inspired by the Franklin paper nearly twenty years earlier, on the question of the practicability of navigation by steam.

Latrobe was presumed to know something about steam engines because he had been the overseer of Philadelphia's pioneering waterworks project, begun in 1800, which used two engines built by Nicholas Roosevelt to lift water from the Schuylkill and to power a downtown pumping station, the first large-scale industrial venture ever undertaken in America. It did not matter that Latrobe was skilled essentially as an architect—his 1801 Bank of Pennsylvania headquarters in Philadelphia was an imitation of the Erechtheum that introduced the Greek revival style that soon plagued all large-scale architecture in America–or that his running of the waterworks was beset by repeated equipment failures and cost overruns that ate up about a sixth of the city budget. He had an affecting English accent and a charming manner, and was assumed to be a polymath of the Jefferson/Franklin mold.

Latrobe's paper acknowledged that in the years after the Revolution "a sort of Mania began to prevail, which indeed has not yet entirely subsided, for impelling boats by steam-engines." But he pointed out that even on land there were, he thought, only five steam engines "of any considerable power" then operating in the United States (the two in Philadelphia, one for water in Manhattan, one at a lumber mill in New York, and one "in some manufacturing" in Boston), and all of them seemed bedeviled by problems. And while those difficulties could eventually be overcome and steam power find increasing use in mills and mines, "there are indeed general objections to the use of the steam engine for impelling boats, from which no particular mode of application can be free."

There certainly were, as every experimenter could attest, chiefly those having to do with the weight of the machinery and the resistance of the water. A steam engine on a boat would require an iron (or copper) boiler large enough to raise a good amount of steam–a chamber of something like 15 feet by 5 would be needed to generate a stroke of 20 to 25 horse-power–and brickwork underneath to protect the deck from its heat, plus a large quantity of fuel, a large piston chamber set on a base thick enough to keep the impact from damaging the deck, an iron condenser, various pumps, pipes connecting everything, and arms and wheels to change the vertical motion to rotary: all of which added up to an undeniably heavy cargo, and the sturdier the boat, the harder to propel. Paddles, or oars, or propellers, or wheels, made for additional weight, since they had to be large and heavy enough to move through water, a very resistant medium, and powerful enough to move a heavy hull creating its own resistance, increasing as the speed of the boat increased. No wonder most steam engines at the time were used on land, as Latrobe noticed, fixedly stationary.

Latrobe did acknowledge that various earlier experiments on water had all faced up to these problems, including Fitch's (which he dismissed as "soon laid aside") and that of "a few gentlemen of New-York," presumably Livingston and Stevens, but he argued that "not one of them . . . appears to have sufficient merit to render it worthy of description and imitation." And with crushing finality: "Nor have I ever heard of an instance, verified by other testimony than that of the inventor, of a speedy and agreeable voyage having been performed in a steamboat of any construction." That would seem to be that.

Except that just months before, yet another steamboat had been launched that defied Latrobe's easy dismissal.

This was the accomplishment of John Stevens, now working alone at his Hoboken estate overlooking the Hudson. He had first begun to think about steamboats seriously in 1788 and for some years had put on paper a number of imaginative designs, though he deemed it beneath a man of his stature actually to build anything to prove their efficacy. In fact, as early as 1791 he was granted one of the three U.S. patents for a steamboat, along with Fitch and the Virginia inventor James Rumsey, without ever having to build a model or a prototype or indeed having to prove in any way that it would work. He moved into a realm of reality in 1793, when he enlisted a mechanic to build a model of a jet-propulsion steamboat he had drawn up, though that failed when the workman, confounded by the design, took to drink instead; and again in 1799, when he experimented with Nicholas Roosevelt on a boat using a set of paddles in the stern, which failed when Stevens's engine proved so powerful that it shook the hull to pieces.

It was not until 1802, while working with his teenage son Robert (named after Livingston), that Stevens finally devised a small boat that not only ran, and stayed intact, but made a journey across New York harbor from the Hoboken estate to the Paulus Hook ferry landing on the west side of Manhattan. Just 25 feet long and 5 or 6 feet wide—Stevens thought of it more as a convenient commuting vehicle for himself than as a commercial venture—it had a high-pressure engine much smaller than the low-pressure types built by Watt and a screw propeller aft that could achieve a top speed of about four miles an hour. Eventually Stevens found that the high-pressure cylinder gave him problems after operating only a short time, but in his account he noted that the boat that summer "was occasionally kept going till cold weather stopped us," proving it was in essence a workable vessel, whatever Latrobe might put forth as his "general objections," and making Stevens another entrant in the list of steamboat inventors before Fulton.

Nor was it a fluke. Stevens decided to revert to a Watt engine for his next effort, along with a boiler for which he got a patent in 1803, and the following year ran a small boat similar to the first as his personal ferry to Manhattan. Like the first, it overcame Latrobe's objections by being compact and narrow, with an efficient boiler, a powerful engine, and torque applied directly to the propellers, but its machinery took up most of the deck and it broke down frequently. How this achievement escaped Livingston's attention is not known, for if he had discovered this infringement on his monopoly he would undoubtedly have protested, but of course the Chancellor had been in Paris since December 1801 and Stevens's desire not to roil things in the family must have outweighed his desire to crow about his success. And besides, not being a commercial venture, it didn't really count.

Not that Stevens cared much for his brother-in-law's monopoly anyway, for he fully intended to challenge it as soon as he could put up a boat that could take on the Hudson. In the spring of 1807, fully aware of Fulton's plans and in fact a frequent visitor to the shop where Fulton's boat was then taking shape, he tested a larger boat, again using propellers, but this time he could not raise enough steam to turn the screws. That only determined him to make another attempt, whether or not Fulton was successful, and he retreated to his little workshop on the estate that summer to draw up his plans. On August 17, it is said, he took a position at a high spot on his property, presumably with his telescope, to have a better vantage point from which to observe the launch of Fulton's absurdly narrow boat from the Greenwich village pier.

Of course, as he probably did not know, there were weighty "general objections" to anybody's using "the steam engine for impelling boats."

3.

1765–1797

THE CHIEF DIFFICULTY in reconstructing the early lives of figures who become famous only in their later years, particularly if they were born to the ranks of the unannaled poor in ages before the ubiquity of government records, is the lack of information for the decades before they come to the world's attention. Once fame arrives, subsequent deeds are chronicled, letters are kept, remarks are recorded, and stories collected, but the previous years remain murky unless the odd youthful diary or a trove of early letters is found. Then the diligent biographer can only hope to uncover childhood friends and schoolroom acquaintances, and extant relatives and neighbors, and hope that the dimly remembered anecdote is approximately accurate and the thirdhand recollection bears some shadow of the truth. And when that proves inadequate or impossible, the temptation simply to make up what *should* have been, à la Parson Weems, complete with childhood details that reveal the adult hero, is easy to give in to.

The first book about Robert Fulton was written two years after his death by a friend and colleague, Cadwallader Colden, who served as Fulton's lawyer for a number of years and would have had occasion to listen to tales of childhood and early career had Fulton chosen to disclose them around a winter fireplace or on some tedious coach ride. But his account of Fulton's early life is quite sparse and unrevealing, not much beyond birth date and parental names, and it seems likely that Fulton was as chary about details of his childhood with his friend as he was in his letters, which have only a few glancing references and a single sentimental anecdote about a brief tussle with two elder sisters. The next biographer, Joseph Delaplaine, who included Fulton in his *Lives and Portraits of Distinguished American Characters,* did no better, and indeed had little to add to Colden other than a few specifics about Fulton's brief time as an apprentice in Philadelphia, where Delaplaine lived and might have been able to consult city directories for accuracy.

No subsequent accounts went further, so it remained for a J. Franklin Reigart to be Fulton's Parson Weems, in his *Life of Robert Fulton* (graced with a frontispiece of the author with quill pen at his desk), published in 1856. Although Reigart was "a citizen of Lancaster," where Fulton grew up, who consulted "many of our oldest citizens" from whom "the most correct accounts and incidents" were obtained, it is doubtful how many people were still alive in mid-century who had *any* recollections of Fulton's childhood years some seventy-five years earlier, much less accurate ones. Moreover, since Reigart was unabashedly determined to prove that Fulton was "the most distinguished inventor the world had ever produced" and the "noblest son a virtuous mother ever bore," he was not likely to have been too scrupulous in insisting on accuracy and verification. Nonetheless, it is here that we find most of the stories later retailed as Fulton's youthful life: how he invented skyrockets and a boat with hand-cranked paddles, how he suggested new designs to local gunsmiths that were "invariably adopted by common consent," how he told his teacher that "my head is so full of original notions that there is no vacant chamber to store away the contents of dusty books." Touching, remarkable, and quite unbelievable.

The facts are unappealingly meager. Fulton by his own testimony was born on a farm in Little Britain Township, some twenty miles south of Lancaster, Pennsylvania, on November 14, 1765, to Robert Fulton, an Irish immigrant from Kilkenny who had bought the property just the year before, and Mary Smith, who from all we can tell lived a life as plain as her name. Fulton senior, who had worked in Lancaster as a tailor and occasional trader, proved very quickly to be no farmer, for in 1772 the farmstead was sold at auction and the family—including three older sisters, Elizabeth, Isabelle, and Mary, and a younger brother, Abraham—moved back to Lancaster virtually penniless ("Y have Nothing to By Land Back," the father wrote, "Nor money to settup with in town"). Fulton senior presumably went back to tailoring, and took on an apprentice, but he died two years later, without a will and without any substantial patrimony.

Because surviving documents do not contain a single word by Fulton junior about Fulton senior—all he later wrote was that he "attached no importance to the circumstances of his birth"—we cannot know how it affected him to have his father fail dismally as a farmer, fall deeply into debt, uproot the family, and die shortly thereafter when the son was only eight, leaving a wife and five children in want. We do know, as will be apparent later, that the pursuit of wealth became a primary interest of his (and he wanted, says Colden, to be "considered, as he really was, the maker of his own fortune") and that he was willing to go to almost any lengths, including what amounts to international blackmail, to ensure that he would not end up as his father had. We also know that as a young man he established at least three close friendships with men substantially older than he was, one of which certainly had an intimacy and a devotion that went beyond the usual. And we can also infer, from the remote relationships he had with his own children—they figure seldom in his letters, and mostly as appendages to his wife—that his relationship to his father was similarly distant, or at least he subsequently chose to regard it so.

Young Fulton lived for approximately ten years in Lancaster, but aside from indications that he took some instruction at the school of Caleb Johnson, a Tory Quaker, there is little information about him in that period and the Fulton name does not appear in any surviving records. It is fair to assume, however, that the solidly artisanal nature of the little town of 4,000, a modestly famous center of craftsmen and mechanics—where, in fact, the dependable covered wagon favored by westward trekkers was manufactured and named after the nearby Conestoga River—made its impression on the boy. Much of his later career was taken up with inventions that called for some understanding of mechanics and with machinery that showed considerable artistry in design, and as that did not come out of his formal schooling, a great deal of it must have been absorbed by him while hanging around, as young boys might, the bustling workshops and manufactories of Lancaster.

Particularly since for eight of those years there was a war going on and Lancaster was an important armaments center, its gunsmiths, the elite of the work force, sometimes working around the clock to meet orders for the Continental Army. War itself, with its ugliness and horror, did not much intrude into Lancaster's life—the British never made it closer than Elkton, Maryland, forty miles away—but the excitement and intensity of it in this fervently patriotic town, considering itself a significant contributor to the war effort, had to have touched all its citizens, even the youngest. In addition to which, American soldiers were a constant presence, stationed as guards for thousands of British and Hessian prisoners of war sent there to be far from the front lines, and the sight of rifles and bayonets, the sound of cannon and musket shot, would have been a regular and stirring part of a boy's existence. It is not hard to find the roots of Fulton's later fascination for, even obsession with, weapons of war and instruments of explosion in this youthful experience.

Sometime in his mid-teens, Fulton, apparently alone, moved to Philadelphia, where by the age of seventeen, according to Delaplaine, he was apprenticed to a jeweler, Jeremiah Andrews, whose advertisement promised "a neat assortment of jewelry of his own manufacture equal to any imported," including "hair worked in the neatest manner." The task of decorating lockets and pendants with human hair, often of a deceased relative, woven into intricate patterns and pictures, seems to have been assigned to Fulton. It is possible that at the same time he worked on miniature paintings that might also grace a locket or brooch, for the first sure record we have of him is a notice in a 1785 directory—"Fulton, Robert, Miniature painter, Corner of 2d and Walnut Streets"—and eight miniatures have been attributed to him, none with certainty, none with any special flair, though all competent enough to have been done by a twenty-year-old with a modest artistic talent. According to Colden, Fulton claimed to "derive emolument" from this venture, but it is hard to believe there was enough there to keep him going, as the trade was not especially well paying and even such a talented painter as Charles Willson Peale, who had returned to Philadelphia after studying in Europe, was forced to hold down other jobs than painting.

What did keep Fulton alive is completely unknown. He was tall and pleasant-looking, with dark curly hair, penetrating eyes, and slightly full lips, and if he was anything like his later self was outgoing and personable, probably making friends—and perhaps patrons—easily. Philadelphia was a bustling and cosmopolitan city, the center of American culture, such as it was, and a place, as a visiting Frenchman put it, "wherein all the speculation of America terminates and mingles." It is not inconceivable in such a world that the young Fulton could have found a few sponsors happy to invest in a rising artistic talent, or simply a patriotic merchant or two willing to nurture the kind of home-grown culture that would honor the new nation. If so, however, Fulton kept the identities to himself, and no such benevolent figure is named in his correspondence.

In any case, Fulton somehow managed to come by enough money as of May 1786 to put down the equivalent of $200 for a farm for his mother in Washington County, on the western frontier of Pennsylvania, where she had gone to be with her brother; a few months later he bought an additional three lots nearby for his siblings to join her, agreeing to pay $5.50 a year "in perpetuity," which it is extremely doubtful he succeeded in doing. It is not known where the money came from, though later correspondence suggests some may have been borrowed within the family, but it was a substantial sum at a time when the farm laborers on Robert Livingston's Clermont estate earned about $100 a year and the average workingman in New York City about $240 a year. Fulton also came up with enough money to treat himself to a health resort, the Warm Springs at Bath, Virginia (now West Virginia), as a cure for some ailment of his lungs involving a racking cough and the spitting of blood. And on his return to Philadelphia he was able to set himself up in a new shop, announcing that "Robert Fulton, miniature painter and hair worker, is removed from the northeast corner of Walnut and Second Streets to the west side of Front Street, one door above Pine Street, Philadelphia."

In his new location Fulton was a block away from the Delaware River, and it was there in the summer of 1786 that John Fitch, armed with a monopoly for steamboat operation from the New Jersey state legislature and $300 from a few credulous Philadelphia investors, began his serious experiments with the mechanics of steam power. With a 45-foot skiff he tried out several means of manual propulsion, finally settling on an arrangement of six paddleboards on each side, moved by a crank, and he operated a model steam engine with a 3-inch cylinder successfully enough to predict speeds of ten miles per hour on a full-scale boat. Whether he actually combined these two into a working steamboat that summer is a matter of historical dispute, but he and his mechanic were certainly active on the river and attracted the attention, and derision, of the sailors and boatmen on the shore, and it is entirely possible that the mechanically minded artist who had just moved into Front Street saw some of these early steamboat efforts.

If he did, he never mentioned it. Then again, throughout his career he never admitted that he had learned anything from any previous inventor.

⁕

According to Colden, it was at the Warm Springs spa that Fulton met "some gentlemen, who were so much pleased with the genius which they discovered in his paintings, that they advised him to go to England" for further study with artists more celebrated than Philadelphia could offer. Again the source of funds is unknown, but sometime probably in the spring of 1787 he bought passage and sailed to England, with, as he later said, "not more than 40 Guineas" (the equivalent of $210) in his pocket.[1]

He also carried a letter of introduction to the distinguished artist Benjamin West, which family tradition says was written by Benjamin Franklin, who would have known West from his earlier diplomatic days in England. West was an American who had practiced art in Philadelphia and New York before being sent by wealthy patrons to Italy in 1760, whereupon he turned his back on America and settled in England, soon becoming an official court painter to George III and in 1768 a founder of the Royal Academy of Arts. Since his monumental works met such approval and commanded such prices, West was little inclined to forgo his royal patronage even when there was a revolution going on, but he did maintain his allegiance to America by going out of his way to be a tutor and sponsor for a great many young American men wishing to be artists ("my adopted sons," he called them), and it would be a particularly fortuitous contact for young Fulton.

Fulton arrived in London sometime in the late spring of 1787 and presumably went straight to West's establishment at 14 Newman Street, where the artist had his residence, his studio, and a gallery to which visitors came to examine, and perchance to buy, the huge dramatic canvases that lined the rooms. William Dunlap, another young American helped by West at just this time, wrote years later about the impression made on him "by the long gallery leading from the dwelling house to the lofty suite of painting rooms—a gallery filled with sketches and designs for large paintings—the spacious room through which I passed to the more retired attelier—the works of his pencil surrounding me on every side—his own figure seated at his esel [*sic*], and the beautiful composition at which he was employed, as if in sport, not labour"—and happy at work, the poet Leigh Hunt once said, because "he thought himself immortal." West would have treated the young man cordially, and Fulton worked his charms on Mrs. West so well that she would later call him her "favorite son," but there is no indication that West considered him adept enough at his profession to take him on as a pupil. He helped Fulton find lodgings with the painter Robert Davy on Charlotte Street, no doubt gave him morsels from the store of advice he always lavished on his American protégés ("Consider that hour lost in which a line has not been drawn, nor a masterpiece studied"), and wished him Godspeed.

It was a difficult time for the would-be artist. Five years later he would recall those days in a letter to his mother: "Here I had an art to learn by which I was to earn my bread but little to support [me] whilst I was doing it and numbers of Eminent Men of the same profession which I must Excell before I Could hope to live–Many Many a Silant solitary hour have I spent in the most unnerved Study Anxiously pondering how to make funds to support me till the fruits of my labours should [be] sifficant to repay them. Thus I went on for near four years–happily beloved by all who knew me or I had long ear now been Crushed by Poverties Cold wind–and Freezing Rain."

Not one of Fulton's works from this period survives, but there is a record of his being allowed to exhibit two paintings, portraits of "young gentlemen," at the Royal Academy's omnium-gatherum show in the spring of 1791, and four others, including portraits of a "young gentleman" and a "young lady," at the less prestigious Society of British Artists later that year. (Fulton told his mother he had had eight pictures accepted at the Royal Academy, but the record shows that this was merely that exaggeration for effect so characteristic of him throughout.) Fulton wrote his mother that his paintings "Recd every posable mark of Approbation that the Society could give but these exertions are all for honor–there is no prophet arising from it," although it is unlikely that the portraits were not commissioned and paid for, however little a price he might command for them. There is no record of Fulton's exhibiting in 1792, but he must have completed at least three historical paintings, because in 1793 they were engraved by other hands and printed–a common way of trying to raise extra money–and a rather revealing trio it is: *Mary Queen of Scots Under Confinement, Lady Jane Grey Before Her Execution,* and *Louis XVI in Prison,* a gloomier genre than which is hard to imagine. In that same year Fulton submitted one last painting to the Academy, a portrait of an unknown Mrs. Murray, and then his career as an artist was pretty much over, save for some later portraits of friends and family and two presumed (but unsigned) self-portraits.

All that seems meager indeed as a means of income, but during more than three years of this period it is very likely that Fulton was supported in some measure by one William Courtenay, Earl of Devon, in and around his ancestral home of Powderham Castle, near Exeter. As Fulton recounted it to his mother early in 1792: "Last summer I was Invited by Lord Courtney [*sic:* after seven months he couldn't spell the name right] down to his Country seat to paint a picture of him which gave his Lordship so much pleasure that he has introduced me to all his Friends–And it is but just now that I am beginning to get a little money and pay som debtt which I was obliged to Contract." (The portrait surely was done, but there is no trace of it even though Powderham and its artistic treasures have been very well preserved.)

What makes this especially intriguing is that William Courtenay was not just a rich young aristocrat: he was one of Britain's most notorious homosexuals and had been involved in one of the era's most celebrated scandals only seven years before Fulton's visit.

Although his coming-of-age portrait shows Courtenay to be a soft and earnest man of no special strikingness, when he was eleven, in 1779, his beauty seems to have completely bowled over the nineteen-year-old William Beckford, another elegant aristocrat and, with £1.5 million by inheritance, reputedly the richest man in England. Beckford declared that he was in love with young Courtenay, whom he called "Kitty" (later, in a novel, describing a character modeled on him as "the most delicate and lovely creature in the world"), and for the next three years they seem to have met off and on, in London and at the Beckford ancestral home, Fonthill, a day's ride east of Powderham. On one of these occasions, according to Beckford, they became lovers: "My dear little C.," he wrote in his diary, "the inclinations he discovered so like my own." Affections cooled, and in 1784, at twenty-three, Beckford married, but on a visit with his wife to Powderham in October of that year he was discovered with Courtenay in the latter's bedroom by a tutor, who reported it to the master of the castle, one Baron Loughborough, Courtenay's uncle by marriage. Apparently to damage Beckford's reputation, Loughborough let the details be leaked to the local papers—one of which commented on Beckford's having made "a grammatical mistake in regard to the genders"—and soon the whole country knew of the affair, particularly serious since at that time in Britain sodomy was punishable by death. Beckford retired to Fonthill with his wife, but the scandal festered and he chose to leave the country the following April and remained abroad until late 1789, after his wife died, whereupon he returned to Fonthill, surrounded himself with young boys as servants and lovers, and lived as an exile from much of proper society thereafter.

As for Courtenay, when he met Fulton in 1792 at the age of twenty-four, he had become the Third Viscount and Ninth Earl of Devon, as well as master of Powderham, where he lived with several of his thirteen sisters—he was the only male child—and as many amusing friends as he could entice within his circle. He was said to be talented as a musician and an artist and is known to have had one of the castle rooms rebuilt by a leading society architect, James Wyatt, so that he could put on plays that he either wrote or translated, with his guests as performers. Whether he gathered to Powderham the same kind of partners as Beckford imported to Fonthill is unknown, but there was no doubt that homosexuality was his mode of life, apparently flagrantly at times, and Fulton could hardly have been unaware of it, if in fact he did not take part in it.

Now, there is no evidence from Fulton or anyone else that he was a participant, but his residence at the castle for a year and a half, presumably at Courtenay's expense since no other income is known, is certainly suggestive. As is part of a 1793 letter in which Fulton declared that "my bachelor ideas still

possess me" and "there is not the most distant prospect" of trying the alternative–which of course could be taken two ways,
though it is relevant that indeed there was no mention of any
women in his life until he was thirty-one years old. And then,
as we shall see, he moved in as a partner with a married couple.

⚜

    William Courtenay, by one account "more actively
and exclusively homosexual" than Beckford, seems to
have eventually become so unsettling to the populace of
Exeter that in 1811 a local magistrate brought charges
against him for "unnatural crimes." His Lordship is said to
have dismissed the accusation with the remark that if he
were to be brought before the House of Lords on this
count, "they most of them were like himself and would
not decide against him," but when he was threatened
with immediate arrest and jail before such a trial, "he lost
all resolution," a contemporary account says, "wept like a
child, and was willingly taken on board a vessel, the first
that could be found." Which happened to be bound for
America.
    Courtenay landed in New York and settled at an
estate in Manhattan called Claremont, overlooking the
Hudson in the village of Bloomingdale (at roughly what
became Riverside Drive and 125th Street), with an annuity of £2,000 a month. (This Claremont of course had
nothing to do with Livingston's Clermont and was said to
be named after its builder's home county in Ireland.) Accounts differ as to how he was received in New York society, whether shunned or lionized, but the most suggestive
version, by a mid-nineteenth-century biographer, James
Renwick, says that "every door was closed against him
except that of Fulton." The then-successful inventor welcomed Courtenay out of feelings akin to those who

"soothe the mental anguish of the last hours of the condemned criminal," according to Renwick (evidently unaware that ordinary feelings of gratitude, or something stronger, might have had earlier roots), which took "a high degree of courage" in the face of a condemnation of the Englishman that "was universally entertained." Fulton's hospitality, of which he himself makes no mention, need not have extended long, however, for soon after the War of 1812 broke out Courtenay chose to betake himself from America, and he was allowed into France, where he bought a house on the Place Vendôme in Paris and died a bachelor in 1835, still shunned by English, but quite acceptable to French, society.

That the artistic and homosexual worlds of Britain overlapped in the late eighteenth century should be no surprise, and Courtenay and Beckford were only two of many who enjoyed, as it were, both circles. Beckford was particularly active in the art world, and one of his favorites, both as painter and as agent for buying artworks in London, was Benjamin West. West painted a portrait of Beckford's mother in 1790, then was commissioned to do a series of seventeen paintings for Fonthill and became a regular visitor, along with such artistic luminaries of the time as J. M. W. Turner, Ozias Humphrey, and James Wyatt. What the thoroughly respectable West made of Beckford's openly bizarre life at Fonthill, or how much he ever saw of the goings-on, he never let on, though it was reported that he thought Beckford innocent of the Powderham affair with Courtenay.

Whatever was occupying Fulton's time during his three and a half years in Devon, the only artistic product we know of is the one portrait he submitted to the Royal Academy in the spring of 1793. It was clear by then, though, that even if Fulton had developed the talent for an artistic career, he did not have the passion to sustain it: there are in his letters no references to works of art that impressed him (his single, listless comment on his trip to France in the summer of 1790 was that he "saw the works of some of the most able masters"), none of the effusiveness that bubbles up in the letters of, say, John Vanderlyn, another young American painter in Europe in this period, no expressions of enthusiasm for this style or that; even his comment on West's work has to do with success, not artistry: "He has stedily pursued his Course, and Step by Step at length Reached the Summit where he now looks Round on the beauties of his Industry." It was obviously time for something different.

That something was, somewhat surprisingly, canals. "I have laid aside my panels," Fulton was to write in September 1796, "and have not painted a picture for more than two years, as I have little doubt but canals will answer my purpose much better." He is not specific about the "purpose," but he is clearly out to advance himself in the world and shows no real attachment to the high calling of art if the latest fashion for canal-building is more likely to serve him. And indeed, England was then undergoing a canal boom, with eighty-one canals authorized by Parliament in the four years after 1791, and the profits on some of them were said to be as high as 1,000 percent, just the sort of thing that would pique Fulton's interest. It was not that he had any known engineering training or experience in any aspect of canal-building, but he must have reckoned that his charm, determination, and a certain Yankee know-how would suffice—and besides, canals would surely be more lucrative than portraits.

Fulton, then twenty-eight, began his canal career with a letter to the Earl of Stanhope in November 1793, criticizing his proposal to use locks on a canal to link the Bristol and English channels through Devon and suggesting instead a series of "in-

clined planes" with counterweights to pull canal boats, a
scheme that would certainly work for Devon, and "I have not
the least Doubt butt, it may be found Usefull throughout the
whole Canal Navigation of England and Scotland." The pre-
sumptuousness was staggering. Not only was the earl a man
whose rank and reputation far exceeded his, but he was among
the leading inventors of the land, known to be no dilettantish
fool, and hardly in need of the advice of a novice who, he
scolded Fulton in reply, had "never made any Experiment on
this, or any like Subject."

Astonishingly, Fulton was not deterred. He kept up a
correspondence, at one point offering to form a partnership
with Stanhope, and when none of his bluster worked he finally threw himself on the lordship's mercy: "I will Candidly
Acknowledge that the tide of misfortune has Run hard Against
me," he wrote just before Christmas 1793, "in Spite of every
Caution which has much Embarrised my Circumstances and
Retarded my Progress. While my Friends will not listen to
my Mechanical Pursuits, But Insist that I should Adhear to my
Portrait Pencil. . . . Should your Lordship be so kind as to favour
me, One hundred Pounds [roughly $500] would Put me
in Motion." Stanhope was not moved. "It will not be convenient to me to afford you at present the pecuniary assistance" requested, he wrote, and added, pointedly, "I doubt
whether you will do well to pursue Mechaniks at present as a
Profession."

A lesser man—or one less convinced of his worth—would
have gone back to his Portrait Pencil. Here he was, presumably
without funds and living at the sufferance of Lord Courtenay
or his friends,[2] decisively rebuffed by a leading canal expert,
and without any experience or particular knowledge of hydraulic engineering. And yet Fulton, some fire working within
him, now began what he later said was three years of studying
various canals in England "to obtain practical knowledge on
the manner of constructing them, and to make myself familiar

with their advantages," as well as to become "acquainted with some of the best engineers."

He did not even wait for that before he went ahead and applied for a patent, complete with thirteen elaborate drawings and six printed pages of description, for his version of the inclined plane, "a simple Machine by which Four Men may with ease raise a Boat of 30 tons to the heighth of 500 feet in Fifteen Minutes." Although the inclined plane was an ancient device and had been used in Britain at least for several years, and although Fulton supplied no evidence that his design would ever work in practice, the Crown granted a patent seal on June 3, 1794, to the man the document described as "late of the City of Exeter, now of the City of London, Gentleman." From whom the newly engentried Fulton borrowed the more than £100 it cost at the time to apply for a patent is unknown, but as Fulton subsequently said he had sold off two shares of his patent right, it is possible that some gullible friend—my guess would be West—had been willing to go in for £50 a share.

⁂

Benjamin West was open to investment ideas at all times and was said by Joseph Farrington, an artist and renowned diarist, to have been shrewd about them. At one point he invested in land in America with one of his young protégés, John Trumbull, the later successful historical painter, buying acreage along the Susquehanna in Pennsylvania and along the Genesee in Ontario County, New York. These two persuaded William Beckford to make a similar investment, and in 1798 the richest man in England bought some 23,340 acres of America alongside West and Trumbull's Ontario County property for £9,400; Raphael West, Benjamin's eldest son (and a friend of Fulton's) was sent out to act as Beckford's agent and live on the property.

It is not clear exactly who was trying to do what to whom. Beckford may have bought this land from West and Trumbull, as one account says, or from James Wadsworth, the man who had originally sold the plot to the two artists. In any case, since West and Trumbull had paid three shillings an acre for their land and Beckford was charged eight shillings for his not dissimilar parcel–"a monstrous price," Farrington called it–it seems that somebody was trying to take advantage of the millionaire. Unsuccessfully. Raphael West spent a little over a year in Ontario County, hated it, and returned in 1800 to tell Beckford that he was being taken; somehow Beckford then backed out of the deal, apparently without losing a shilling.

If Benjamin West was in fact guilty of trying to bilk Beckford, it bothered his patron not at all. He continued to use West as an artist for the huge faux abbey he was building at Fonthill–designed by James Wyatt, who had also worked for Courtenay–and as an agent scouting artworks for him in London.

❧

Having embarked on a career of invention, Fulton was suddenly afire with ideas. He contrived a marble-cutting saw and built a small model that was honored by the Society for the Encouragement of Arts in 1794. He designed a canal-digging machine to be drawn by four horses that he was sure could remove a cubic yard of earth faster than a human and at a third of the expense. He drew plans for prefabricated iron bridges and aqueducts for canals, intended to cut down on the time and expense of building waterways. And he even thought about steamboats.

Just when Fulton entered the steamboat lists is a matter of some uncertainty. He probably knew James Rumsey, the American inventor who had gone to England to raise capital for a steamboat and was in London on and off from 1788; if so, he might well have known about Rumsey's first attempt with a boat on the Thames in December 1792 and, after Rumsey's death that month, a second trial early the next year, neither of which was completely successful but both of which confirmed the promise of steam propulsion. Fulton also knew that Lord Stanhope not only had received a patent for a steamboat in March 1790 but had persuaded the British navy to begin building a full-scale version in the fall of 1792. So it is possible that he tried some steamboat experiments in Devon in the summer of 1793 and that he even used side paddles, as he later claimed, though the letter to Stanhope asserting this was in dispute during Fulton's lifetime and remains questionable today. What is not in doubt, however, is a letter from Fulton to Boulton, Watt & Co. in November 1794 asking about a 3- to 4-horsepower steam engine and what size boat it should go in—filed without a reply, as the firm was not in the boat business—proving that by then he had at least a passing interest in steam navigation.

Only passing, however, for canals were still his passion. That was what led him, in the fall of 1794, to travel to northern England, where the most successful waterways had been built, and to settle in Manchester in a boardinghouse where, with some fortuity, a fellow lodger was a young Welshman named Robert Owen. Owen, then twenty-three, had been a manager of one of the huge cotton mills of Manchester for the past four years and was starting to formulate the principles that would guide him a few years later in turning the cotton mills of New Lanark, Scotland, into the world-famous models of large-scale production, labor harmony, and benevolent welfarism that they became in the nineteenth century. Though from a humble background, he was now making at least £300 a year and was typically generous with his money to his new companion: he invested £65 in December 1794 in Fulton's canal-digging machine and inclined-plane system, for half the profits he was assured would be forthcoming, and another £173,8s. the following spring, though he later claimed that he thought the ventures to be "very problematical." In that assessment he was right, for Fulton had no success in advancing his schemes, and it was not until May 1797 that Owen saw any return on his generosity, a meager £60, all he was ever to receive.[3]

Fulton's one modest success during this period was somehow impressing the directors of the Peak Forest Company, who were building a canal southeast of Manchester. Now with a new vision of small-scale canals using small-tonnage boats, Fulton produced a report for the directors, including a series of drawings and plans, on how they could make the Peak Forest system conform to this vision, which they immediately discarded but were good enough to pay him £105 for; he next persuaded them to underwrite the £210 cost of printing up two hundred copies of a treatise to be distributed to the canal's investors in which he would expand on his small-canal ideas. No explanation for this unusual generosity was ever given, and Fulton did not even acknowledge it in the document he produced, but at least one biographer has surmised that Fulton must have had a special patron on the board on whom he was able, as he had for the past eight years, to work his charm.

The document that appeared in March 1796, *A Treatise on the Improvement of Canal Navigation . . .* by "R. Fulton, Civil Engineer," is a long (158-page) and elaborate (seventeen engravings) argument for small-scale canals, complete with his inclined planes and now boats with wheels to ride those planes, which he puts forth here as the answer not only to all transportation and communication problems of virtually any country but as the means of eventually preventing war by making each canal nation strong and self-sufficient. Rodomontade aside, the treatise is interesting chiefly in ways that would not have interested the Peak Forest investors in the least. For one thing, though it asserts it is "deserving [of] the attention" of English planners, it is aimed largely at America and concludes with a long letter to Thomas Mifflin, governor of Pennsylvania, telling him of the "great importance to the States of America" of small canals; in fact, its argument for water transport as the basis for industrial development is quite prescient in predicting America's nineteenth-century course, although that was achieved not so much through canals as through the steamboat. For another, it is an elaborate defense of Fulton's mode of "invention," by which he had regularly appropriated old ideas and mixed them into new forms ("a particular arrangement [that] will produce a new and desired effect . . . is usually dignified with the term Genius"), coupled with a bitter attack on those, like Stanhope, who had dismissed his earlier work as having nothing new ("men of the least genius are ever the first to depreciate, and the last to commend").

Predictably, the Peak Forest directors paid no attention to the book they had commissioned, nor were any other canal companies moved to adopt Fulton's ideas or hire him on to administer them, an oversight that must have rankled an author of such enthusiasm and conviction, not to mention arrogance. Fulton returned to London sometime in the middle of 1796, perhaps to be near the Wests, but his fortunes did not improve. In late December he was desperate enough to write Stanhope again:

> *I am now Sitting Reduced to half a Crown, Without knowing Where to obtain a shilling for some months. This my Lord is an awkward sensation to a feeling Mind . . . Who on Looking Round Sees thousands nursed in the Lap of fortune, grown to maturity, And now Spending their time in the endless Maze of Idle dissipation. Thus Circumstanced My Lord, would it be an Intrusion on your goodness and Philanthropy to Request the Loan of 20 guineas Which I will Return as Soon as possible.*

There is no evidence that Stanhope responded.

Fulton next tried to interest West in investing £1,500 in his canal schemes, however tenuous they may have been, and through him William Beckford, promising that it "will soon be considerably productive and in time yield an important fortune" and be "the means of gratifying the predominant sensations of men[,] *that of Riches and Fame,*" which says a good deal about Fulton but was not persuasive to either West or Beckford. Shortly after this, though, he hit pay dirt. In an excited letter to Robert Owen on April 28, 1797, Fulton announced that he had sold "one fourth of my canal prospects for £1,500 to a gentleman of large fortune," evidently having forgotten (or hoping Owen had) that he was ostensibly still in partnership with Owen. He would be obliged "to go to Paris and obtain patents for the small canal system," he said, without explaining why, but he expected the following spring to sail for America, "where I have the most flattering field of invention before me, having already converted the first characters in that country to my small system of canals." From his initial payment he promised to send Owen £60, which he did, and to send "the remainder in six months," which he did not.

The "gentleman of large fortune" was one John Barker Church, an Englishman who had made money in America during the Revolution in a somewhat suspicious fashion but returned unscathed to England in 1784 and set himself up as a high-living member of the rather dissolute set around the young Prince of Wales. Among his other beneficiaries were West's protégé John Trumbull (though Trumbull complained the Churches "were in the habit of seeing a little more company than pleases me"), who painted the portraits of his wife, Angelika, and son Philip, and Whig leader Charles Fox, who was counted on to provide tips for various investment schemes in which Church was usually an intemperate speculator. It is not hard to imagine how the practiced Fulton enticed him into his plans for a country full of small canals yielding "an important fortune."

⁘

Among the investments made by John Barker Church at about this same time were six pairs of handsome dueling pistols he found in a London shop and took with him when he returned to America in 1798.

In New York he settled down at 52 Broadway with his wife, a member of the illustrious New York Schuyler family, and became friendly with Alexander Hamilton, who was married to her sister Elizabeth. The friendship solidified to the point where Church professed Hamilton's Federalist policies and Federalist antipathies, including a dislike of Aaron Burr, an enmity that led the following year to a duel with Burr at a secluded bluff in New Jersey, in which Church used his fine pistols but neither man drew blood.

When, in 1801, Hamilton's son Philip was drawn into a duel, on a bluff in New Jersey, he naturally chose to use Church's guns, which, alas, were insufficient, and he died of his wounds. Three years later Hamilton himself was on that same New Jersey bluff, again with Church's pistols, again with unhappy result.

❦

The arrangement with Church, sealed with £500 down that spring–the equivalent of $2,500, probably the most money he had ever known–marked a new way for Fulton to think about canal schemes. Until then he had generally talked of canals, particularly in America, as the appropriate undertakings of state or national governments, and in his *Treatise* he saw the federal government as the agency to subsidize a Philadelphia–Pittsburgh canal; as he put it in a letter to President Washington, to whom he had, unbidden, sent a copy of his *Treatise* and a note asking his "sanction" for small canals, "I first Considered them as National Works." Now, however, with the prospect of investors, he had second thoughts: "Perhaps an Incorporated Company of Subscribers . . . would be the best mode," he wrote, "as it would then be their interest to Promote the work: *And*

Guard their emoluments." And since, as he figured it, investors would easily bring in forty percent on their money and America could easily be filled with canals, the prospect of making $2 million a year in profits was easily in sight. Filled with the wisdom of that, and the benefits of putting private cupidity over public enterprise, he set about finding other investors for his project.

Just why Fulton now decided that he had to go to Paris is unclear, since his new partnership was aimed at promoting canals in America, and why he thought he could use his small-canal patents there to finance private canal companies is harder still to understand, since the French government had nationalized almost all canals in 1791. Perhaps he planned to drum up new investors for his American schemes, perhaps he knew of some specific sources of wealth, or perhaps he hoped to find political as well as financial support from the sizable American colony in Paris; he does not say. Something led him across the Channel in June 1797, and, for the next decade, into a completely different world.

4.

1797–1803

It may have been small canals and a search for investors that impelled Robert Fulton to Paris in 1797, but aside from taking out a dilatory patent on his idea early in 1798, he seems to have ignored the subject almost entirely thereafter (and John Barker Church is not heard from until much later, demanding his money back). Another fire, another career, left to smolder. What occupied Fulton's attention for most of the next decade was not his marble-cutting saw, which he never attempted to build for operation, nor his ditch-digging machine, which he probably realized shortly after dreaming it up would never work, nor the designs for steamboats he said he had experimented with in Devon, and not even the two devices that he would poach from English inventors and patent in France as a means of making money. No, his interest was fixed on a new contrivance, something he described as "a curious machine for mending the system of politics," indeed for annihilating the British navy and establishing "the liberty of the seas" and "a guarantee of perpetual peace to all maritime nations": a submarine, armed with "torpedoes." Never mind that this was a weapon of war regarded as so terrible that the navies of civilized nations had rejected it out of hand, there was nothing that rose to the level of importance in his mind as much as this "curious machine" that absorbed so many of his days.

When Fulton arrived in Paris, he chose to stay, as many Americans did, at Madame Hillaire's *pension* on the Left Bank. There, too, was Ruth Barlow, a pretty, self-possessed woman in her early forties, reckoned witty and winsome, worldly, frail, and perhaps a little risqué, well armored when it came to parlor repartee and even serious philosophy, but by her own account "a child . . . in everything that affects my heart," the "weakest part" that is "always most strongly attacked." Fulton, a tall and handsome thirty-one, his charm honed by a decade of English survival, attacked. She was to be the most important love of his life.

Ruth Barlow was the wife of Joel Barlow, then thought to be among America's most eminent poets, whom she had married in 1782, not long after his graduation from Yale. One of a group of literary men who fancied themselves the "Connecticut Wits," Barlow had written a huge and tedious patriotic epic, *The Vision of Columbus* (1787), that won him a certain reputation in America, and a comic poem, *The Hasty Pudding* (1793), and then had gone to Europe to make his fortune as an agent for an Ohio land-speculating company. The company collapsed in scandal in the 1790s, but Barlow escaped untainted, with money enough to invest in various ventures, among them trading French bonds and running goods through Britain's blockade of Europe, from which he emerged, by his own account, with $120,000 in his estate. In 1795 he had been tapped by President Washington to serve as a special ambassador to Algeria to negotiate the release of Americans taken prisoner by Barbary pirates, leaving Ruth to fend for herself in Paris. She had grown used to this kind of separation in their marriage, and it apparently did not diminish her admiration for her husband as, so she had said just that January, "the best of men and of lovers."

There is no way to know how close Fulton and Ruth Barlow became over the summer of 1797, but by the time Joel Barlow returned to town in September, they were intimate enough—and the husband approving enough—that the three of them left Madame Hillaire's and moved into a set of rooms together in a Left Bank *hôtel*. And here, as Ruth years later told Cadwallader Colden, "commenced that strong affection, that devoted attachment, that real friendship, which subsisted in a most extraordinary degree between Mr. Barlow and Mr. Fulton during their lives." For the next seven years these three would be intimate and loving companions, living quite openly in that arrangement to which the French, naturally, have given the name.

For Fulton the arrangement may have been unique, but the evidence in Ruth's letters is that the couple had had other *"grand garçons"* before and were used to such triangles of affection. Ruth Barlow had taken lovers previously and had boasted to her husband of the men she had enticed and "how happy & bad" she had been, and the suggestion is strong that they had shared lovers in the past. Fulton, though, was different for them: this was a long-term friendship, going beyond whatever sexual dalliances they had entwined in before, and there is little doubt about the genuine love that existed among the threesome, almost certainly to the exclusion of any other partners during their years in France. Analysis is essentially futile: sufficient to infer that, in addition to all else, the Barlows, childless, might have delighted in being able to tutor this still-unpolished fellow American a decade younger—in their family, Ruth told Colden, "he learnt the French, and something of the Italian and German languages" and "also studied the high mathematics, physics, chymistry, and perspective"—and that he in turn found two elder figures who embodied the suave sophistication, not to mention the fame and fortune, that had always been his ideals, and in Joel perhaps the successful Yankee go-getter he was determined to, as his father had not, become.

Joel Barlow was also a dabbler, somewhat above the dilettante level, in mechanical arts and inventions—he had taken out a French patent around 1792 for a boiler he thought could be used for steamboats—and it was undoubtedly he who, over brandy or port in their rooms, first lit the submarine spark in Robert Fulton.

The submarine was actually invented in 1775 by a Connecticut mechanic, David Bushnell, and even used to launch floating mines against British ships in New York harbor at the start of the Revolution in 1776, though without effect. Its essentials were known to many in the American army, and Bushnell sent a full description of the boat and his experiments to Thomas Jefferson in 1787 and the following year submitted a similar account to the Yale faculty for his master's degree. When Barlow came to learn of it is not known, but he had served in the war as a chaplain in Connecticut; his friend and fellow Connecticut Wit David Humphreys worked with Bushnell during that time; he would have known Bushnell when they were at Yale together and might have seen his thesis; and he was a friend of Jefferson's and shared with him an interest in inventions. We may imagine Barlow regaling Fulton with his knowledge of this intriguing machine, and the young inventor seizing upon the idea as a natural extension of his interest in water navigation—and if handled right, a money-maker besides.

Fulton would later argue that he was interested in a lethal submarine because, by his logic, it would guarantee the openness of the oceans and thus perpetual free trade among nations, an ideal that had recently become his passion. (He even sent a twenty-two-page essay, "Thoughts on Free Trade," to the French Directory, the latest of France's revolutionary governments, in October 1787, lecturing the directors on how nations "would peaceably enjoy the Fruits of their Virtuous Industry" if they would follow his recipe.) In his view, it was the warships of Europe's navies that stood in the way of free trade, and so, he later wrote, "I turned my whole attention to find out means of destroying such engines of oppression by some method which would put it out of the power of any nation to maintain such a system, and would compel every government to adopt the simple principles of education, industry, and free circulation of its produce." After thinking about it a bit, he related, he realized he needed two things: "First, to navigate under water, which I soon discovered was within the limits of physics; second, to find an easy mode of destroying a ship, which after some time I discovered might be done by the explosion of some pounds of powder under her bottom." *Voilà*, the submarine and its mines–for him, "torpedoes"–just as Bushnell had devised them.

Fulton wasted no time in trying to get a sponsor for the submarine. On December 13, 1797, he sent a proposition to the Directory: he would form a company to create a "Nautulus or Submarine" that could be used to destroy British warships and "annihilate their Navy," and in return he wanted some 3,500 francs (roughly £160, or $800) for each gun on any ship over forty guns he destroyed, and half that for guns on smaller ships, except if the government wanted to build its own submarines at his direction, which it could do by paying him nearly 80,000 francs per ship. He added, wanly, that he hoped France would never use this weapon against "the American States."

Nowhere in his proposal did Fulton describe (if in fact he knew) what his "Nautulus" would look like, or give any reason for assuring it would work as he said–it was dismissed as impractical by those who did not regard it as contemptible and cowardly–and the fact that this offer was considered by the French government at all, and sent for serious perusal to the Marine Ministry, suggests that Fulton may have had a friend at court, most probably Barlow himself, an honorary French citizen who had skillfully remained on good terms with each succeeding government in the revolutionary cavalcade since 1789. It was, however, to no avail. After some dickering, the Marine

Ministry informed Fulton in early 1798 that the government was not interested.

For some, it is said, ninety percent of genius is perspiration, but in Fulton's case it would more likely be perseverance: rejection generated determination, or, as he once said, "Friction brings forth the sparks of latent fire." First he appealed to Citizen General Bonaparte, in his third year as commander of the army and back from the successful Italian campaign, whom Fulton astutely determined was an important locus of power in France, and pushed his multiple arguments for international free trade. Less astutely, he suggested to this consummate soldier that it was to be achieved "only by eliminating as far as possible the causes of war," an idea so ill placed that it generated no response. Next, in late July, he resubmitted his submarine proposals along with some plans and a small model he had had built, again promising "the destruction of the English Navy" and the rise of France to be "alone and without a rival" as the leader of Europe.

This time, for reasons unspecified, the Directory approved the proposal and had the Marine Ministry appoint a committee to examine Fulton's plans. On September 5, 1798, the committee submitted a very detailed and essentially favorable account of Fulton's work—"the first conception of a man of genius"—and urged the government to let him proceed: "It cannot be doubted that, with the same brains that have been put into its conception, the elegance and solidity of the different mechanisms comprised in it, he who has executed the model would be able to construct the full-sized machine in a manner equally ingenious."

Fulton must have been sure success was his at last. He drew up and sent in a formal agreement, offering to try out an experimental "Nautulus," which, if it destroyed one English vessel, "there should be paid to me or my order five hundred thousand francs [$114,000]," with which he would proceed to build a fleet of "Nautuli" and "put into execution my plan against the English fleet." Bureaucratic silence. He wrote an angry note to the Marine Ministry, complaining that he deserved a prompt answer. Ministerial silence. He fired off individual letters, the first in French in his hand, to the members of the Directory, denouncing the "monstrous government" of England and promising destruction "so novel, so hidden and so incalculable" that it would lead to nothing less than a state of "terror" in the English fleet and a republican uprising in the land. Directorial silence.

Nothing seemed to move the revolutionary establishment. Some years later Barlow would praise Fulton for having warned him about French bureaucrats that "you must have as much patience with them as with a piece of wood or brass." This fortitude Fulton no doubt learned during this most trying period.

In his frustration Fulton turned to a new idea for making money: he would build and patent in France two devices he had seen in England, a method of "invention" that, however morally dubious, was approved and indeed encouraged by French law as a way of expanding the country's economy.

The first was a panorama, the original of which Fulton must have seen in London, a large circular building, on a raised platform, on the inside of which is painted a scene of such realism and fascination that the public is persuaded to spend a few pence to see it. Fulton took out a French patent in April 1799, built a forty-six-foot-wide tower near the Boulevard Montmartre (presumably with Barlow's money), painted the interior with a grand view, and–*quelle surprise*–success.[1] "A stranger greets it with a sigh and takes leave of it regretfully," a local guidebook enthused, and it quickly became popular at a franc and a half (thirty-three cents U.S.) a ticket. No one has left a record of just how popular, but in July, Fulton felt flush enough to send some money to his mother (a futile gesture, as she died that year) and eight months later he sold the rights to the panorama to a fellow American, James Thayer, keeping a share of the annual profits, and the patent was in effect, and the public gratified, until 1815.

The second device was a rope-making machine, modeled on one invented in England by the Reverend Edmund Cartwright, the man who had in 1785 created the power loom that effectively mechanized the English weaving industry. Fulton had become acquainted with Cartwright in London in his last year there, had spent evenings talking over inventions and projects (including steamboats and rope machines), and had urged the somewhat otherworldly cleric that he ought to "convert the overflowings of his mind to cash," which is what Fulton now proposed to do. He found an angel for a rope-making factory in one Nathaniel Cutting, a Boston businessman then serving as the American consul at Le Havre, who offered to put up some 20,700 francs (about $4,700), 4,500 down, if Fulton would design it, patent it, and have the machines built; they took out a joint patent, all Fulton's work, in May 1799.

Seldom has a partnership gone more awry. Fulton took the down payment and employed the skilled mechanic Jacques Périer to make the first machine with a portion of it, but with the rest, he had to confess to Cutting later, he paid off an old debt that had caused him "much shame" (to Richard Codman, an American, but for what is unknown), and this he justified on the grounds that "it is not reasonable that I should wreck my imagination, run after workmen and take on myself the expense of improvements without being supported in the undertaking." Cutting waited awhile and then asked for an accounting; Fulton replied that he was at work and said he needed more money; the tone of the letters is acrid and angry. Things seem to have been patched up later in the year, with Barlow and Codman as mediators, and Fulton paid some intermittent attention to the rope machine, but as late as June 1800 he had not set up the factory and was demanding another 9,000 francs to get the engines running: "Poor Fulton, says Cutting," Fulton wrote sourly that month, "not money, that is a pity by god, then I will find it, or the engines cannot move." There is no indication that Cutting was goaded by the sarcasm or wasted another sou on the project, and all that was ever produced by the affair was a lifelong enmity.

But the submarine idea still burned, and Fulton apparently grew a little desperate. After a pleading letter in July 1799 to the Directory's military committee that received no response, he stewed a bit and then in October resorted to thinly disguised blackmail: "I sincerely hope for the honor of France," he told the Marine Ministry, "that I will not encounter petty objections or intrigues that will make it necessary for me to publish the principles of the *Nautilus* and its happy consequences or to seek in Holland or America the encouragement that I would hope to find in France." This was entirely unscrupulous, but Fulton was serious: when he received no reply to his threat, he approached Holland, then under French oversight as the Batavian Republic, first through its representative in Paris and then through a private Dutchman named Vanstaphast, with whom he must have been quite close, to judge from a letter ("how sincerely I love and esteem you") written several years later. The Dutch government showed no interest—it could hardly undertake what its French sponsors had rejected—but Vanstaphast appears to have put up some serious money, because Fulton hired Jacques Périer again and was well along in the construction of the submarine in April 1800, without any help from the French treasury; Colden is quite straightforward in saying that Vanstaphast "furnished him with the necessary funds, and he proceeded to construct his machine."

It is curious, indeed. What was it that inspired Fulton to go ahead with this project, without any support from the French or indication that they would let him effect it, entirely on his own? What passion, what zealotry, drove him to construct this awful instrument of death and destruction that was considered in many quarters immoral even according to the lax principles of warfare? Come to that, why was he driven to destroy the ships of a nation whose hospitality he had accepted for a decade and against which he had no animus, and why would he provide his deadly apparatus to any nation but his own?

The record supplies no answers. There was, to be sure, that high-minded rhetoric about the liberty of the seas and such, and Colden argues in his defense that Fulton believed so deeply that his inventions "would annihilate naval armaments [and] the war system of Europe," to the obvious benefit of "all nations," that he wanted to prove them "without reference . . . to the merits of the then existing contest" or "feeling a partiality or enmity to either of the belligerents"; he was merely "introducing a new military science, which he wished to prove, and in which he had a desire to perfect himself for the benefit of his country, and mankind." All very well, but even if sincere such motives seem inadequate to explain Fulton's compulsion to develop weapons of war, of unknown or uncertain efficacy, in a foreign country for a government that showed no interest, all by himself.

❧

Joel Barlow arrived in Paris in 1788 as an agent for the Scioto Associates. That was a company created by the Continental Congress in 1789, through the conniving of William Duer, secretary of the Board of the Treasury, in a shady backstairs deal that gave, as he put it, "a number of the principal characters of [Washington] City" title to 3.5 million acres of land between the Ohio River and Lake Erie for speculation. The Scioto Associates did not have to pay anything for the land, which they planned to do only after they sold it—a scam even then—and that is where Barlow's venture came in.

Barlow established a French company, Compagnie du Scioto, sold shares to prominent Frenchmen, issued brochures describing "the garden of the universe, the center of wealth" that awaited the prescient investor, and waited for French aristocrats, fearful of the revolution and anxious to find a place where they could export their capital, to sign up. By the middle of 1790, some 100,000 acres had been sold and several hundred French families set forth in five ships to make their homes in paradise four thousand miles away.

At that point the Scioto officials had to do something to back up the boasts Barlow had made about the acreage, so they rounded up fifty farmers from Massachusetts, settled them along the Ohio near the Kanawha River (a place they named Gallipolis, in honor of their French marks), and had them quickly put up a few hundred log cabins in the wilderness as emblems of the promised "center of wealth." The French families arrived in considerable dismay, but, powerless, they settled in and awaited the benign climate they had been assured of— instead of which came harsh winters and malarial summers, killing off a third of the settlers in short order and sending another third to the relative civilization of Eastern cities or New Orleans. By 1800 no more than sixteen families were left.

Barlow suffered no repercussions. He made a good deal of money and invested it in French bonds that accrued value with Napoleon's ascendancy. Whatever the French in America thought of him, the French in Paris made him a French citizen.

❦

In any case, Fulton sailed determinedly on. On April 10, 1800, he notified the Marine Ministry that his submarine was nearly finished and indicated he was optimistic that the new revolutionary government that had taken power the previous November—the Consulate, with Napoleon as the First, and only meaningful, Consul—would come to terms with him: "I have every reason to hope from Bonaparte the welcome, the encouragement that I have so long been refused by Directors and Ministers." Napoleon, however, had his coup d'état to secure and some recalcitrant foreigners to conquer; in May he left Paris to fight the Austrians at Marengo, without giving a reply. Consular silence.

And on. On June 13, Fulton decided to test his *Nautilus* before an audience of Parisians, including, he made sure to effect, the new marine minister, Pierre Forfait, a naval architect who had already reviewed Fulton's plans favorably for the government two years before and could be expected to act as a forceful internuncio if the experiment went well now.

The boat was docked in the Seine, not far from the Périer factory where it had been built, an odd-looking tubular affair 20 feet long and 5 feet in diameter, with a kind of bubble toward the front through which Fulton and a compatriot, Nathaniel Sargent, slipped themselves to ready the craft. It moved on its own out into the middle of the river, then slowly sank beneath the water; for some twenty minutes it was out of sight, and then it rose some distance downstream; it dived again and after another twenty-five minutes reappeared where it had begun; it maneuvered to shore, and out came the two triumphant experimenters, none the worse for it. Forfait, in his enthusiastic report to Bonaparte, said that "everything that could be desired was completely achieved" and there was hope that "in a month the Nautilus could be in the sea and ready to act."

Perhaps there was an official letter from the Consulate, though none survives, perhaps no more than a favorable word from Forfait, but the government must have given some sign of approval, for Fulton proceeded immediately to make trial runs in preparation for blowing up a British warship in the open seas. In July he took the boat down the Seine to Rouen, had it fitted with a snug platform and sails that gave it the look of an ordinary boat when it was on the surface, and made several tests with a crew of two in which, as he reported to Forfait, the *Nautilus* "succeeded to sail like a common boat and plunge under water when I think proper to avoid an enemy." He then took the boat farther downriver to Le Havre, to experiment in Channel waters, where he would actually go after one of the British ships then blockading French ports, and after a number of tests there at the beginning of August he reported delightedly that "all my experiments on submarine navigation have fully succeeded." Thus, finally, nearly three years after he first proposed the idea of submarine warfare, Fulton could claim that he had a boat that would sink and rise and maneuver and attack underwater, just as he had all along promised. What's more, he had tried out his torpedo (though using an ordinary boat, not the submarine), and with some backing and forthing managed to work it at the end of a rope under a barrel he had anchored in the harbor, which, when contact was made, "was reduced to fragments."

So now he was ready for war—and never mind that he was taking on the indomitable navy of the mightiest nation in the world with a craft about the size of a whaleboat that had never been used to plant an underwater mine and, for all he knew, might not even be able to navigate in the open sea. On September 12, armed with explosives supplied by the Marine Ministry and a full store of arrogance and courage of his own, he set sail for Cherbourg, the harbor on the northern Normandy peninsula off which a substantial number of British ships were regularly cruising.

For thirty-five days Fulton and his crew remained at a little harbor near Cherbourg, most of the time confined to the shore because of what he called "equinoctial gales." Twice he set out to attack two English brigs anchored a few miles away, but both times, "whether by accident or design," he reported, "they set sail and were quickly at a distance"; both times, in fact, alerted by the Admiralty that the *Nautilus* was in the area– British spies seem to have had no trouble keeping track of Fulton's moves–they spotted the boat as soon as it came near. It wasn't that the submarine could not stay submerged for long periods–in one of these attempts the crew was underwater for six hours, breathing through a little tube while waiting for a change of tide on which to approach the brigs–but it presumably needed to break water to be able to steer effectively toward a target, thereby alerting a sharp-eyed enemy. Such a problem, however, worried Fulton not at all. In mid-October he quit the harbor and returned to Paris, confident that "the most difficult part" of proving his invention had been accomplished: "Navigation under water," he wrote in November, "is an operation whose possibility is proved, and it can be said that a new series of ideas have just been born as to the means for preventing naval wars or rather of hindering them in the future; it is a germ which only demands for its development the encouragement and support of all friends of science, of justice and society."

That encouragement came at last, in a report on November 19 from a committee Napoleon had appointed to assess Fulton's achievement: "We do not doubt his success especially if the operation is conducted by the inventor himself who combines with great erudition in the mechanic arts an excellent courage and other moral qualities necessary for such an enterprise"; it recommended a payment of 52,800 francs ($12,000). A few days later Fulton was granted an audience with the First Consul himself, the only time on record the two men ever met. It was surely a cordial meeting–no account from either side exists–but somehow the copious Fultonian charm and persuasiveness did not have the usual effect, and of course there was not much in the way of actual achievement he could lay before the highly practical soldier; Napoleon listened, but he made no promises.

Fulton, however, waited in Paris for the assumed go-ahead. When he had heard nothing by December 3, he fired off a most intemperate letter to Forfait threatening that "the cold and discouraging manner with which all my exertions have been treated during the past three years will compel me to abandon the enterprise in France if I am not received in a more friendly and liberal manner." Forfait could not have been unmindful of the implications of "in France," and he pressed the First Consul for some kind of answer. Finally, in late February 1801, it came, confirmed in a formal agreement the following month: the government would pay Fulton 10,000 francs ($2,250) to equip and arm the *Nautilus;* it would establish a table of payments to be made if any enemy vessels were destroyed, ranging from 60,000 francs for the smallest to 400,000 for the largest; and it would put the naval base at Brest, on the far western edge of Brittany, at his disposal.

In truth, it was not a generous pact. Fulton had already paid out some 20,000 francs for the boat's construction (and still owed, according to Forfait, another 8,000), had paid for three months of experiments and upkeep for a team of three, and now was expected to repair the *Nautilus* after a winter's layup, fit it with appropriate explosives, haul it two hundred miles to Brest, and maintain the crew for another summer of attacks. Of course, there was the teasing possibility of 400,000 francs–$90,000, a veritable fortune–for a thirty-gun ship of the line, but all Fulton was being given for three years of thought and effort was 10,000 francs and the complete responsibility to see the job through on his own.

That was enough. The fire was unquenchable. On March 3, 1801, Fulton accepted.

One other fire–or perhaps more likely two–burned in Robert
Fulton's soul at the time as well: his affection for Ruth and Joel
Barlow.

The record we have of their entanglement comes from
only one side of the triangle, but it is plentiful, and revealing.
During the summer of 1800, while Fulton was at Le Havre
testing his *Nautilus* in Channel waters, he was living with Ruth
at the fashionable Hôtel du Bienvenu, and they were in regular
touch with Joel, left behind in Paris to tend to Fulton's dealings
with the Marine Ministry and busy himself with his dinner parties and his investments. Nothing from the Le Havre lovers remains, but a dozen of Joel's letters survive, and the picture they
provide of the threesome, though filtered through the kind of
baby talk one would not have thought a distinguished poet capable of, suggests a *ménage* of intimacy and passion in all three
directions.

Joel, who generally called himself "hub" in these documents, was secure enough in the durability of what he would
term their "happy trinity"–"Hub noes bote ove [love] hub and
hub noves bote"–that he was content to be a sideline patron of
the summertime affair of the two others. He gave them the use
of a handsome little carriage and two white ponies, and he
wrote that he could imagine Ruth swimming every morning
"and then driving around the countryside with her sweetheart"
in the afternoon. To Fulton–for whom his nickname was
"Toot," never explained–he urged that he "tate dood tare of
nitten wifey [take good care of little wifey]–sant [mustn't]
tweeze too ard–jus ov properly," and to his wife he declared
how pleased he was that she had "run away from hub" to be
with their younger charge and explained that he loved her
more than ever "because I think wifey is happy": "I love your
happiness before all things, independent of the idea of its de-
pending on me."

Of his love for Ruth there was no question, as maudlin as
his words might be–"You are my flesh & my blood, my life and
my soul"–and of his sexual feelings also no doubt: "How hub

ants [wants] de big beautiful hard warm sweet moutens [mouth] to lie in lap." Similarly for Fulton: "Always repeat to him how much I love him; you cannot tell him too much of it," and "Tell toot . . . that the machine of his body is better & more worthy his attention than any other machine that he can make . . . and that unless he could create me one exactly in the image of himself with the materials now in his power, he had better preserve his own automoton *[sic]*."

Two portraits of Joel Barlow exist from about this time, a pencil drawing by John Vanderlyn, carving out the career Fulton had abandoned, and an oil by Fulton. They show a man more self-assured than handsome, with full and sensuous lips, intelligent eyes without much sparkle, and, in his mid-forties, a shock of white hair receding from a very high forehead. One biographer of Fulton says Barlow resembles "an aging satyr," but that is reading too much in; he actually resembles an aging businessman wishing to be a young satyr.

At the end of October, when Fulton and Ruth returned to Paris, the "happy trinity" moved into an elaborate mansion that Joel had purchased for them at 50 Rue de Vaugirard, across from the Jardin du Luxembourg, in one of the finest parts of town. It was a huge affair, occupying most of a block, that Barlow managed to purchase on the cheap from an aristocrat who had lost his wealth in the revolution, and he did not much worry about trying to furnish more than a few of the twenty-two bedrooms, just those that served to meet their purposes, as he put it, "now we are three and must have so many rooms separate and yet compact, adjoining each other so as to be convenient." Fulton was to stay there, happily, for the next three and a half years, the first home he had had since childhood.

Contract in hand, Fulton spent the summer of 1801 in another attempt to destroy the British fleet. It was a fiasco.

First he dutifully transported the *Nautilus* from its layover harbor near Cherbourg, had it repaired from the ravages of the winter, and tested it again, underwater for as long as an hour and forty minutes with the aid of a compressed-air tank he had devised. And then he abandoned it. Without warning, without explanation. Just as David Bushnell himself had discovered twenty-five years earlier, Fulton obviously decided that it was not so easy to maneuver a boat underwater, at least in the open seas, and anyway it should be possible to deliver floating mines to enemy hulls with an ordinary boat, provided it could move essentially undetected. And so, only a year after it was created, the submarine was discarded, never again to be part of Fulton's naval armory.

Then Fulton persuaded the Brest navy yard to build him a 36-foot boat to be propelled by cranks on each side so that neither sails nor oars would be visible. It succeeded in delivering a mine to a stationary hulk anchored in the harbor, but it was too slow and unmaneuverable, and the cranks made a noise that would alert the sleepiest British watch. He abandoned that boat, too.

Next he decided to go with three ordinary longboats that could be rowed to their targets, and he went out with them once in August to attack a small British armada anchored in the Channel. But when the ships came into sight, Fulton concluded that the task was too formidable for his inexperienced crew—and besides, he had not tested the mines and was not sure that they would work. The longboats returned to harbor.

On September 6, the would-be warrior conceded defeat. In a letter to the committee reporting on his progress to Napoleon, he confessed that the *Nautilus* was not fit for underwater warfare and his floating mines needed more work. But, he quickly added, he had a new idea: if the government would build him some *larger* submarines, and stock each with twenty or thirty better mines, he could sneak to the major harbors of England, release the mines (some of which would be timed to explode, others that would go off at impact), and the commerce of the entire nation would be destroyed: "No vessel could pass without the utmost danger of running on one of them and Her instant destruction." That was indeed a peculiar way to ensure the freedom of the seas and promote international commerce, but Fulton was clutching at any straw at this point. Surprisingly, it took the First Consul's fancy, and he asked Fulton to let him see the *Nautilus* so he could better judge what the inventor had in mind.

Here the foxy Fulton had finally outfoxed himself. He had destroyed the submarine—because, so he said, "she leaked Very much and being but an imperfect engine I did not think her further useful," but actually because he was now determined that France would not enjoy any more free ride and should pay him full fare for the construction of new submarines; he assured himself of the job by seeing to it that the *Nautilus* could not be copied by some agent of the Marine Ministry. He argued that the submarine was, after all, his private property that he was free to destroy, and lest they "construe this into an avaricious disposition in me"—as they certainly would—he asserted that he had "now laboured 3 years and at considerable expense to prove my experiments" and thought it only fair to receive the "sufficiency I conceive this invention should secure to me." And he added, as if to explain the sorry record of his summer's trials, "I find that a man who wishes to cultivate the Useful Arts cannot make rapid Progress without sufficient funds to put his succession of Ideas to immediate proof."

When Napoleon heard the news that there was no boat, not only was he convinced of Fulton's "avaricious disposition," he reportedly accused the American of being a fraud and a swindler, trying to extort money on the basis of a nonexistent vehicle and a record of unrelieved failure. No "sufficient funds" from this quarter. Fulton was informed that fall that France had no further interest in his "plunging machine."

It must have been a very dismal winter for Fulton that year. He would not forget the submarine and the floating mines, but he had precious little to show for his nine-year career as mechanical inventor and civil engineer, other than an outdoor *divertissement* that he no longer owned and that hadn't been his idea in the first place. He was now thirty-six years old: where should he turn next? Canals? Maybe, though not in France—perhaps in America, where, as it happened, the Barlows were planning to return soon. The rope-making machine? He had alienated Cutting, who was through backing him on that—and again, it hadn't even been his own idea.

It is probable that the Barlows entertained at their regular pace during this winter, especially to show off their new mansion, and with Fulton went to the usual round of dinners and soirées, where they kept company with such as Lafayette, Kościusko, the Montgolfier brothers, Count Constantin de Volney, most of the American expatriate crowd, including Vanderlyn and Thomas Paine, and many of the important politicians and ministers of the successive French governments. Fulton, charming and enthusiastic, would likely have talked of the mechanical arts, perhaps canals, certainly the submarine, and the subject of steamboats might have come up, for that idea was still very much in the air.

It was at one such gathering, sometime in February or March 1802 (though no one recorded the momentous event), that Robert Fulton, as he later described it, "accidentally met" Robert Livingston—the encounter that would change history.

Livingston, imposing and patrician, growing increasingly deaf at fifty-five, had arrived in Paris the previous December as Jefferson's agent to negotiate the New Orleans matter and maybe buy up a bit of the Spanish territory that Napoleon had acquired. Most of his time was spent fruitlessly waiting around for answers and offers from various Napoleonic henchmen, and he would have been open to the kinds of ideas and passions that Fulton would espouse, particularly those that touched on the "useful arts" and manufactures, and most particularly the one about boats navigating by steam. He would have seen in the younger man the talent and enthusiasm that could bring to life his dream of a steamboat on the Hudson, and Fulton would have been at his most charming and persuasive once he sensed a much-needed patron for an enterprise that would at last put him on the path to his still-abiding dream of "Riches and Fame."

How and when they came to an agreement is not known, and at first it must have been no more than a promise and a handshake, but Fulton set immediately to work. Both having agreed that it would be wisest to purchase an engine in England, preferably from Boulton, Watt, Livingston was left with the diplomatic job of getting permission to export one to America, while Fulton was free to concentrate on the size of the hull and the means of propulsion, the real problems that had beset previous experimenters.

Fulton by now had decided, who knows how, that the solution to the propulsion problem lay in "endless chains," belts with boards that would move in a repeated oval like a tank tread, and he commissioned the craftsman Étienne Calla to make a three-foot model with chains powered by clockwork springs. His plan was to test the model, derive the calculations for the hull, and then, when they got the engine, supervise the construction of a full-scale version, using Livingston's money the while. At the end of April he took his notebooks and went to the fashionable resort town of Plombières, in the Vosges mountains near the German border, to wait for the model to be sent.

Thomas Paine, who, though an Englishman, had done so much to fire the American Revolution, continued his pamphleteering career in England in the years after the French Revolution began until his radical ideas displeased the British establishment, and, after being charged with sedition in 1792, he fled to France. There he lived mostly in Paris, became a member of the revolutionary legislature, and worked diligently on the manuscript he believed would be his most enduring contribution to political thought, to be called *The Age of Reason.*

Among his circle of friends none was closer, at this time, than Joel Barlow, with whom he shared ardent republican and antimonarchical views. It is indeed thanks to this friendship that the manuscript of *The Age of Reason* survived, for after one of the many turns of the French Revolution Paine was held in disfavor, and on Christmas Day 1793 the police came to arrest him. It happened that Barlow was his houseguest at that time, and after being interrogated for several hours Paine managed to thrust his manuscript into Barlow's arms before being bustled off to Luxembourg prison. Barlow, who visited Paine there regularly, tended to the manuscript and was largely responsible for the first part's being published in 1794; Paine, released in November of that year, oversaw the publication of the second part in 1796.

Paine stayed in Paris until 1802 and had occasion to meet Robert Fulton several times. As an inventor himself, he took a marked interest in Fulton's schemes, though he never thought much of the submarine project. In fact, as late as 1807, when he was living in New York City and heard rumors about Fulton's planning a blow-up with his mines in New York harbor, he wrote to Barlow: "What is Fulton about? Is he taming a whale to draw his submarine boat?"

That year, the year of Fulton's triumph, Paine was living on Partition Street—later to become part of a new Fulton Street.

Fulton also took Ruth Barlow to Plombières, and the real reason for picking that town was that it was a resort famous for its curative waters, and Ruth just then had come down with unexplained rashes and tumors on her buttocks and genitalia, what one might assume to be signs of some sexual disease. So once again the two of them got into the little phaeton, and jogged off to the mountains, leaving Joel behind to pursue Parisian nightlife–with, once again, his fond blessings: "What you are about," he wrote, "is a party of pleasure, a summer's recreation," two happy people "turned out like a couple of colts to pasture, romping in the woods, dashing in the water, without a care, breathing the fragrance of spring and tasting the innocence of nature."

Barlow's Plombières letters are even more erotic and explicit than those of two years before, but they convey the same triangularity of affection. Of the complex relationships of the "little holy trinity," he wrote to Ruth: "What a charming toot it is; must always tell him how much hub nubs (loves] him and ipey [wifey] must love him too." And: "Tell toot I love him more than ever man was loved by man. His goodness to little one will not be forgot. Perhaps I shall owe my wife to him at last." Lauding Ruth for her regimen of douching and soaking in the baths to cure her sores, he exulted about her sex: "Praise it! I shall praise it and love it & adore it and flog it & kiss it & fold it up in my soul till it comes, and then in my arms. I shall tell toot to reward it for all its good deeds as it goes along."

Although he approved of Ruth's "fooling with toot," he also thought of Fulton as "playing the rogue" among the elegant women who frequented the spa and even using his sexual charms as the medieval Franciscan monks were reported in ribald tales to have done to supplicants using the spa as a cure for infertility: "I reckon all those fine ladies who come for the purpose of making babies may find the same instruction and sprititual edification from toot as they used to from the barefoot brothers of St. Francis." And he pretended to be jealous for Fulton's affections, warning him that if he didn't "haave [behave] better" he would "sharpen up knife and tut tok [cut cock] off . . . smack smooth goes im toks."

Whether Fulton's roguery was ever as developed as Barlow's imagination made it out to be is doubtful, but he was undoubtedly happy through the summer and he stayed with Ruth at Plombières until the end of the season.

Though it clearly was not the obsession it might have been and his proofs of progress were insufficient to placate Livingston back in Paris, Fulton did not neglect the steamboat. The Calla model was sent to him at the end of May, and he proceeded to make experimental runs with it in a sixty-six-foot basin he had created in a small streambed, some of them apparently under the amused eye of Josephine Bonaparte and her coterie. The results convinced him, as he was always ready to be convinced, that he could build a full-scale boat, 90 feet by 6, that would go at eight miles an hour and make the New York–Albany run in eighteen hours, with a profit of $198 for each trip carrying a full load of fifty passengers; not even a week later he envisioned a boat 120 feet by 8 that would do twelve miles an hour and carry a hundred twenty passengers; and shortly after that he calculated that he could build a boat 200 feet by 12 that would do sixteen miles an hour and make it to Albany in twelve hours.* And so he wrote to Livingston in June, adding that as he saw it their partnership should be based on equal parts of the Chancellor's money and "my time . . . And my knowledge of the Subject," and hence an equal share of the profits, an arrangement decidedly more generous than Livingston had had in mind.

Livingston allowed that he was "perfectly satisfied" with

* Fulton obviously did not know the distance from New York to Albany: his first calculation would make it 144 miles, his last 192 miles. By river it is about 160 miles.

Fulton's calculations, worrying only that the pounding of the engine might shatter the elongated boat Fulton had in mind and that it would not be possible to patent the "endless chain" device since it had already been used in America. According to Barlow, who was negotiating for Fulton in Paris, Livingston seemed "desirous of bringing the thing forward" and there was "no danger of his trying to do this thing without you," since by now the statesman was no doubt persuaded he did not want to repeat his experience with Nicholas Roosevelt. As to a fifty-fifty partnership, however, Livingston made it clear, "the demand you make of half the profits without any risk upon an untried scheme" was "much too great a compensation for the labour & time it will cost you."

Fulton spluttered—not about the partnership but the patent. The endless chain was certainly patentable, he persisted, since just having an idea or even a prototype was not true "invention," but making something work, over and over, was—and "I have no doubt but the patent in America can be made good, that is, if the patent law means to secure to a man a movement of mind or discovery which is commonly called Inventions." Thus began the turmoil over patentability and inventiveness that was, sadly, to bedevil Fulton, often unnecessarily but with endless rancor and exhausting persistence, for the rest of his life.

The futility of which was underscored less than a month later, when Fulton decided that the chain was *not* the best means of steamboat propulsion and was now convinced that "wheel-oars"—paddlewheels, as he came to call them—worked better than chains, leaves, paddles, propellers, or any other device. He contrived a rationale by which they, too, could be patented, even though he knew that others before had used them: "Although the wheels are not a new application," he would write a few months later, after more tests, "yet if I combine them in such a way that a large proportion of the power of the engine acts to propel the boat in the same way as if the purchase was upon the ground[,] the combination will be better than anything that has been done up to the present and it is in fact a new discovery."

On the strength of his new conviction, Fulton returned to Paris in September and continued his haggling with Livingston, which resulted in a signed agreement on October 10, 1802, setting up a company to take out a patent in the United States "for a new mechanical combination of a boat" designed "to run between New York and Albany [at] 8 miles an hour in stagnant water and carry at least 60 passengers." Livingston gave in on the fifty-fifty deal, agreeing to share all profits equally, but he also insisted that Fulton invest equally, each of them taking fifty shares of the company. He agreed to put up the initial £500 for Fulton to go to England and build a prototype, with the hope that they could borrow the engine itself from Boulton, Watt or some other designer, and if trials there succeeded, Fulton was to go on to the United States to oversee construction of a boat to ply the Hudson. If Fulton failed, he would reimburse Livingston half his investment.

Fulton went diligently to work with the new year, but the real achievement that spring was Livingston's.

With his secret acquisition of Spain's possessions in America, Napoleon had hoped to establish an empire in the Americas, but had not had much luck at it. The black colony of Haiti rebelled and overthrew French domination, the army he sent to quell the rebellion in 1801 was destroyed by yellow fever and the fierce resistance of the former slaves, and the fleet he planned to send to retake it was iced in over the 1802–03 winter. How was he going to control the vast territory along the Mississippi if he could not even establish dominion over the little half-island of Haiti? And was it worth it? Perhaps Europe should be the focus of his attention, and another attempt to invade that annoying nation of shopkeepers on the island to the north—with which he was now technically at peace, though he was using the truce merely to assemble the wherewithal to reopen the war at the earliest opportunity.

In his bath on the morning of April 11, 1803, Napoleon was struck by a forcible thought: he could get the money to mount an invasion of Britain by selling not just the New Orleans entrepôt but the entire Louisiana Territory to the Americans, who would have to find the necessary sums by borrowing from (and thus depleting) British banks—and if the invasion was successful, he would end up owning the banks the Americans would owe money to, thus being paid twice for land that was, after all, a trackless wilderness and that France owned only nominally and could not control. He sent word by his foreign minister, Charles de Talleyrand, who startled Livingston one night by asking, "What would you give for the whole?"

Livingston, then joined by James Monroe, whom Jefferson had sent out to speed up the protracted negotiations, had no good answer, since he was not authorized by Congress (or, for that matter, the Constitution) to buy "the whole," whose extent no one was sure of in the first place, and since he knew that whatever France would ask for was far more than the American treasury contained. Long nights of dickering ensued, but finally the Americans offered to pay the equivalent of $15 million, and the French, who had not expected to reap that much, accepted. It was, despite its fundamental illegitimacy, the greatest real estate deal in history; as Livingston said to Monroe, "We have lived long, but this is the noblest work of our lives."

The purchase agreement, dated April 30, was signed on May 2. Two weeks later Napoleon resumed his war with Britain.

⚜

Although contractually obliged to build a steamboat to ply the Hudson, Fulton knew from the outset that it would be on the Mississippi and its major tributaries that the steamboat would have its most consequential impact: "My first aim in busying myself with this," he wrote to the French Conservatory of Arts and Trades in January 1803, "was to put it in practice upon the long rivers of America where there are no roads suitable for haulage." Now that what his colleague Livingston had accomplished made it certain that America would own and develop those long rivers, he must have been even more energized in his steamboat work.

Fulton never admitted that he had learned anything from his many predecessors, but as he continued his experiments in Paris that spring he was in a singular position to have had access to more steamboat information than probably anyone else before. He had studied a model that had been exhibited in Paris the previous year by a French inventor named Desblancs (and pointed out why he was sure it would not work), he could well have seen the plans of Jouffroy's first steamboat in Jacques Périer's possession, he knew of Lord Stanhope's experiments and possibly of James Rumsey's in London, he was reported to have studied for "several months" drawings and specifications John Fitch had left in Paris, and of course he had a partner who had tried his own boat and was familiar with the work of Nicholas Roosevelt and John Stevens. In addition, he made use of two studies available in Paris, an account of underwater resistance published by Marc Beaufoy in 1798 and a work on ship resistance by the mathematician Charles Bossut, and with them calculated the water pressure one might expect from various kinds of paddlewheels or oars, and what hull shapes would be most efficient for them. In this he went well beyond the abstract calculations Lord Stanhope had made and far beyond the trial-and-error methods of most other steamboaters: his was an attempt to provide a scientific basis for mechanical development, a theoretical substructure for his designs, and though there was much imperfect in his reckonings and analysis, the effort may well have been the first time that such a process–now considered the hallmark of modern invention–was ever applied to the creation of boats of any kind.

Early in the spring of 1803, Fulton and Livingston gave up on the plan to borrow an engine from Boulton, Watt and turned to Jacques Périer again, and Étienne Calla for the boiler, while Fulton oversaw the construction of the hull. The machinery was installed in the frame sometime in May and lay tied up in the Seine near Périer's factory for all to see–"two large wheels mounted on an axle like a cart," said the *Journal des débats,* and behind them "a kind of large stove with a pipe"–and perhaps to consider for some sabotage. One night, at any rate, the boat was broken apart and the machinery sank to the bottom of the river, according to the papers the work of "evil-minded persons," most probably some of the sailors and bargemen who saw the steamboat as a threat to their future and chose a Luddistic response. Fulton later recounted that he was awakened that night by a messenger from the docks exclaiming, "Oh sir, the boat has broken in pieces, and gone to the bottom," and said that at that moment he felt a greater despondency than he had ever known before. He rushed down to the river nonetheless and worked through the night and the next day without food or rest to raise the machinery, an exertion he subsequently blamed for a permanent effect on his health, particularly a dyspeptic and increasingly delicate stomach.

At the end of July, when a new hull had been built and the machinery reinstalled, Fulton announced that he was ready to have the public, including a delegation from the eminent National Institute, witness the boat's initial run. In the late afternoon of August 9 he fired up the engine and, with three helpers, moved out into the river, towing two boats behind, and headed upstream. The boat went against the current for about a mile, at a speed one newspaper account guessed to be almost three miles an hour, then turned and went with the current at a slightly faster speed, and "for an hour and a half," the *Journal des débats* reported, "he afforded the curious spectacle of a boat moved by wheels like a cart, these wheels being provided with paddles or flat plates and being moved by a fire engine." It was, the paper exulted, *"un succès complet et brillant,"* and if it were properly applied to France's rivers "would be fraught with the most advantageous consequences to our internal navigation."

Though "the author of this brilliant invention" left no record of his own—nor were Livingston and Barlow on hand to register their responses—Fulton must have been well pleased with this first trial, for everything had gone without a hitch. The basic steamboat problems that Benjamin Latrobe had laid out just four months earlier to the American Philosophical Society had been solved—much as Fitch, by trial and error, had solved them—by capturing most of the steam power in the cylinder and applying it directly to the wheels. The speed was a good deal less than the sixteen miles per hour Fulton had promised, but the success of the design principles—a long and narrow hull (about 75 by 8 feet), shallow and tapered at the bow to minimize resistance; extra-large paddlewheels (12 feet in diameter) with ten arms to maximize propulsion; a powerful engine (24 horsepower), kept from damaging the deck by resting on a beam that distributed its force across the hull—indicated that this might be bettered in the future. Especially as he was sure that with top-grade machinery from Boulton, Watt, he would be able to achieve the speed he needed to satisfy the Livingston contract. And he decided then to discard the idea of the steamboat as a freight barge, finding the tow-boats too much of a drag on the boat's momentum, and he never tried that arrangement again.[2]

One person who was keenly interested in this trial was Napoleon, now made Consul for Life, who had resumed war with Britain and was planning the invasion of perfidious Albion from the proceeds of his sale of Louisiana. On July 21, having received an account of the goings-on at the Périer works, Napoleon had demanded that a commission from the National Institute immediately report on "the project of Citizen Fulton," which he complained he had heard about, strangely, "too late to permit it to change the face of the world," though he obviously saw its potential as the means of conquering the Channel. A delegation from the Institute was duly dispatched to the trial, and its report, which does not survive, must not have been nearly as favorable as that of the *Journal des débats,* for Napoleon did not contact the inventor and never referred to the steamboat again.

One account of dubious veracity has Napoleon again assessing Fulton as a charlatan and impostor,[3] but it is more likely he figured that a boat that could do only four miles an hour on a calm river going with the current would never make it across the choppy Channel—an accurate assessment, which even Fulton would probably have agreed with—and after the submarine fiasco he had no reason to put much trust in Fulton anyway. But how history might have been changed had Napoleon had a little more patience and enthusiasm, for it was not more than six years later that a steamboat proved it could handle the (not too rough) open seas.

Napoleon's lack of interest is understandable, but what is quite peculiar is that almost nothing substantial was done by either Fulton or Livingston for the whole next year to put their project into effect. Fulton did write to Boulton, Watt in August, specifying in some detail what kind of engine he wanted the firm to build and ship to New York (a request he repeated in September), but when the company replied in October that it could not get an export permit from the British government (understandably uninterested in helping a man who had been trying to destroy its fleet), Fulton seems to have laid the matter aside. He also sent off two rather hapless letters to James Monroe, then the American ambassador in London, asking for help that never came, but thereafter nothing indicates that he tried to find some other manufacturer, not even the dutiful Jacques Périer, to build his engine. Livingston, for his part, was not heard from at all: he and his family spent August in Switzerland, so he missed the demonstration, but there is no record that when he returned to Paris he heaped praise, or money, on his younger partner or even that they celebrated the achievement. He was preoccupied primarily with trying to establish the primacy of his role over Monroe in the Louisiana negotiations, to which his part in steam navigation might now seem largely secondary, and he did not even mention his involvement in the Fulton steamboat to his friend Lafayette. He did nothing in the one area where his experience might have been valuable—using his diplomatic contacts in England to secure an export license—and of course be had no intention of asking Monroe for assistance in that.

It is wondrous strange, and there is no good explanation. The two men, seemingly on the verge of success in a project by which they had both set so much store, were not fired with the possibilities, did not hold heated meetings or exchange urgent letters, did not engage Périer or consider alternative manufacturers. Indeed, through the long and desultory winter and into the spring of 1804, it looked as if the steamboat on the Hudson might never be built.

Two portraits of Fulton survive from this period. One is a sculpted bust in marble (paid for by Barlow) by the eminent Jean-Antoine Houdon, aptly renowned for his psychological insights in stone, showing a handsome and confident figure fixing a rather steely gaze on the world, the shadow of a smile that might almost be sardonic on his lips, a face not untroubled but with a willful force behind it. The other is a self-portrait in oils that shows something of the same confidence, almost arrogance, but only hints at inner strengths and instead bears unmistakable traces of sorrow and fright, and an aura of what might be despondency. Looking at them side by side, it is the self-portrait that seems better to reveal the Fulton of this period–and the sculpture that reveals the man that will be.

5.

1804–1807

ONE TANGIBLE REASON for Robert Fulton's haphazard approach to getting a steam engine and launching a steamboat might have been the rekindling of his old passion for his submarine and his underwater mines, this time around from the most unexpected source: the government of the nation whose fleet he had built the submarine to destroy.

The British knew all about Fulton's earlier efforts with the *Nautilus* and probably knew that after the French government had turned him down in 1801 he had done nothing more with it. But since the Peace of Amiens had broken down in May 1803 and France had resumed its preparations for an invasion of England with an ever-growing fleet at Boulogne, it occurred to someone in the Admiralty Office that it might be a good idea to be sure that the French did not resurrect the "plunging machine" and its fiendish "torpedoes" to assist them. Consequently, an agent of the British secret service named only "Mr. Smith"–an American, perhaps a friend of Fulton's, but never identified–turned up in Paris sometime in mid-1803 to see whether Fulton would be open to coming to London and building his devices there for the British to use against the French.

Fulton, apparently without hesitation, said that he would, and he was ready with his terms (as he later recounted): £10,000 ($50,000) for going to England, £10,000 more to build a submarine capable of carrying thirty hundred-pound mines, and £100,000 for showing the British how to build and use the weapons: "As these inventions are the product of my labors for some years, I now consider them as rich gems drawn from the mines of science and which I and my friends have a right to convert to our own advantage." (Advantage indeed: £10,000 was twice the $25,000 salary of the president of the United States at the time.) Smith carried the terms to London, but because of weather and the war could not get back to the continent until December, when Fulton met him in Amsterdam; no agreement was reached, Fulton revised his demands somewhat, and finally the two met again secretly in March 1804 in Paris, where Fulton agreed to £800 for traveling expenses and some vague terms of Britain's "utmost liberality and Generosity."

Fulton then wrapped up his affairs in Paris in great haste, suggesting to both Livingston and Barlow that he was on his way to New York and was stopping only briefly in England, and perhaps would be able to go to Boulton, Watt personally about the engine. In fact, he was consumed with the possibility that at last his submarine dream would be realized and he would have the riches he deserved. On April 29 he left Paris.

Britain's motives in this are not hard to ascertain, even its willingness to hire a man who had tried to attack its fleet, but Fulton's seem particularly tawdry and amoral, perhaps traitorous. It is true that he was the citizen of a technically neutral country and theoretically was free to sell his ideas to any nation willing to pay for them; it is also true that France had had an opportunity and had refused. Yet he was now to build a serious weapon of war to be used against the country that had been his host for the past six years and whose revolutionary government, even in its Napoleonic phase, was close enough to his republican beliefs that he continued to support it and indeed commit acts of war on its behalf. He was also materially helping the country that had shown open hostility to his native land, blocked American ports, and occasionally boarded American ships, and arming it with weapons that could effectively destroy the fledgling U.S. navy and place a chokehold on every American harbor. And if they really did succeed finally in eliminating warships and securing that "liberty of the seas," as he claimed to believe, the effect of that would be to ensure the primacy of the massive British merchant fleet over the meager American one for generations to come.

Worse still, it no longer seemed that the grandiose notions of open seas and free trade were uppermost in his mind, for he did not believe that the British actually intended to put his weapons into operation—because they would understand that if the method of unfailingly blowing up warships became widely known, it would be more disastrous for the dominant British navy than anyone else. Fulton went to England, as he later wrote candidly, to "exhibit the principles of my engines to the government, and should they conceive that the introduction of them into practice in France, America, or elsewhere to be injurious to the interests of Great Britain, I proposed to take the value of one ship of the line of £100,000 to let the discovery lie dormant." Dormant: in other words, he simply intended to blackmail the British into buying up his invention so that they could suppress it, and was content to see his professed dream of freedom of the seas and perpetual peace be squelched for £100,000 in his pocket. "I came here," he told the British frankly, "to acquire wealth by communicating a new system to the government."

In the event, Fulton did not wrest that kind of money from Britain, but he did arrive at a deal that gave him more money than he had ever had—and, remarkably, without even proving that his inventions could work.

Arriving in London in the middle of May, after a circuitous route and with a cover name of "Robert Francis" that he would use for his stay in England, Fulton drew up a set of plans and drawings for the submarine and water mines, which he submitted to the government of William Pitt. A commission was duly appointed and in June reported that it saw promise in the mines but regarded the submarine itself as expensive, unproven, and unnecessary; as Pitt later told Fulton directly, it would be "some years" before the submarine would be perfected, and Britain had no appreciable need of it, since "those who command the seas" would be able to deliver the mines by ordinary rowboat. Fulton professed outrage that his invention had been so dismissed, particularly because it meant he would not be paid for its suppression, but he submerged his anger at the prospect of at least getting to use his mines and making, for the first time, some real money. The terms he set were stiff (though milder than his original demands), yet he must have sensed the government's eagerness: £200 a month in salary, £7,000 for expenses to build and demonstrate the mines against the French, £40,000 for proving the superiority of his weapons against all other methods of destruction, and one-half the value of any ship destroyed under his supervision, one-fourth if he was absent, for fourteen years, during which time he pledged not to divulge his secrets to any other nation. The British government agreed, and on July 20, 1804, Robert Fulton was on his way to becoming rich.

As a favor to Fulton, the Pitt government agreed to let him have a permit to have his steam engine built, though it stipulated that be would need a further permit before he could export it. Fulton seized on the offer and went to Birmingham in early July to meet with Matthew Boulton—Watt had by then retired from the business—and to place an order in person for a £380 engine, with condenser and air pump. Boulton was apparently cold to this American intruder, rebuffing his notions about some kind of partnership "to promote useful improvements," but he was willing to build the devices according to Fulton's drawings and instructions. The work was completed in December and sent to Fulton in London in February 1805, the cost having escalated to £548 to execute the air pump in brass instead of copper, as Fulton had directed; together with a 4,399-pound copper boiler, made in London for £477, the working parts of what was to become the first successful steamboat operation were ready for shipping in March, and Fulton was given permission to send them to America.

Fulton's mind, however, was elsewhere.

In the summer of 1804, Fulton attended to the building of an arsenal of his underwater mines at the Portsmouth navy yard on the Channel, and by October he was ready to make an attempt to cripple the invasion fleet at Boulogne. On the night of October 2, a number of rafts with seamen dressed in black, along with five small boats, were dropped from an Admiralty ship and paddled into the outer harbor, where they set loose a flotilla of twenty mines—wooden boxes packed with gunpowder and stones and sealed with tar, some as long as eighteen feet and weighing as much as two tons—designed to be carried by the tide under the anchored ships and to explode by contact or by clockwork detonator. There is some dispute as to how many of the mines actually blew up that night, and at least some did go off, but it was not many and the only casualties seem to have been a small pinnace and her crew, a loss the French kept secret; Fulton himself, who spent the night waiting at the British base in Dover, acknowledged that of the 130 gunboats under attack, "my opinion is that very few were destroyed and the others made their escape." Another attack was made in December, against a fort in the Calais harbor; here only one of three mines exploded, doing minor damage to an outer wall. Thus, after six months and a £8,200 investment, Britain learned that Fulton's mines could explode underwater—which, from monitoring Fulton's activities at Le Havre, it already knew—and that they were not really so efficient at destroying enemy ships.

Having proved a failure, and opposed by a good many naval officers and conservative politicians as a scurrilous departure from the just principles of war, the mine project might reasonably have ended there and then and Fulton been sent packing. Nonetheless, Lord Pitt, perhaps not wanting to deprive his naval quiver of any arrows, however flawed, as long as Napoleon had a sizable fleet at the ready just thirty miles off the English coast, continued to keep Fulton on salary into the next year, though he ordered that the mines already made be stored at the Portsmouth base and refused to sanction the building of more. Fulton, for his part, while saying he was "fully satisfied" with the government's "liberal mode" of salary, chafed at the inactivity as the next year stretched on and kept pressing officialdom for another chance to prove his worth. Not once, evidently, did he ever think to abandon his ill-fated experiment and go off to America to try his hand at something he knew would work.

Springtime came and the Channel was passable again, but Pitt sent no word. Summer came and the French fleet expanded to 1,800 invasion barges, and still no word. Finally, in August, Fulton shot off a most intemperate letter to Pitt demanding that he be given a squadron to carry his torpedoes up and down the French coast, or else he would be "willing to retire" and accept the £100,000 "to let the discovery lie dormant."

Perhaps it was this letter, perhaps it was the failure of the British fleet to penetrate Napoleon's defenses at Boulogne, but at last the government authorized another mine attack and permitted Fulton to construct a hundred new copper bomb cases. On the night of September 30, 1805, with Fulton again confined to dockside, several small boats made their way into the Boulogne harbor, attached mines to the anchor cables of two French brigs, and successfully rowed away under musket fire. At least one of the mines exploded, but without result: no ships were damaged, none was sunk, and the French reported no casualties except one wounded seaman. "The torpedoes," Fulton wrote with wry understatement, "did not produce the desired effect."

And still the game went on. Somehow, after all this, Fulton managed to extract permission from the British government to demonstrate the power of his mines by blowing up a captured Danish brig lying at anchor in the harbor at Deal, north of Dover. On October 15, in front of a crowd of naval brass and excited onlookers, Fulton set the clockwork on a 180-pound mine, had it carried out and grappled to the ship's anchor cable, and then thrown into the water at a depth of about fifteen feet. The tide carried the box under the brig, and in minutes, as Fulton proudly wrote, "the explosion seemed to raise her bodily about six feet; she separated in the middle, and the two ends went down; in twenty seconds nothing was to be seen of her except floating fragments; the pumps and foremast were blown out of her; the fore-topsail-yard was thrown up to the crosstrees," and so on in the same excited vein. And then, almost as if the explosion made him realize for the first time what a powerful device he was playing with, he wrote that the demonstration was "the most tremendous and frightful and carries with it the reflection which gives me some pain that in vessels thus attacked it will be impossible to save the men—and many a worthy character must perish."

Even though Fulton had now demonstrated that his mines could really do considerable damage—if, as Ichabod Fungus might say, they could be put in place in daylight, with the right tide, below an unmanned and defenseless ship riding at anchor—there was very little enthusiasm at the upper levels for continuing the enterprise. One high-ranking officer expressed the navy's consensus that despite the fact that Fulton's mines had proved able to blow up ships, "placing them is a perilous business; his boats are too ticklish for these seas"; and another more bluntly denounced them as "a mode of war which they who commanded the seas did not want, and which if successful would deprive them of it." The one notable exception was Robert Stewart, Viscount Castlereagh, then secretary of war and beginning a long ministerial career, who authorized a handsome reward of £10,000 to Fulton for providing a means "of annoying the enemy in their own ports with little comparative risk to ourselves." But when, in late October, Horatio Nelson annihilated the French fleet at Trafalgar and Napoleon withdrew his troops from Boulogne to fight on the eastern front, the danger of invasion was over and the diabolical inventions of the clever Mr. Fulton were no longer needed. Early the next year, his £200-a-month salary was canceled.

Some men might have given up at that point; Fulton, seemingly obsessed with his "tremendous and frightful" weaponry, did not. For the next entire year, in letter after increasingly threatening letter, he badgered the government to let him show off his mines again, and to pay him the tens of thousands of pounds he was worth—or else, contrary to what he had pledged in his original agreement with Pitt, he would go public with his inventions and let the whole world build underwater mines. This letter to Pitt in January 1806 suggests the tone:

> I will not disguise that I feel the power which I possess is no less than to be the means of giving to the world a System which must from necessity sweep all military marines from the ocean by giving to the weaker maritime powers Advantages over the stronger which the Strong cannot prevent. . . . It must be observed I did not come here so much with a view to do you any material good as to Shew that I have the power and might in

> *the exercise of my plan to acquire fortune, do you an Infinate In-*
> *jury, which Ministers, if they thought proper, might prevent by*
> *an arrangement with me.*

The "arrangement" he was asking for was £60,000 and £200 a month for life. Fortune, indeed.

That the various men of government to whom Fulton appealed did not respond to this rather unscrupulous blackmail, or dismissed him curtly, did not lessen his ardor, or his avarice: "Let any man place himself in my situation," he wrote in April 1806, "and then ask himself if he has not a right to convert his labours into fame and emolument, for what other objects do men labour?" On and on the demands went, until finally by the summer Fulton was threatening to make all of his weapons material public, a move that the government so decidedly wanted to avoid, having conducted the affair in secrecy, that it agreed to an arbitration hearing in August. At the session Fulton defended his schemes in great detail, even claiming he needed money because he had "two friends who have been kind to me and are more governed by the hope of gain than I am"—if they really existed, we have no idea of who they were—and then proceeded to read a statement with the surprising assertion that there was no amount of money that would persuade him to suppress his inventions "should my Country at any time have need of them." Why Fulton would undermine his case with this display of newfound patriotism is a mystery, after so long trying to exact a fortune to buy his silence, but the arbitrators took it seriously and regarded it as reason enough not to award him anything at all for his ideas. The importuning inventor would get an extra £1,000 above the £4,000 salary he had already received, he would be allowed to keep the £10,000 from Lord Castlereagh, and he would be given £647 he had requested for expenses. Nothing more.

Not ungenerous, especially given that Fulton's devices remained unproven in warfare, but not the fortune he had spent the last two and a half years expecting and pleading for. He denounced the arbitrators and began a correspondence with Lord Grenville, who had become prime minister after Pitt's death in January, demanding a hearing before the full cabinet and promising (as he had no power to) that the mines would never be used against Britain if he were granted his proper reward and annuity. It is clear from these letters that he was planning to publish them all, since he now painted himself as an American patriot who first had offered his underwater scheme to Jefferson and only when rebuffed had turned to Britain–for which there is no substance–and who in any case was more interested in offering his nation a steamboat, "of more immediate use to my country than submarine navigation." And indeed, in late September, Fulton had the correspondence printed in a small book he said he was giving to a few individuals close to the negotiations, affording them one last chance to come up with his reward before he went public with his devices; at the same time he told the arbitrators that if he did not receive his due–now it was £40,000 down and an annual fee of £3,000– he would take measures that would end with the subjugation of the entire British Isles.

Presumably the government regarded these intemperate threats as evidence of an increasingly unstable mind and not worth taking seriously, for it made no response to Fulton's booklet at all. (One of the men who dealt with Fulton at this time, the maritime engineer John Rennie, later said of him, "I consider Fulton, with whom I was personally acquainted, a man of very slender abilities though possessing much self confidence and consummate impudence.") Fulton was sent his £1,647 and, much to his chagrin, thereafter ignored. That meant, in his eyes, that he was now free, as he wrote Barlow in September, "to burn, sink, and destroy whom I please, and I shall now seriously set about giving liberty to the seas by publishing my system of attack." It mattered not that this violated his previous promises, that its reasoning was not coherent, that no nation around wished to support him, or that all his various experiments with his "system of attack" against a real enemy had failed: this was a flame that would not be extinguished.

⁂

Although the British dealings with Fulton were done in secret and the public had no knowledge of the details, it would have been no surprise to George Gordon, Lord Byron, that it was Castlereagh who was the single official to reward Fulton for his underwater mines and with a generosity that amounted to thirty times what the French government had been willing to pay him. For Castlereagh was probably the most militaristic and coldhearted of a generation of ruthless British leaders, for whom war had no scruples and the suppression of dissent no limitation, which made him fair game for Byron at his satirical best. In *Don Juan* he termed him an "intellectual eunuch" and pictured him thus:

Cold-blooded, smooth-fac'd, placid miscreant!
*   Dabbling its sleek young hands in Erin's gore,*
And thus for wider carnage taught to pant,
*   Transferr'd to gorge upon a sister shore,*
The vulgarest tool that Tyranny could want,
*   With just enough of talent, and no more.*

Percy Shelley was even more lacerating. In his *Mask of Anarchy* he imagines Castlereagh in a dance of death:

I met Murder on the way–
He had a mask like Castlereagh–
Very smooth he looked, yet grim;
Seven blood-hounds followed him . . .
He tossed them human hearts to chew
Which from his wide cloak he drew.

It is fitting that Castlereagh was the one to reward
Fulton, for he was a man who bore a great measure of that
ability to understand the world in terms of interests rather
than principles that characterized the American's dealings over the torpedoes. It is further fitting that it was
Castlereagh, as foreign minister, who helped bring on the
War of 1812 with the United States, thus giving Fulton
the opportunity to use his inventive weaponry on behalf
of his native land—and to try to use his underwater mines
in a little private war against the British.

※

While he was going through his rounds of entreaty and com-
plaint during his two and a half years in England, Fulton seems
to have lived a full social life, including dinner parties and the
opera, without any pretense of actually being the "Robert
Francis" he was officially supposed to be.

The winter of 1804–05 was spent with the Barlows at lodgings on Bedford Square while they sought treatment for the
still-ailing Ruth, and Joel worked on his massive *Columbiad,* an
expanded version of *The Vision of Columbus* that had won him
modest fame in 1787. For the new edition, he wanted a series of
New World scenes illustrated by the English artist Robert
Smirke, which he asked Fulton to have engraved in London
and sent to his Philadelphia printer; as the frontispiece for his
epic he wanted a portrait of himself, which Fulton dutifully executed, in properly flattering fashion, that winter. Though the
Barlows set sail for America in May, the "happy trinity" fully
expected to continue their *ménage* in the near future, even
though Fulton would be obliged to start out in New York while
building his steamboat and Joel wanted to be near the seats of
power in Washington City, as it then was called; as Fulton en-
visioned it in a letter to his Dutch friend Vanstaphast in 1806,
he intended to "settle down comfortable" with a friend (presumably Barlow) among "the pleasures of our Athenian

garden in America," and he invited the Dutchman to join them.

Barlow continued to be a faithful friend to Fulton, though by then he had obviously soured on the whole water-mine scheme and probably told him so. He took pains to write a letter to several influential Americans, including President Jefferson, effectively disavowing "my friend Fulton's European projects" and offering the explanation that, "convinced in himself that he is right, his mind has taken a strong hold of his subject and presses forward to the completion of his views, in whatever country he can find a footing for his machines, regardless of the momentary opinions of his friends or enemies"–a very good description of Fulton's obsessiveness. But Barlow did not abandon his younger companion and ended with praise for "his humane views, his facility in the useful arts . . . & his excellent moral character."

As for the other partner in the trinity, there is little evidence as to how she felt about the inventor or his project or even whether the closeness that had been achieved in the Plombières summer of 1802 survived; if she wrote to Fulton while they were apart for six months in 1804 or after she settled in America in mid-1805, no letters survive. One tantalizing indication of her and Joel's feelings at this time is an imploring letter from Joel trying to talk their "very dear and excellent friend" out of marrying a wealthy Englishwoman whom Fulton apparently was courting in January 1806: "We see in it at least the wreck of our most brilliant projects of domestic happiness, if not of public usefulness. . . . Is the mighty fabric vanished? It seems forever gone." Whether Fulton was moved by this plea there is no way to know, and no other reference to this woman exists, but he did not marry her and was still single when he returned to America.

Another couple close to Fulton during those days in London was Benjamin West and his wife, Elizabeth, who seem to have provided a hospitable hearth, especially after the Barlows left. Two years earlier Fulton had done something to affront

West deeply, perhaps during the Wests' visit to Paris in 1802, and it was serious enough for Joel Barlow to visit West in London shortly thereafter to mediate with him; the nature of the offense is unknown, Barlow referring to it only as "a certain proposition" at which the painter was "very much offended" (sexual? financial? political?), but he was apparently successful in smoothing things over, because the rift had healed by 1804. West even agreed to paint Fulton's portrait in 1806, a generous act for a man so busy–the painting shows an intense dark man almost arrogant with satisfaction, sitting before a window through which a ship, an image of the Danish brig at Deal, is being blown in two–and he also gave Fulton a double portrait of himself painting his wife, done probably the same year.

Of the one other elder figure in Fulton's life there is almost no trace. Robert Livingston had left England in May 1804 and returned to America, but there is no surviving evidence in the archives that he was in touch with his ostensible partner or that Fulton informed him he had a steam engine ready to go in early 1805. The Chancellor must have been stewing in anxiety, especially since by his monopoly arrangement–which he had already used his influence to have extended past its 1804 expiration date–he had to have a boat running successfully by April 1807. He could not have been pleased that, if he had any word of Fulton's doings in England, it was all about his infernal water mines.

With the handsome sums from the British government, Fulton could count himself a man of substance even if he never got the full rewards he felt were due. And he spent like one.

According to a reckoning he made in September 1806, Fulton invested some £2,000 in paintings (including two of Benjamin West's that he acquired at auction for £341), some of which he allowed would be the nucleus of a museum of fine arts that Charles Willson Peale was establishing in Philadelphia. Later that year he paid out £2,000 more for the engraving of Barlow's *Columbiad* plates, bearing the whole cost, he said, to return the Barlows' generosity during the years in Paris. He sent at least $900 to his brothers and sisters in Pennsylvania, which seems a bit skimpy, though of course he had not had any contact with them for years. And he managed to put together a rather stunning wardrobe that bore out Beau Brummel's remark at the time that a gentleman in London could not spend less than £1,000 a year to dress properly; it included, according to his "memorandum" of April 1806, "23 fine shirts, 11 night shirts, 50 cravats, 27 pocket handkerchiefs," no fewer than twenty-one waistcoats of different colors, eleven pairs of breeches, three pairs of pantaloons, five coats and three "great coats," one "swimming waistcoat and pantaloons," "5 pair shoes, 3 pair half boots, 3 pair whole boots," two pairs of sheets, and thirteen towels.

In a letter to Barlow after the arbitration procedure, Fulton reckoned that he had been given £15,000 in all by the British government—the equivalent of $75,000—including his salary and the £10,000 bonus, and what he had left from that, plus the nearly £2,000 Barlow somehow owed him from their Paris days, would give him an annual interest income of £500. Including the £200 he had left over from expenses on the water mines, the steam engine now sent to New York, and his £2,000 worth of paintings, there was every reason for him to write, "Therefore, I am not in a state to be pitied." And to add, "I am in excellent health—never better and in good spirits."

It had taken him twenty years, but finally, at the age of forty, Fulton had arrived at the position of life that he had so long aspired to. Only one thing was lacking: he had not yet *done* anything, or anything consequential, had not yet achieved the renown he knew he deserved. Perhaps best to return to America, see the steamboat project through—and try to sell torpedoes to the United States.

In 1806, the year that Fulton became a man of means, Patrick Colquhoun, an English scholar, wrote *A Treatise on Indigence,* in which he attempted to lay out the distribution of wealth in England according to income per family for what he termed "Aristocracy," "Middle Ranks," and "Lower Orders." As he calculated it, there were only 2,854 families with incomes greater than the £2,400 annual salary Fulton had enjoyed: 2,000 well-to-do merchants, 540 baronets, 287 peers, 26 bishops, and the royal family itself. Not even the ordinary English gentleman, of which he estimated there to be 20,000, enjoyed that sort of income, for his was calculated to be closer to £700 a year on average.

As to the annual income of £500 that Fulton anticipated would be his lot in the near future, that placed him on the same rank in Colquhoun's chart as some 5,000 shipowners, 1,000 upper clergy, and 40 "lunatic keepers." It was substantially above the income of ordinary lawyers (£350), those in the arts and sciences (£260), surveyors and engineers (£200), and fourteen times as much as the average income of the million or so families who made up the "lower orders" and constituted half the population.

In American terms, that £500 was $2,500, and it probably placed Fulton in an even more rarefied category in a land where wealth was more widely spread. Although it was Robert Livingston's belief that a gentleman had to have an income of at least $15,000 a year, there were probably not more than a few thousand families with that kind of wealth, and most of that was inherited.

The Fire of His Genius

It was sometime shortly after the disappointing arbitration hearing that Fulton decided to sail back to America at last, and he booked passage on a packet ship leaving from Falmouth at the end of October. It was not an especially good time to cross the North Atlantic—Fulton decided to leave a copy of his submarine and steamboat plans with the American consul in London in case anything should happen to him and arranged to have his paintings shipped in the spring, when the passage was safer—and the stormy voyage ended up taking seven weeks. When he docked in New York on December 13, 1806, he returned to very different circumstances from those he had left twenty years before.

A Washington newspaper, the *National Intelligencer,* greeted Fulton's arrival a week later with a notice, probably instigated by Joel Barlow, citing him as the "author of various improvements in *civil engineering* and the *mechanical arts* which have secured him a lasting reputation in Europe," something of an exaggeration, and asserting that "his return will be an important acquisition to our country in the various branches of public improvement," especially through "his system of *submarine navigation* [that] may be advantageously united with our *gun boats* to form the cheapest and surest defense of our harbors and coasts." There was no mention of steamboats at all.

Fulton certainly knew how important steamboats might be in the development of America, and in fact in February had calculated down to pennies per pound just how successful a boat on the Mississippi would be, hoping to persuade Livingston to invest in that project. He also believed that he could establish a passenger line on the Hudson that would be popular enough, by his calculations, to bring in more than $30,000 a year. And yet steam navigation always seemed to be a secondary consideration for him, as if he could not really imagine what a transformation, not only of transport but of economic and social life, it would be able to effect. As he wrote Barlow that spring, "I will not admit that it is half so important as the torpedo

112

system of defense and attack," because, as he still professed, "out of this will grow the liberty of the seas, an object of infinite importance to the welfare of America and every civilized country."

It was this persistent belief that must explain why Fulton was so dawdling about setting to work on the Hudson steamboat, although he knew the deadline for securing the monopoly was in April and he would need to start passenger operations in the early summer to maximize the travel season, and profits, before the river froze. Although he wrote to Livingston immediately after landing in New York, declaring he was "now ready to carry" the project forward, he nonetheless went off to Philadelphia to be reunited with the Barlows, who were living there temporarily so that Joel could supervise the printing of his *Columbiad,* and after that the three decamped for Washington. Fulton stayed there a month, enjoying a fast-paced social life–whose high point was a triumphal banquet in honor of Meriwether Lewis, recently returned from his epochal trip to the Pacific–and his only steamboat work seems to have been an examination of the twelve patents that had so far been granted for American steamboats, "not one of which," he told Livingston, "approaches to practicability." Back in Philadelphia, he carried on long-distance negotiations with Livingston about who was to pay how much to whom and when, and still tried to interest the Chancellor in a steamboat on the Mississippi, where, he was now predicting, they could soon net $500,000 a year.

Livingston, a New Yorker body and breeches, had little interest in the Mississippi and a good deal at stake–and a monopoly besides–on the Hudson, and he must have conveyed that with some little heat because Fulton moved up to New York with dispatch and started to fulfill the contract the two men had made four and a half years earlier. By mid-March he could report that "the boat is now building" at the shipyard of Charles Brownne at Corlear's Hook, the part of lower Manhattan that projected into the East River at about Grand Street, and soon afterward he paid the customs duties to retrieve the steam engine that had been lying in storage.[1] Later in March he wrote that "I have now Ship Builders, Blacksmiths and Carpenters occupied at New York in building and executing the machinery of my Steam Boat" and estimated that it would require four more months before it was finished. "Like every enthusiast," he added, "I have no doubt of success." That was of course well past the monopoly deadline, but Livingston took care of that with a two-year extension, and indeed, by July 14, Fulton could boast, "I have all the wheels up; they move admirably," and he was planning his first test the following week.

Only one problem: money. Difficult as it is to figure out from the scattered letters that remain, it is clear that Fulton and Livingston, despite their original fifty-fifty arrangement, had severe disagreements about how much each was to put into the project, and Fulton was for some reason chary of spending much of his British windfall. He appears to have paid $5,122 for shipping and storing the engine, in addition to the $2,750 for the engine itself, and perhaps another $2,000 in New York for the hull and ironwork, and it is natural that he expected Livingston to contribute a like amount; Livingston apparently paid $2,000 in March and another $3,800 by August, and Fulton told him on August 2 that another $1,530 was due to "cover all expenses." This suggests that both men initially invested about $10,000 each in the boat, plus sharing Fulton's living expenses at a fashionable boardinghouse at 13 Broadway, though of course Fulton in addition was actually supervising the work for no salary. In any case, as Cadwallader Colden noted, Fulton found that the boat expenses, which he had originally pegged at $5,000, "would greatly exceed his calculation," and he looked around for someone who would take a third of his share, but when "he made this offer to several gentlemen . . . no one was then willing to afford this aid to his enterprise." There is even the story that at the last minute he could raise a critical thou-

This sketch by Fulton of the enlarged *North River* of 1808, somewhere in the Hudson Highlands, accompanied his first application for a patent in 1809. Note the two sail masts, seldom used and abandoned on subsequent boats, the foremast capable of being lowered horizontally so as to make a bowsprit when not in use.
(©Mariners' Museum, Newport News, Virginia; used by permission of the American Society of Mechanical Engineers.)

John Vanderlyn, like Fulton, one of the young American artists whom Benjamin West called his "adopted sons," arrived in Paris shortly after Fulton in 1797, and the following year made this charcoal drawing of the inventor, then 32. It is the earliest known portrait of Fulton. (©Collection of the New-York Historical Society.)

Charles Willson Peale, America's foremost painter at the time, created this oil portrait of Fulton early in 1807, while Fulton was in Philadelphia with Ruth Barlow. The inventor, just 41 at the time, has aged considerably since the Vanderlyn portrait. Peale, though a friend and admirer of Fulton, is unsparing. (©Independence National Historical Park, Philadelphia.)

This miniature portrait of his wife, Harriet, was painted (on ivory, 4⅜ by 3¼ inches) by Fulton sometime between 1810 and 1814, probably on the earlier side. Fulton had previously done miniature paintings during his first years as an artist in Philadelphia in the 1780s. (©Collection of the New-York Historical Society.)

This oil portrait of Joel Barlow was done by Fulton probably when the two were in London in 1805 and Fulton had some time on his hands. It was used as a frontispiece for Barlow's *Columbiad,* published in 1807 and dedicated to Fulton. (©National Portrait Gallery, Smithsonian Institution.)

A watercolor of Ruth Barlow, presumably by Charles de Villette (a note beneath the portrait claiming credit is signed "C. de V."), who was Fulton's and the Barlows' neighbor on the rue de Vaugirard in Paris, and whose sister was painted by Fulton in 1802. (©The Connecticut Historical Society, Hartford, Connecticut.)

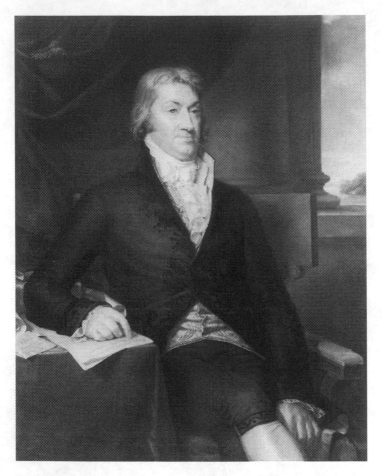

Robert R. Livingston, painted by John Vanderlyn in Paris in 1804, shortly after the "Chancellor's" negotiations with the French government for the purchase of Louisiana. His success is amply evident. Vanderlyn was born and raised in Kingston (then called Esopus), New York, a few miles downriver from Livingston's Clermont estate. (©Collection of The New-York Historical Society.)

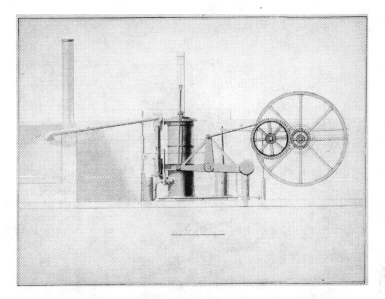

These two sketches by Fulton, showing both sides of the machinery of the *North River,* one in a slight perspective, were attached to his 1809 patent application. In his written description he details how steam passes from the bricked-in-boiler to a condensing cylinder, and then to an air pump that moves the large central beam and thus the paddlewheels. (©Mariners' Museum, Newport News, Virginia; used by permission of the American Society of Mechanical Engineers.)

Although this lithograph of the *North River*, at an unspecified part of the upper Hudson, was done sometime around 1830–35, it is a fairly accurate depiction of the boat around 1813, except that there was no ornamental bowspirit. And of course the sail (rarely used in any case) was not capable of blowing one way while the smoke was blowing in another. (Miriam and Ira D. Wallach Division of Arts, Prints, and Photographs, The New York Public Library.)

sand dollars only by keeping the names of the donors secret, "as they feared that their folly would become a matter of public ridicule."*

Money, which both partners should have had in sufficient abundance, continued being an embranglement for them, even after their enterprise began making it. A matter perhaps more of temperament than finances.

***

In a nation hungry for heroes, Meriwether Lewis was the first, other than Washington and a few military figures, to be widely acclaimed. A handsome, self-possessed, maybe even brilliant individual, he was a man of letters and science as well as of accomplishment, and when Americans learned in the fall of 1806 of his incredible two-year, four-month journey to the Pacific and back, traversing almost eight thousand miles of implacable wilderness to point the way that America's future would lead, they greeted him everywhere with cheers and celebrations. Across the newly settled territories–in St. Louis, Vincennes, Cahokia, Louisville–Lewis and his colleagues were treated to banquets and balls and bonfires, and as he made his way across his native Virginia to the nation's capital there were more festivities. The grandest event of all, however, would be the dinner in Washington City on January 14, 1807, where no fewer than seventeen scheduled toasts were drunk and what the *National Intelligencer* called "a well spread board" was enjoyed by the elite of the city, though not including the man who had sent Lewis on his mission, Thomas Jefferson.

* One minor though unexpected expense was the $20 a week that Fulton had to start paying in June to "the men who guard the boat" after some vessel had smashed into it–no doubt a deliberate act by New York boatmen who, like those on the Seine, saw in it an unwelcome form of competition.

At this grand banquet, with his wife and dearest friend in tow, Joel Barlow pressed his campaign, already begun with the president, to honor Lewis the way a true hero should be honored, by having the Columbia River he traversed renamed for him. This was a slightly odd request from a man whose most famous poem had been about Columbus and whose reworking of that poem was to be issued later in the year, but Barlow used the occasion to have read to the diners a verse of his that explained:

Columbus! Not so shall thy boundless domain
Defraud thy brave sons of their right;
Streams, midlands and shorelands illude us in vain,
We shall drag their dark regions to light. . . .
With the same soaring genius thy Lewis descends,
And, seizing the car of the sun,
O'er the sky-propping hills and high waters he bends
And gives the proud earth a new zone. . . .
Then hear the loud voice of the nation proclaim,
And all ages resound the decree:
Let our Occident stream bear the young hero's name
Who taught him his path to the sea.

Jefferson's ears were deaf to this plea—the diners might well have regretted that theirs were not—and the campaign got no further than that.

Barlow also treated the audience to a toast that night that, while exaggerated, rather neatly encapsulated one crucial element of the American dream that Lewis had aroused in all who heard of his feat: "To victory over the wilderness," the poet sang out, his glass high, "which is more interesting than that over man." And it was followed by an expansive toast offered by one Robert Fulton: "The American Eagle—when she expands her wings from the Atlantic to the Pacific ocean, may she quench her thirst in both."

This was not the last time that Meriwether Lewis enjoyed the company of the "happy trinity." Planning to write a three-volume account of his epic journey, he had selected as his publisher John Conrad, in Philadelphia, who was then suffering though Barlow's last-minute emendations to the *Columbiad* galleys. In April, Lewis visited Philadelphia to work with Conrad in planning the volumes and selecting artists for its engravings, and he stayed at the fashionable boardinghouse of Mrs. Woods, where the Barlows had been staying for some time and where, in late March, Fulton had joined them to offer solace to the grieving Ruth, whose brother had just died. There is no mention by either man of their meeting, but since Fulton did not leave Philadelphia until April 10 or so, the two undoubtedly crossed paths and, one likes to think, talked of ways in which the West would be won.

Lewis left Philadelphia in June and, though he had been appointed governor of the Upper Louisiana Territory, traveled around the East on amatory and authorial chores for the better part of a year before taking up his duties in the territorial capital at St. Louis. He spent only a year and a half there before a quarrel with the new secretary of the army appointed by James Madison became so heated that he decided to return to Washington to press his case. In September 1809, with a small party, he began a journey down the Mississippi and then across Tennessee, until October 10, when he stopped for the night at a cabin in the woods about seventy miles from Nashville. That night he suffered two gunshot wounds, probably self-inflicted, and he died the next day.

America's new hero, then only thirty-five, was dead, and by such means that tarred his reputation among a public regarding suicide as cowardly. No matter. By then

America had a newer hero, the "inventor" of the steamboat.

⚜

One other problem, also: the torpedoes. How much he told Livingston is unclear—perhaps nothing at all—but Fulton was simultaneously preparing for his "blow-up" off the Battery, which he decided would take precedence over the steamboat trials.

While in Washington in January, Fulton had pressed the case for his underwater mines on Secretary of State Madison and Navy Secretary Robert Smith, stressing that they would be considerably cheaper than any other method of protecting American ports, and probably neglecting to mention that he had already offered them to the nation whose increasing interference with American shipping made them necessary. No objections seem to have been voiced to the moral impropriety of using such weapons or of Fulton's shopping them around, and authorization and money for a demonstration were forthcoming that spring. By July, Fulton had built at least three copper-cartridge mines, each with a clockwork detonator and 170 pounds of gunpowder, and secured a derelict brig in New York harbor to use them on. Eager to show off his weaponry to compatriots for the first time, particularly after ill-feeling toward Britain grew fervent with an attack on an American ship by the HMS *Leopard* in June, he postponed a steamboat trial scheduled for July 20 and used that day for his demonstration instead. That it took three tries before the ship exploded, and then only after six hours of laboriousness in plain sight before a defenseless vessel, did nothing to deter the promoter's enthusiasm, but it did not inspire the government to encourage further experiments. Fulton was free to concentrate on the steamboat at last.

The first trial, on August 9, 1807, four long years to the day after his original trial on the Seine—was all its designer could hope for. "I ran about one mile up the East River against a tide of about one mile an hour," he reported to Livingston the next day; he added another paddle, and then, "according to my best observations, I went 3 miles an hour," then "turned the boat and ran down with the tide—and turned her neatly into the berth from which I parted. She answers the helm equal to anything that ever was built, and I turned her twice in three times her own length. Much has been proved by this experiment." An adequate speed was not proved—the monopoly called for a vessel at four miles an hour—so Fulton reassured the Chancellor: "I beat all the sloops that were endeavoring to stem tide with the slight breeze which they had; had I hoisted my sails I consequently should have had all their means added to my own." And the account ends with that profound observation, even if a bit inapposite under the circumstances, that "whatever may be the fate of steamboats on the Hudson, everything is completely proved for the Mississippi, and the project is immense."

He planned to make a few corrections, he told Livingston, and then "I shall start on Monday next"—August 17, 1807—"at 4 miles an hour" on the maiden voyage to Albany.

6.

1807–1812

B<small>Y HIS OWN LACONIC REPORT</small>—a letter to the *American Citizen* the day after the journey ended, and the only account to appear in the New York City press—Robert Fulton's maiden voyage was extraordinarily uneventful:

"I left New York on Monday at 1 o'clock, and arrived at Clermont, the seat of Chancellor Livingston, at 1 o'clock on Tuesday, time 24 hours, distance 110 miles. On Wednesday I departed from the Chancellor's at 9 in the morning, and arrived at Albany at 5 in the afternoon, distance 40 miles, time 8 hours; the sum of this is 150 miles [actually 160, Fulton still guessing] in 32 hours, equal near 5 miles an hour."

Others did not perceive it quite so nonchalantly. "She excited the astonishment of the inhabitants of the shores of the Hudson," Cadwallader Colden reported, "many of whom had not heard even of an engine, much less of a steam-boat. . . . She was described by some who had indistinctly seen her passing in the night, to those who had not had a view of her, as a monster moving on the waters, defying the winds and tide, and breathing flames and smoke." Those on other boats in the river "saw with astonishment that it was rapidly coming towards them; and when it came so near as that the noise of the machinery and paddles were heard, the crew . . . in some instances shrunk beneath their decks from the terrific sight, and left their vessels to go on shore, while others prostrated themselves, and besought Providence to protect them from the approaches of the horrible monster."

One spectator, writing years later, remembered as a small boy being in a crowd of villagers on a hill across from Poughkeepsie, and when they saw this "strange dark-looking craft . . . some imagined it to be a sea-monster, whilst others did not hesitate to express their belief that it was a sign of the approaching judgment." By the time of the return voyage, "the whole county talked of nothing but the sea-monster, belching forth fire and smoke. The fishermen became terrified, and rowed homewards, and they saw nothing but destruction devastating their fishing grounds . . . wreaths of black vapour, and rushing noise of the paddle-wheels, foaming with the stirred-up waters."

The passengers themselves were apparently not similarly discomfited, for one young man in a sloop near Newburgh, though he thought the craft looked like "a backwoods saw-mill mounted on a scow and set on fire," was surprised to hear people on board singing. The song he said he heard was an old Scottish tune, "Ye Banks and Braes o' Bonny Doon," described by a Fulton descendant as being one of Fulton's favorites, though the Robert Burns lyrics are so extremely dour ("departed joys, departed never to return") that it does seem an odd choice for such a joyous occasion. On the other hand, since this was well after midnight and there were no real berths on this first craft (as there would be on later ones), the passengers may have been using their entire repertoire to stay awake. Besides, the night was balmy, and there was a full moon over the water.

Livingston family tradition has it that in the early afternoon of August 18, as the steamboat made its way to the dock at Clermont, just down from the imposing white mansion Livingston had built fourteen years before, the Chancellor himself gave a little speech, over the noise of the engine, in which he announced the betrothal of his cousin Harriet Livingston to the inventor whose name "would descend to posterity as that of a benefactor to the world" because of his now successful creation on which they all stood. Highly imaginative, and unlikely: in the first place, the Chancellor was probably at Clermont awaiting the boat, as seems clear from his later account of his leg of the journey on to Albany; in the second, it is hard to see when Fulton would have had time that year to court Harriet, and there is no evidence in the correspondence around this period that he did so.

It is probable that Fulton did meet Harriet on this journey and possible that the two became somehow enamored during the layover at Clermont before the journey resumed the next morning. Harriet was by no means a pretty woman, but she was said to be elegant and spirited, she had two years of a seminary education, she was young (twenty-four, seventeen years Fulton's junior) and, as a Livingston, rich. If Fulton were to spurn the Barlow trinity for a conventional marriage, which his residence in America and his impending success might necessitate, she could be regarded as a sensible sort of choice.

Harriet and most of the Livingston clan were left behind at Clermont when the steamboat continued on its journey upriver to Albany at nine A.M. Wednesday. One account, written three weeks later, reported:

> *The excursion to Albany was very pleasant, and represented a most interesting spectacle. As we passed the farms on the borders of the river, every eye was intent, and from village to village, the heights and conspicuous places were occupied by the sentinels of curiosity, not viewing a thing they could possibly anticipate any idea of, but conjecturing about the possibility of motion. As we passed and repassed the towns of Athens and*

Hudson, we were politely saluted by the inhabitants and several vessels, and at Albany we were visited by his excellency, the governor, and many citizens.

And it ends with this interesting reaction to the conquest of time:

She is unquestionably the most pleasant boat I ever went in. In her the mind is free from suspense. Perpetual motion authorises you to calculate on a certain time to land; her works move with all the facility of a clock; and the noise when on board is not greater than that of a vessel sailing with a good breeze.[1]

The other is from the Chancellor, who wrote that "our steam boat has acted wonderfully well," and added:

At every publick landing the sight was amusing. All the people of the town [Albany?] were upon the prospect that faces the river–upwards of twenty boats filled with men and women came to meet us having seen us at a great time coming down. They all make the utmost efforts to keep up with us, and though there was in the number a fine sail-barge double masted, they could not by all this effort keep near us more than ten minutes. She has exceeded Fulton's and fully justified my calculations.

It was at Albany that Fulton decided to turn the voyage into a commercial one, placing a placard over the side of the boat announcing a departure for New York on the following day at nine A.M., passenger fare $7. There were not many takers–two Frenchmen, one of whom reported that "so great was the fear of the explosion of the boiler that no one dared to take passage in it," and three other gentlemen. According to one account, the chief engineer went off on a bender as soon as the boat landed Wednesday evening, so Charles Dyck, the assistant engineer, was elevated to that post, and it is from him that we get a later description of Fulton's reaction to the first passenger to come aboard Thursday morning, who remembered:

> *I inquired the amount to be paid, and after a moment's hesitation, a sum, I think six dollars was named. The amount in coin I laid in his open hand, and with his eye fixed upon it, he remained so long motionless, that I supposed there might be a miscount, and said to him, "Is that right, sir?" This roused him as if from a kind of revery, and as he looked up at me, the big tear was brimming in his eye, and his voice faltered as he said: "Excuse me sir; but memory was busy as I contemplated this, the first pecuniary reward I have ever received for all my exertions in adapting steam to navigation. I would gladly commemorate the occasion over a bottle of wine with you; but really I am too poor, even for that, just now."*

But it so happened, this fanciful account continues, that four years later, on another steamboat trip, the two men recognized each other and Fulton bought the bottle he supposedly could not afford previously. Then, speaking of the first meeting, Fulton is rendered as saying, "That seemed, and still does seem to me, the turning point in my destiny—the dividing line between light and darkness, in my career upon earth, for it was the first actual recognition of my usefulness to my fellow-men."

With how much salt that story needs to be taken is hard to say; though Dyck was a faithful employee of Fulton's for several years after, another tale has Fulton "so exhausted" when he got to Albany that "he could scarcely walk without tottering," and the records do show that a Mr. D. E. Tyle did pay $6 on that return voyage. The concluding remark, at any rate, sounds very much like the kind of high-flown sentiment that Fulton so often professed. And there is no doubt that this voyage did indeed mark the turning point in his destiny.

❦

Just before steaming into Clermont, Fulton would have passed an imposing mansion built in the style of a French château, with moat and high brick wall around, which until that summer had been the home of a French aristocrat, Pierre De Labigarre, a man of wealth and dreams.

Labigarre had come to the United States to flee the French Revolution, married into the Livingston clan, and from the Chancellor purchased some 150 acres of land south of Clermont on the river at a spot he named Tivoli, after the site in central Italy famed for its villas and gardens. There he planned to create a model community, with a public basin and a park called the Pleasure Ground and streets named Peace, Friendship, Plenty, Commerce (intersecting one called Bargain), Flora, Dream, and, with a nod north, Chancellor. But after he erected his own château, around 1795, he seems to have had no success in attracting the populace he expected, and in 1807 the Chancellor was forced to foreclose on the mortgage (with sorrow, for he and Labigarre had been fellow tinkerers) and reclaim the property. Labigarre by that time had cut and run to New Orleans, where he would undoubtedly have kept company with another of the Livingston clan, Edward, a former mayor of New York City who had left town under a cloud in 1803, after having put up his fortune to cover a theft from the New York Customs Office by a subordinate. Labigarre died shortly thereafter; Edward would be instrumental in helping Fulton bring steamboats to the Mississsippi.

Labigarre failed, but he could count himself part of a long line of people who dreamed of community in the Hudson Valley over the years. Quakers from Connecticut had established the town of Hudson a few miles above Clermont and made a thriving whaling port of it. The

Livingstons themselves planned a town on the other side of the river a few years after the Tivoli fiasco that they hoped would be a commercial rival to Hudson and maybe even the endpoint of a canal to come from Lake Erie; it attracted a modest few and became a quiet country backwater. Two separate groups following the principles of Fulton's old friend Robert Owen later established utopian villages on the river, one at Haverstraw in Rockland County, the other at Coxsackie in Greene County. Then Shakers, Mormons, Oneida Perfectionists, Jews, and even vegetarians came to live out their ideals at new communities in the valley, most of them lasting only a few years before melting and dissolving themselves in the light of reality or becoming absorbed by ever-growing towns around them.

The Hudson River had inspired dreams from the beginning. Fulton's was one of the few to come true.

❦

The return voyage was, in Fulton's words, as uneventful as the outgoing one: "On Thursday at 9 o'clock in the morning I left Albany and arrived at the Chancellor's at 6 in the evening; I started from thence at 7, and arrived at New York on Friday at 4 in the afternoon; time 30 hours, space run through 150 miles, equal 5 miles an hour."[2]

Apparently there was less consternation from the riverside onlookers this time, for the French passenger reported that "from every point on the river whence the boat, announced by the smoke of its chimney, could be seen, we saw the inhabitants collect; they waved their handkerchiefs and hurrahed for Fulton." At West Point the entire cadet garrison turned out, it is said, and shouted huzzahs over and over as the boat went by.

Nothing is recorded about how the boat was received

when it put into the Greenwich village dock on Friday after-noon—we may presume huzzahs—but then nothing was re-ported in the New York papers other than Fulton's own letter in the *American Citizen,* accompanied by a cursory editorial: "We congratulate Mr. Fulton and the country on his success in the steamboat which cannot fail of being very advantageous. We understand that not the smallest inconvenience is felt in the boat, either from heat or smoke." There were no banquets or fireworks, no toasts or speeches, no ceremonies or parades. No government officials at any level strode forth to announce how city, state, or nation would take advantage of or prosper from a development that was bound to change the nature of water transportation forever.

This lack of response to what many perceptive people must have known was indeed a "very advantageous" achieve-ment—particularly in promoting that ideal of commerce that was the foundation of the American dream and ligature of the American nation—is hard to explain. Henry Adams deliberated on this puzzle in the 1880s when he came to write his history of the Jefferson presidency: "A few whose names could be mentioned in one or two lines hailed the 17th of August, 1807, as the beginning of a new era in America—a date which sepa-rated the colonial from the independent stage of growth. . . . The problem of steam navigation, so far as it applied to rivers and harbors[,] was settled, and for the first time America could consider herself mistress of her vast resources," and yet a proper assessment of this "passed the genius of the people." It even appears, at least initially, to have passed the considerable genius of the president himself, a man who in his previous in-augural address had called for "new channels of communica-tion [to] be opened between the states," which Fulton's new machine would seem to have done rather neatly, but who had nothing publicly to say about it.

Perhaps the genius of the people was merely cautious: one voyage of less than four hundred miles does not make a transportation revolution; best wait and see whether this will turn out to be anything lasting and significant or just another amusing pastime, like the craze for those hot-air balloons then in vogue.

Fulton himself, however, knew what he had done. In a letter to Joel Barlow shortly after the maiden voyage he assessed his work frankly: "It will give a cheap and quick conveyance to the merchandise on the Mississippi, Missouri, and other great rivers, which are now laying open their treasures to the enterprise of our countrymen; and although the prospect of personal emolument has been some inducement to me, yet I feel infinitely more pleasure in reflecting on the immense advantage that my country will derive from the invention."

First things first, though; Fulton set immediately to work to modify the steamboat so that it could be suitable for passenger service in the remaining weeks before the usual November freeze on the river. At the end of August he reported to Livingston that he was working at "boarding all the sides, decking over the boiler and works, finishing each cabin with twelve berths to make them comfortable, and strengthening many parts of the ironwork." On September 2 he placed advertisements announcing that regular service to and from Albany would begin on September 4:

THE NORTH RIVER STEAM BOAT

Will leave Pauler's [Paulus] Hook Ferry on Friday the 4th of September, at 6 in the morning, and arrive at Albany, on Saturday, at 6 in the afternoon.

Provisions, good berths and accommodations are provided.

The charge to each passenger is as follows:

To Newburgh	$3	time 14 hours
To Poughkeepsie	4	17
To Esopus [Kingston]	4½	20
To Hudson	5	30
To Albany	7	36

. . . The Steam Boat will leave Albany on Monday the 7th of September at 6 in the morning and arrive at New-York on Tuesday at 6 in the evening.

She will leave New-York on Wednesday morning at 6, and arrive at Albany on Thursday evening at 6 in the evening.

She will leave Albany on Friday morning at 6, and arrive at New-York on Saturday evening at 6.–Thus performing two voyages from Albany and one from New-York within the week.

The next day Fulton enrolled the boat officially at the New York port as the *North River Steam Boat,* its only name and the one by which he always called it.

John Wilson must have been a young man when he went on that first regular commercial voyage on September 4, defying a friend who accosted him in the street and told him he would be risking his life in a boat that was "the most fearful wild fowl living," and "thy father ought to restrain thee." Years later he left this account, and, if he remembered correctly, the populace if not the officials of the city seems by then to have given the steamboat its due:

When Friday morning came the wharves, piers, housetops, and every spot from which a sight could be obtained, were filled with spectators. There were twelve berths, and every one was taken. The fare was $7*. . . . Thick, black smoke issued from the

---

* There is no record of how Fulton came up with this fare, but it worked and stayed in effect for some years. The stagecoach, which took about sixty hours for the New York–Albany trip, charged $10.

*chimney—steam hissed from every ill-fated valve and crevice of
the engine. Fulton himself was there, his remarkably clear and
sharp voice was heard above the hum of the multitude and the
noise of the engine. All his actions were confident and decided,
unheeding the fearfulness of some and the doubts and sarcasms
of others. . . .*

*When everything was ready, the engine was started, and
the boat moved steadily but slowly from the wharf. As she
turned up the river and was fairly under way there arose such
a huzza as ten thousand throats never gave before. The passengers returned the cheer, but Fulton stood erect upon the deck, his
eye flashing with an unearthly brilliancy as he surveyed the
crowd. He felt that the magic wand of success was waving over
him, and he was silent. . . .*

*As we passed West Point the whole garrison was out and
cheered us. At Newburgh it seemed as if all Orange County
had collected there; the whole side-hill city seemed animated
with life. Every sail-boat and water craft was out; the ferryboat from Fishkill was filled with ladies. Fulton was engaged
in seeing a passenger landed, and did not observe the boat until
she bore up alongside. The flapping of the sail arrested his attention, and as he turned, the waving of so many handkerchiefs
and the smiles of bright and happy faces, struck him with surprise. He raised his hat and exclaimed, "That is the finest sight
we have seen yet."*

At the end of the voyage, the passengers, as was often the custom at the time in attesting to new ventures, signed a statement
about the length of the journey (a fast "twenty-eight hours and
forty-five minutes") and the comforts ("the accommodations
and conveniences on board exceed their most sanguine expectations").

The *North River* was a success from the start and stayed
in service until November 19, when the Hudson south of
Albany "froze entirely across," according to the New York

Post, and during most of that time was able to maintain a two-round-trips-a-week schedule. There were occasional accidents that threw the schedule off and, worse, occasional "intentionals," deliberate Luddistic attacks by sailing boats and scows trying to damage the steam-powered competition that, as Cadwallader Colden observed, "it was soon perceived would interfere with the interest of those, who were engaged in the ordinary navigation of the river." Nonetheless, ridership increased, from the twelve passengers of the first trip to as many as ninety on certain rides in October, and Fulton reckoned the average was a hundred passengers a week and a weekly income of around $700. He complained, however, that "our Hands are too numerous, their Wages too high, our fuel more than half too dear," and he estimated that the profit for the two-and-a-half-month stint had been only $1,000–though, as he explained to the Chancellor, "after all the accidents and delays, our boat cleared 5 per cent on the capital expended." What's more, he anticipated $700 a week in fares for the next year, $300 a week in expenses, and a profit of $400 a week for thirty weeks, or $12,000–"an excellent thing."

The figures are important because they demonstrated to the partners, and would soon prove to the world, that this Hudson River steamboat would be a resounding commercial success. Fulton's craft had not yet traveled as far as the one John Fitch had on the Delaware in 1790–perhaps 1,400 miles that summer, compared with Fitch's 2,000 or so–but it turned out to be far more popular and did not drive its operator into debt, vindicating Livingston in his decades-old belief that the Hudson was just the right sort of river–it is, after all, flat from ocean to Albany–to demonstrate the virtues of steam transportation. Now, with the assurance of profitability and durability for the next year and probably years to come, the steamboat may truly be said to have been invented at last.

In the singular year of 1807, New York State established a Streets Commission of three men—Gouverneur
Morris, John Rutherford, and Simeon De Witt, the last a
surveyor—to draw up a street plan for the future settlement of Manhattan Island, with instructions "to unite reg-
ularity and order with the Public convenience and
benefit." For two years it took surveys of each of the
11,400 acres of the island, ninety percent of which was
unsettled, and in 1811 it announced its plan: a grid pattern
of twelve avenues, each 100 feet wide, cutting north from
Houston Street for some nine miles, crossed by regular
streets, varying from fifty to a hundred feet wide, from
First to 155th. No considerations of nature were allowed
to interfere with the geometric rigidity, and hills, rocks,
streams, ponds, valleys, springs, and forests were all alike
subdued under a surplus of plusses for the length of the island, some two thousand blocks in all.

New York was a commercial city from the beginning,
with none of the moral and religious overlays that might
have affected a Puritan Boston, a Catholic Baltimore, or a
Quaker Philadelphia. Its business in 1624 was business—
trade, mostly in furs—and its business in 1811 was business. The best thing for business was a city of long,
regular thoroughfares with rectangular plots for, as the
commission put it, "strait-sided and right-angled houses,"
the cheapest to build and the most efficient in occupying
every square inch of space. There would be no "circles,
ovals, and stars" in the plan, such as L'Enfant had designed for Washington City, and there would be the
fewest possible interruptions of such public amenities:
"So few vacant spaces have been left, and those so small,
for the benefit of fresh air," the commission explained, because "those large arms of the sea which embrace Man-

hattan Island render its situation, in regard to health and pleasure, as well as to the convenience of commerce, peculiarly felicitous." In all, the scheme allowed for the nearly unimpeded progress of structural development, with untold opportunities for "buying, selling, and improving real estate," that would, like a hidden hand, let the commercial elements of New York control the future of the city for a century to come.

The grid plan, adopted enthusiastically by city and state, was, like the steamboat, the utilitarian and highly commercial triumph of man over nature.

Fulton did not stay in New York for the entire fall season of the steamboat. In the middle of October he went to Philadelphia for a few days, probably to see to the final printing of the engravings for Barlow's *Columbiad,* then coming off the presses in a sumptuous volume that cost an immense $20, a price as elevated as the poetry. (It was dedicated to Fulton in pretentious prose: "A monument to our friendship; you cannot need it as a monument to your fame.") He was in Washington City with the Barlows by November 1, staying with them at a grand house near Georgetown that Barlow had bought as the "Athenian garden" for the continuation of the happy trinity and, in keeping with the Greek motif, named Kalorama ("good view").

Fulton ought to have been in New York tending to badly needed revisions in the steamboat for the 1808 season, but, in addition to the reunion with his lovers, he was of course bent on pressing various official figures to give him another chance with his torpedoes. He wrote both the president and the secretary of the navy, suggesting that for $2,000 he would be glad to put on another demonstration of his mines against a brig and show them how to blow up the British navy. He also had a new scheme, a harpoon gun by which he would shoot a rope carrying a mine into an enemy hull, whose plans Jefferson said he had read over with "great satisfaction."

It was not until the end of December that Fulton returned to New York, making plans to spend much of the winter at Clermont to oversee the refurbishing of the *North River* at a boatyard nearby. What he had in mind was a substantially new boat built from the machinery of the old, four feet wider and seven feet longer, with a new deck and windows, and cabins holding fifty-four berths, plus a kitchen, larder, pantry, bar, and stewards' room below deck, and a new boiler and ironwork to provide increased pressure for the extra load.[3] The paddlewheels would be covered, to keep water from splashing onto the deck, and a permanent awning would run most of the length of the deck from the smokestack aft, where "the passengers will be sheltered from rain and Sunshine" and "can dine in fine weather," a place "so spacious it will be charming," as Fulton promised Livingston. Fulton supervised the work at Clermont during the winter but decided to take the boat to New York when the ice broke in March so that he could take on additional experienced workmen; "I am working as hard as I can," he reported to Livingston in April, "and at so many parts great and small that I cannot detail them." By the end of that month a handsome and elegant *North River*, with $4,000 in new fittings and fixtures—so altered, indeed, that it was newly registered in the New York port as "the North River Steamboat of Clermont"—was ready for its first trip to Albany.

Fulton made the decision to offer accommodations of some taste and luxuriousness, rather than the somewhat spartan conditions of the earlier boat, with calico curtains in the windows and mahogany furniture below, polished oak railings and plush sofas in the cabins, and a well-stocked bar and three tidy meals a day included, setting a fashionable example that was followed by almost all succeeding steamboaters. "As the Steam-Boat has been fitted up in an elegant style," Fulton admonished the public in regulations he posted on board, "order is necessary to keep it so," and gentlemen were urged to "observe cleanliness, and a reasonable attention not to injure the furniture"; smoking was forbidden except in the fore cabin and on deck, and "cards and all games are to cease at 10 o'clock in the evening, that those persons who wish to sleep might not be disturbed." That this was a wise decision was proven by the brisk custom that came to the boat from the first, even in a year in which trade in general had fallen in the New York port as a result of Jefferson's Embargo Act of the previous year; by July, Fulton noted, "her reputation is growing on her regular departure and return" and it was clearing $1,000 a week. That pace did not continue through the entire season, but he calculated later that he and Livingston had ended the year with a profit of $16,000, one-third more than he had predicted and some two-thirds of the investment they had made so far, with the prospect of the boat's running for years.

While Fulton was busy with the *North River,* Livingston was holding up his end of the partnership by expanding their monopoly rights with the New York State legislature, which voted in April to extend their privilege for five years for every new boat they put in the water, up to thirty years, in effect a gift of another ten years of exclusivity over the previous act of 1807; with the steamboat docking twice a week practically within the legislators' view, there were no gibes about the Chancellor's "hot-water bill" this time around. Thus inspired, the partners decided to build another boat for the Hudson on the lines of the *North River–*in October a contract was let, again, to Charles Brownne, for a grandiloquently named *Car of Neptune–*as well as a steamboat ferry for the New York–New Jersey run, to be operated by the Chancellor's younger brother, John R. Livingston.

Fulton did not spend the summer of 1808 attending to his

steamboat business, however, for he had another project on his mind. That January he had acquired, after a courtship so whirl-wind as to be almost overnight, a wife, in the person of Harriet Livingston, and he wished to add her to the happy trinity at Kalorama, hoping that the charms of a woman he clearly still loved would be absorbed, perhaps by osmosis, by a woman for whom he betrayed no signs of passion. The fact that not one letter survives with the least intimation of love between him and his bride, nor any correspondence in which he refers to her in any but the most abstract and indifferent terms, suggests that the marriage was an entirely pragmatic one, but Fulton apparently had some idea that he could effect a *ménage à quatre* in Washington that would be idyllic. As he told Joel Barlow: "Shall we unite our fortunes to Make Kalorama the center of taste, beauty, love and dearest friendship or by dividing Interests never arrive at that comfort, elegance or happiness for which our souls are formed[?] There Shall the Sage [Joel], enjoying every blessing, prosecute with tranquil mind his literary pursuits, the artist [Fulton] his plans of Improvement. Ruthlinda, dear Ruthlinda, heart of love, and Harriet, receiving Information by her example[,] acquire all that is the most endearing."

The Fultons went to Kalorama in July and stayed there until the following February; the *ménage,* not surprisingly, did not happen. Ruth was (or pretended to be) sick most of the time; Harriet was preoccupied with pregnancy and giving birth (in October) to a baby boy, named Robert Barlow, called Barlow; Joel managed a long visit at Monticello with Jefferson, escaping the city's heat; and Fulton busied himself working up a patent application for the steamboat and apparently taking up oil painting again. The "comfort, elegance or happiness" seems to have been quite out of the question, and the Fultons left Washington in February having learned, as Fulton wrote Joel, that two couples with very different "ideas of interior arrangement" in their marriages would not be able to live together. The Fultons' "interior arrangement" did not grow visibly warmer over the years, and the experiment was not tried again.

⚜

That Harriet Fulton did not subscribe to the unconventional marital arrangement her husband had in mind for her is hardly unexpected, given her decidedly aristocratic background.

Her mother, Cornelia Schuyler, was a direct descendant of Peter Schuyler, the seventeenth-century mayor of Albany and land-patent grantee, who was married to a Van Rensselaer and whose sisters married into the Livingston and Van Cortlandt families, in the sort of incestuous mingling fancied by New York's finest families. In the same line was Philip Schuyler, the Revolutionary War general, whose daughter married Alexander Hamilton and who had built himself a mansion just south of Albany, overlooking the river.

Harriet's father, Walter Livingston, cousin to the Chancellor, owned several thousand acres of the Livingston manor in addition to the five-hundred-acre parcel on which his mansion, Teviotdale, was situated. A lawyer by profession, he was a speculator by instinct, and in the Revolution he operated as a supplier to the American army, netting a neat profit. After the war, like a great many rich Americans, he invested in real estate schemes in the territories to the west, where land was cheap and could be sold to settlers and speculators, many from Europe, at inflated prices (as Joel Barlow had discovered). One of his partners was the same successful William Duer who had established Barlow's Scioto Associates, but the two suffered enormous losses in 1792 when the Bank of England stopped specie payments. Both men had to declare bankruptcy, and Walter was forced to put his Livingston manor property up at auction. The Livingston family, however, always able to take care of its own, arranged that the only bidders at the auction were Walter's brothers, who bought the land back and shortly after returned it to Walter's hands. Walter died at Teviotdale in 1798.

In matters financial, the Livingston clan was not always aboveboard. In matters marital, however, there was, there would be, no deviance.

❦

Over the next four years, Fulton would add to his steamboat fleet, but not with the alacrity and determination one might have expected in someone so keen on emoluments, and not with the enterprise one would have thought from someone bent on "carrying steam to the optimum of its powers," as he had once promised Livingston. The *Car of Neptune,* longer and wider than the *North River* but costing about the same $24,000, was not finished until August 1809–$4,456 worth of copper from Paul Revere's shop in Massachusetts was delivered late because the ship bringing it to New York was frozen on Long Island Sound until March–and saw only limited service that fall. The ferryboat for John Livingston, the *Raritan,* also started service that fall, mostly on the Manhattan–New Brunswick run. But it was, unaccountably, three more years before any other boats were built for the Hudson, a lacuna for which there is no good explanation.

The boats that finally were launched in 1812 suggest what could have happened earlier. The first was a large and sumptuous *Paragon,* a "floating palace" nearly twice the tonnage of the *North River* (331 tons, one of the largest Fulton ever built) and twice the cost, with nearly $20,000 spent on "outfitting" it so that, as Fulton would brag, "my *Paragon* beats anything on this globe": mahogany staircases, a kitchen with two ovens and broilers capable of preparing dinner (served on china) for 150 people, 104 berths wide enough to contain two (when "it is agreeable to the parties"), carpets and mirrors in the cabins, curtains of muslin and silk that swiveled out to allow passengers to dress in privacy, four rooms for captain and crew (seamen, cooks, chambermaids, waiters, stewards, and "boys in the kitchen"), and a large barroom. The other boats were smaller, the 81-foot *Firefly* for the New York–Poughkeepsie run and an ingenious new catamaran ferry, the 78-foot *Jersey,* for the Manhattan–Jersey City run.

Fulton's tardiness in expanding to rivers beyond the Hudson was even more egregious. For all his talk in 1807 about how the steamboat was "completely proved for the Mississippi," it was not until mid-1809 that he took any steps to start anything there, a deal with Nicholas Roosevelt, whose various engineering projects had turned sour, to examine the Ohio and Mississippi currents, measure the velocities, calculate the trade, and determine when and where to build and launch a boat. It was not until mid-1810 that Fulton finally told Roosevelt to go ahead with a boat, to be built on Fulton's design in Pittsburgh, where there were able workmen and good facilities, but to be taken down the river to New Orleans, where Fulton and Livingston would acquire a monopoly from the Orleans Territory in April 1811, and be used for a Gulf-Natchez run. And it was not until September 27, 1811, that Roosevelt set out from Pittsburgh in the *New Orleans* on a trial voyage that lasted nearly four months and had to maneuver through the devastating effects of the huge, eight-plus-Richter earthquake centered at New Madrid, Missouri, before arriving in New Orleans on January 12, 1812.

Shortly after this maiden trip, the *New Orleans* began a schedule as a "regular trader" between New Orleans and Natchez, allowing Fulton to boast to Barlow that "the Mississippi . . . is conquered" and to anticipate a profit of $20,000 a year, but in fact he had conquered–upstream–only some three hundred miles of the immense river system and did not dare the trickier run up the Ohio to the falls at Louisville and beyond them to Pittsburgh. It had taken him four years to get this far, and it showed only how much might have been done, and won, had he started earlier.

Nor did Fulton launch, or allow an agent to launch, a steamboat on any other river during those four lost years, though there were several Eastern and Southern waterways where a *North River* equivalent could easily have prospered, particularly the Potomac to Washington and the James to Richmond. Part of what held him back was his insistence on having monopolies in other states of the same sort he and Livingston enjoyed in New York, and though he picked some slick operatives for his efforts in the South–Benjamin Latrobe, that charming polymath, in Washington City, and a glib young lawyer, John Devereaux Delacy, in Virginia–he could not persuade any other legislatures to give gifts to a Yankee entrepreneur.

Even more vexing, because it made attracting subscribers elsewhere more troublesome, was the difficulty in establishing a patent for the steamboat with enough authority that it would prevent competition and ensure a lucrative investment. Fulton had indeed taken out two patents, in January 1809 and October 1810, and submitted several dozen pages of documents and drawings to prove he had been the first to use side paddles and devise the extra-long and narrow shape that enabled them to get a proper purchase; but a dozen other people had been granted steamboat patents of their own, and, in the American patent system (modeled after Britain's), it was up to the courts to decide among competing claims–always likely to be a long and costly process involving, in Cadwallader Colden's nice summary, "perpetual legal contentions and ruinous expenditures." On top of which, as even Fulton realized, his steamboat may have been new, but "the whole is composed of old parts and looks as though different persons who have attempted Steam boats had tried the whole of them," and it would be hard to have the courts recognize that Fulton's combinations were sufficiently unique to be exclusive.

Had Fulton truly been driven by the idea of "carrying steam to the optimum," and not overpreoccupied with ensuring monopoly rights and patent superiority for his invention, he might well have gone ahead and built vessels for Southern and Western waterways anyway, trusting simply to their obvious virtues to make them a success regardless of what competition might rise to challenge them. But somehow he saw himself, perhaps unconsciously, as something akin to the English nobility, for whom the steady collection of rents, secured by government laws, was considered superior to the accumulation of profits in the helter-skelter of the unregulated market, and hence as deserving the protection of monopoly and patent, secured by government laws, rather than being subject to the uncertainties of head-to-head business rivalry.

Besides, he was driven instead by the need to prove his weapons of war. Steamboats were, to be sure, "useful and honorable amusements," as he was to write, but the "favorite offspring of my scientific pursuits" was the underwater mine.

During his months in Washington in the winter of 1808–09, Fulton continued to lobby for his torpedoes and even gave a demonstration of his harpoon gun on the pond at Kalorama in February for the new president, James Madison. Official Washington, however, was now cool to his devices, and the Navy Department, he complained, treated him with "coldness and procrastination." And so, impelled against all temperance, he once again offered his weapons to France, in a letter to François de Barbé-Marbois, a French minister whom Fulton had met through Robert Livingston. Despite the facts that France was still interfering with American ships that tried to trade with the Continent and the United States was at least nominally at peace with England, Fulton again proposed to provide Napoleon with enough torpedoes to "destroy the whole British fleet" at a cost of 1,000 francs ($225) for each gun put out of service. His justification for what was on the face of it both an act of treason and an act of war—even if Napoleon were to disregard the fact that he had been trying to blow up the French fleet—was the contention, unknown in international law, that as "a citizen of a neutral nation" he was "free to act in any country." Just as well, no reponse came from France.

Throughout the fall and early winter of the next year Fulton redoubled his efforts with Washington officialdom, writing a tract that he hoped would prove that a full-scale adoption of his underwater weapons, now including an unsinkable boat to carry the harpoon gun and anchored floating mines, was an essential means of protecting U.S. harbors—and of course ending naval warfare, establishing free trade, and allowing America to develop its "real grandeur of character." This was published in January 1810, as *Torpedo War and Submarine Explosions* (with his new slogan, "The Liberty of the Seas will be the Happiness of the Earth," on the title page), sixty pages of heated prose, and a number of handsome drawings, which Fulton immediately took to Washington and passed around in any corridor of power he could find, accompanied by a series of impassioned speeches to anyone who would listen. He praised torpedoes as "our best protection and hope" and defended them as "humane" if they could prevent "barbarous" acts like the British shelling of Copenhagen, but his principal argument was economic, aimed at a generally parsimonious Congress, the burden of which was that torpedoes for all of the nation's harbors would be far cheaper than building up a navy of "fifty ships of 80 guns" and that for the price of two gunships he could produce 650 torpedo boats and explosives. The navy was not convinced—in fact, Commodore John Rodgers called it the most impractical scheme "to have originated in the brain of a man not actually out of his mind"—but most of the Congress was impressed by Fulton's charm and energy, and his plan was cheap enough to test out. On March 30, 1810, Congress voted (with all Federalists opposed) to supply $5,000 for another public demonstration of underwater mines deployed against a protected navy brig.

With the arrogance of someone who in his Washington speeches compared himself to Galileo, having invented a project whose magnitude was "beyond the limits of vulgar understandings," Fulton demanded that the test be postponed until summer and take place in New York rather than Washington, and asserted that he would be able to defeat "every plan of booms, ropes, chains, nets etc." the navy could come up with to defend its ship. By June, having thought it necessary to spend only $1,500 of the allotted money, he announced that he was ready. Commodore Rodgers, who was to serve as a navy observer on the official evaluating committee, replied that he did not intend to stay in New York in its typically broiling and unhealthy weather, and the demonstration was put off until September.

Instead of using the extra time to perfect his equipment, Fulton continued on his misbegotten—and probably treasonous—campaign to try to interest *some* other government in his torpedoes. He wrote again to French officials, enclosing his tract and sent ten copies (and a threatening letter) to Lord Stanhope and copies to the Russian ambassador in Washington and an agent of the Dutch government (with models and drawings), telling them all to urge their nations to adopt the system, as if he was somehow determined that the whole world would end up with torpedo defenses—thus ensuring that there would be no liberty in any harbor and none upon the seas. There is no indication that any of the recipients responded to the offer.

When the demonstration day finally came, Fulton found that the navy brig was so well defended with grapnels and a net supported by sail booms that he "was taken aback" and had to ask for a delay. To fill the time, he showed off his harpoon gun, but discovered it would work only at an impractical range of fifteen feet; he then tried a test of an underwater cablecutter he had devised, which failed even to find the intended cable; and he then showed off a model of his unsinkable harpoon boat, which he admitted he had not built to full scale and thus was not sure how it would operate in harbor waters. A month later he allowed that he had not been able to devise a scheme for penetrating the brig's netting and planting his mines. There could be no demonstration.

Commodore Rodgers was scathing in his scorn for Fulton, the navy immediately decided to proceed with building ships for harbor defense, and the official torpedo committee reported that the United States should not plan to rely on underwater mines for protection.

A different kind of man would have been humiliated. Fulton admitted nothing more than that his experiments had been badly conducted and vowed that in the end his methods of marine warfare would prove themselves to the world. And probably without telling anyone, he went ahead and contracted with his friend William Lee in Paris to act as his agent with the French government to persuade it to experiment with his torpedoes until proven successful, in return for half the profits if done in eighteen months.

By the end of 1812, despite his failure to convince any nation in the world of the efficacy of his underwater mines, Robert Fulton could count himself an authentic American success.

From beginnings in rural poverty, without even the benefit of proper schooling, he had become a polished and cultured gentleman with a patina of European sophistication and acknowledged charm and flair. His public reputation was high, for he had proven the ingenuity and superiority of the new republic in the matter of steam navigation, which he showed would serve to make money besides. His social standing was of the best, settled as he was with a family connected to the manorial Livingstons, four servants (and one slave girl he promised in his will to manumit, though by New York State law she would be free on her twenty-fifth birthday anyway), and a splendid carriage and a house on Manhattan's fashionable Marketfield Street (later Bowery Lane). His civic commitment and patriotism had been made manifest by his treatises on public affairs and his recent service on the prestigious committee assessing the desirability of building a canal from Lake Erie, the contribution recognized that December by a "Freedom of the City" ceremony honoring his services "to the interests and accommodation of the city." And he could consider himself one of the richest men in the republic, certainly among the self-made rich, with an annual income of now close to $20,000, and a partner in a steamboat company that might be reckoned to be worth several hundred thousands of dollars.

Above all, like a true American, he had done everything, at least in his perception, on his own, with his own skill and pluck and perseverance.

The American dream.

7.

1813–1815

I̲t̲ ̲w̲a̲s̲ ̲e̲a̲r̲l̲y̲ ̲i̲n̲ 1813, when Robert Fulton was just beginning to realize the full potential of the invention he had so long slighted, with six steamboats at work and no fewer than six more ready to be launched and working before the year was out, that his personal life was dealt a blow deeper than anything he had experienced before.

Robert Livingston, who had been ill since the previous summer and nearly incapacitated during the autumn, suffered a fatal stroke on February 25, 1813. A man with whom Fulton had more difficult, even stormy, relations than smooth and affable—they both were proud, self-assured, self-willed—he was nonetheless an important complement and balance, absolutely forthright and trustworthy, and they shared The same vision. Fulton could not have had a better partner and colleague, as he immediately, if reluctantly, acknowledged.

On the same day that he received this grievous news, Fulton learned that Joel Barlow, who had reluctantly gone to France two years before as a special minister to try to release American shipping captured by the French, had died in Poland of fatigue and fever while seeking an audience with Napoleon on his retreat from Moscow. Although their relationship had cooled some since the unfortunate *quatre* attempt in 1808–09 and Barlow had studiously avoided visiting the Fultons in New York thereafter, the two men had been linked for fifteen years by an irreducible friendship and a true affection, and Fulton felt this additional blow deeply.

"My good friends the Chancellor and Mr. Barlow are dead," Fulton wrote to Harriet's brother, (another) John Livingston, who was then building a boat for him in Pittsburgh. "This melancholy news arrived to me on the same day, to me it is an immense loss, and to the nation, America has not 5 more such men to loose, they were the 1st order of mind and usefulness. . . . Few men have lost 2 such companions and sincere friends in the short space of 2 months. . . . I am much oppressed with sorrow."

The loss of Robert Livingston had, of course, the more immediate consequences. The Chancellor had been crucial in the legal maneuvers the partners mounted to protect their New York and New Orleans monopolies, a thicket the two had been thrashing about in for more than two years. The most important challenge had come from a company in Albany of "22 pirates," in Fulton's words, "who have clubbed their purses and copied my boats and have actually started my own invention in opposition to me": a steamboat called *Hope,* built almost exactly like the *North River,* that had begun its Hudson run in June 1811 and another, *Perseverence,* that had started operating in September. Livingston mounted an immediate attack, signing up a legal team of the eloquent Thomas Addis Emmet (brother of the Irish patriot Robert Emmet) and the meticulous Cadwallader Colden and then pushing a suit through three successive New York courts, seeking an injunction and triple damages. The decision did not come down until April 1812, but when it did it fully supported the Fulton/Livingston case (on the basis of the legitimacy of the monopoly, leaving the question of patent infringement aside) and ordered the confiscation of the two Albany boats. In December, after protracted negotiations, Fulton actually bought the *Hope* and put it on the Hudson run under his own management for 1813 and 1814. Livingston took full credit for the court decision–"Your law suit could have been carried on by no one but myself," he told Fulton, "nor could the necessary funds have been raised as we wanted them without my credit"–and Fulton did not demur.

Other challenges came while Livingston was there to advise–on Lake Champlain, on the St. Lawrence, on the Mississippi, and on the New York–New Jersey ferry route–and both partners wasted many hours with letters, threats, depositions, affidavits, summonses, lawsuits, injunctions, and litigious rigmarole, with only indifferent success. Bitter battles were waged with the New Jersey entrepreneur John Stevens, for example, beginning when he launched his *Phoenix* in 1808 as a New Brunswick–New York ferry–and though he backed off under threats of lawsuits from the Hudson partnership and took the boat by sea to the Delaware for the Philadelphia–Trenton trade, he enraged Fulton all the while by refusing to concede that he was copying the *North River* and infringing on its patent. The constant wrangling finally ended in December 1809, when the three men agreed to divide up steamboat rights on various Eastern rivers, but just two years later Stevens began another steam ferry between New York and New Jersey and it took another two years of threats and suits and injunctions before he gave that up. And Stevens, mind you, was a putative *friend* of Fulton's and Livingston's, a former partner with the Chancellor and his brother-in-law besides.

With Livingston gone, Fulton would have to bear the brunt of such challenges, and they would multiply as others saw not only the profitability of steam transport but, more threateningly, the vulnerability of Fulton's patents. For all of Fulton's fulminations ("I am the Inventor of Steam boats, it is my property for the whole United States") and his invective against "pirates" and "picaroons," his patent rested on shaky grounds indeed. His steamboat was an ingenious combination of old devices, fit together with a knowledge of "proportions and velocities," but the U.S. patent law was designed to protect new and original objects and mechanisms, not reworkings and reconfigurations, and it specifically denied the patentability of proportions and such. Fulton's ego was heavily, even obsessively, invested in asserting the originality of his invention—a perfect example of what Tocqueville saw as Americans being led by their "pride and self-confidence" to "seek the light of truth in no one but themselves"—but nobody knowledgeable in the area, including the learned William Thornton, head of the U.S. Patent Office, supported him. And many were prepared to challenge him.

The burden of defending against new lawsuits and simultaneously keeping an expanding steamboat operation profitable exacted a heavy toll on Fulton, both mentally and physically. He suffered from a recurring facial boil, at times so enlarged it blocked one eye; in early 1813 he was so sick he could eat "no solid food" for some time; that August, he confessed, "my health is bad." His weakened lungs made him susceptible to winter colds, so bad in January 1814 that he took to bed with a harsh cough and was treated by his doctors with such drugs and purgatives as they could devise; that summer his stomach, according to his friend and doctor David Hosack, "became so much deranged" and his bowels so "torpid" that he was put on a diet of "animal foods" and "a glass of weak brandy and water" and still did not go out in company. He attended to his boat-yard regularly, but was so burdened by his multiple responsibilities as designer, contractor, foreman, and auditor on projects from New York to New Orleans—this "state of slavery," he complained early in 1813, "has hardly allowed me to eat my victuals for the last four months"–that his poor health continued to drain his energy. In December 1814 he thought it prudent, at the age of forty-nine, to make out a will, leaving $9,000 a year and child support to Harriet ($3,000 if she should remarry) and the bulk of his estate to his children.

One might regard $9,000 a year as a handsome settlement, and it was not niggardly, but cutting Harriet out of an estate that might be worth a quarter of a million dollars or more, from which Fulton was taking out $12,000 a year from his North River Steamboat Company alone, could well be seen as reflecting a growing distance between the two marriage partners. Fulton seems not to have developed any particular affection for his wife in the years after the Kalorama experiment, and his references to her in surviving letters are curt and cold ("Harriet has a little girl," is how he wrote of the birth of his fourth child in 1814). She in turn showed herself bitter about his neglect of her and his "thoughtless way" with money she felt was due her, at one point sarcastically referring to him as "my lord and master" when acknowledging a promissory note she received from him. A portrait that Fulton painted of Harriet at about this time, a miniature, betrays little feeling of warmth on the part of the artist and none of love, and depicts a woman stern-jawed and unamused, looking resolutely into the distance, with little sign of warmth and none of love.

The Fultons seem to have had few guests and–aside from one lavish party on a new boat in 1812–entertained in only a desultory manner. Fulton was described by a friend as "very generally" good company, but "sometimes . . . he would become silent and distracted, his mind away upon his boats," and in this mood "would sit for perhaps half an hour." Another friend allowed that the inventor could be removed and silent even among people, sometimes staring "at the tablecloth so intensely he seemed to be counting the threads."

❧

Harriet Fulton's perturbation with her husband for not providing her with the money she felt she needed had at least one legitimate ground. Fulton had promised as her quarterly "pin money" the profits of his *Jersey* ferryboat, but when Robert Livingston heard of this he wrote angrily to his partner that it was not reasonable "that you should shut me out of the ferry" and warned that if he did not get his full share it would make their accounts "very troublesome." Fulton backed down but failed to tell Harriet, and when she found out months later, she took out her anger at the Chancellor for being "involved in the horrible sin against a defenseless woman." Livingston, however, did not budge, even for his cousin, and Fulton's half-share was all she ever got for "pin money."

Harriet's predicament was typical for a married woman in early-nineteenth-century America: she had no rights whatsoever. She was essentially her husband's property, her body regarded in law as owned by him, much as a slave's would be. She could not have an independent bank account or invest whatever money she might earn or be given, could not sign contracts, could not carry life insurance, could not inherit or own property independently of her husband. Having no property, she could not take part in politics, as either a voter or a candidate. She could not attend college (though she might, as did Harriet, attend an all-female boarding school) or apprentice for or join any of the acknowledged professions, unless prostitution be regarded as one. She could not be the legal guardian of her children.

Mary Wollstonecraft's *Vindication of the Rights of Woman*, published in 1792, was known to many women in America, and indeed a women's rights journal had been published with some success in New York City in the

The Fire of His Genius

1790s. But in the early nineteenth century the concept was essentially a playground for polite debate or dinner-party cleverness rather than the impetus for a serious movement. That, however, would come, and it would come in New York State, even if it took another two generations.

❧

Perhaps realizing (though perhaps not admitting) that the best way to defend against challenges from other steamboaters would be practical, not legalistic, Fulton threw himself in earnest in 1812 and 1813 into the project of expanding his steamboat holdings.

He began construction of a drydock, the first in the nation, and up-to-date marine works in a three-building complex in Jersey City, at a cost of some $25,000. For the 1813 season on the Hudson he rebuilt the machinery of the *Car of Neptune* and added the *Hope* and two sleek new boats, the 370-ton *Richmond* and the 275-ton *Washington,* which as the names implied were intended for eventual use on the James and the Potomac, but which kept from their assigned destinations when the British navy blockaded most of the East Coast harbors after war broke out in June 1812. He also built three new steam ferries, the *York* and the *Jersey* for the New Jersey runs and the *Nassau* to begin a Manhattan–Brooklyn service, this last enterprise given over to Harriet's brother-in-law William Cutting (no relation to Nathaniel), who successfully raised $68,000 capital for it the next year, a measure of New York investors' confidence by now in steam transportation. And to cap off that extraordinarily productive period, Fulton launched an elegant 327-ton boat, a round-bottom seagoing vessel designed to ply the Long Island Sound to Connecticut ports (also blockaded) of which he was so proud, and there being no one to object, that he named it the *Fulton.*[1] That made eight steamboats on the Hudson, including the three blocked by the British, one reason Fulton's North River Company made $119,000 in 1813, perhaps clearing as much as $50,000, although so much money was now being plowed back into building boats that at the end of the year Fulton claimed poverty.

The following year was even more successful, and the somewhat jumbled records suggest that the Hudson boats cleared at least $85,000. Accounts for the *Car of Neptune* for the first third of the season, for example, indicate that gross receipts were $16,966.30 from 3,505 passengers, that expenses in "provisions wages washing Liquors") were $4,863.62, and that fuel (260 cords of wood) cost $1,430, leaving a profit of $10,672.68; projecting it for the year, minus "winter expenses" of repairs and wharfage, Fulton figured a profit of $30,473.04—and this on an investment five years earlier of $24,000 to build the boat, or an annual return on investment of 125 percent. Not all the other boats ran up such figures—Fulton estimated the *Firefly* and *North River* would clear no more than about $7,200 for the year—but the North River Company partners (Fulton with one half, the Chancellor's widow and two sons-in-law with the other) took out at least $24,000 from the operations that year.

The Fulton ferries were also running successfully and making money. There are no extant figures for the *York* and *Jersey* for the cross-Hudson service, though Fulton, very proud of the latter's catamaran design, predicted a moneymaker, with upward of twenty-four trips a day to and from Jersey City. The figures for the *Nassau* suggest the possibilities: when it began in May 1814, it was making forty trips a day, carrying about five hundred fifty passengers and several horse-and-carriages, with passenger rates at four cents a trip and freight according to size; if it kept to that rate, it would make something like $1,000 a day and $250,000 a season, with expenses only of fuel, salaries, and boathouses. It seems to have been not quite that successful, for five years later the Cutting company pleaded that it could not afford a second boat, despite the demand, but it obviously was a profitable enterprise.

Fulton's grand plans for steamboats on the Southern waters and along the coast from Norfolk to Savannah were not so easy to realize. The British blockade and effective control of the coasts was one problem, compounded by Fulton's prohibiting anyone to build a steamboat without his exact plans and under his direction and without acknowledging his patent, even if they could find mechanics for the job. But more serious was the failure to attract investors along the various routes to back the steamboat ventures, despite the efforts of John Delacy and Benjamin Latrobe and advertisements in major cities, because moneymen were inevitably wary of Fulton's patent and the likely legal challenges to it, and in no state was there a legislature as compliant as New York's in granting a monopoly to protect them. Fulton boasted to Benjamin West in July 1813 that he would have steamboats running from "Lake Champlain to Charleston South Carolina distance 1500 miles" in a year, but he never succeeded in establishing a single company in the South.

The Mississippi operations, where there was a New Orleans monopoly and a prospect so rich that Fulton and the Livingstons were willing to put up a large portion of the money themselves, were far more auspicious, despite Nicholas Roosevelt's slow start. In 1813 the *New Orleans* regularly ran the New Orleans–Natchez route, and, though trade in the Gulf was also hampered by British ships, the boat was said to have made $20,000 after expenses, repairs, and interest that year, half of the initial investment and a return to Fulton's Mississippi Company that a local newspaper editor said was "superior to any other establishment in the United States." A second vessel, the *Vesuvius,* which John Livingston was building in Pittsburgh, ran behind schedule and over budget but made its maiden voyage down to New Orleans in May 1814 and was put on the New Orleans–Louisville route immediately, proving to be as profitable as the first boat.

Fulton, tardy about realizing the Mississippi's potential,

tried to capitalize on those successes: he put John Livingston in charge of building another full-size boat, the *Aetna,* and he sent Latrobe out to oversee a smaller vessel, the *Buffalo,* designed for the Pittsburgh–Louisville run. But a string of bad luck, combined with the difficulties of long-distance communication and the ever-present temptation of land speculation, almost jeopardized the western ventures. The *New Orleans* hit a tree stump and sank in July 1814, the *Vesuvius* ran aground off Tennessee not long after, the *Aetna* was still unfinished as late as February 1815, and a run-amok Latrobe, after wasting unaccountable time and money, put the *Buffalo* up at a sheriff's auction in November 1814 as security for his mounting debts. The *New Orleans'* engine was eventually salvaged and installed in a new hull in 1815; the *Vesuvius,* freed after six months, was grounded again for several months near New Orleans but returned to service by March 1815; and the *Aetna* finally began regular and successful New Orleans–Louisville runs later that year. What really saved the enterprise, however—and this in the grand American tradition as old as the Revolution—was the contract Fulton arranged with the U.S. government in November 1814 to pay him $40,000 for the use of the *Vesuvius* to transfer troops from Tennessee to New Orleans for the battle against the British that Andrew Jackson was preparing. (It was while in government service that the *Vesuvius* went aground for the second time, leading to a later suit by Fulton interests seeking to recover for lost revenue at the $800 a day they said the boat could have earned; though as a result of this accident no troops were actually transported, the $40,000 was never returned.)

It may have been too little, and certainly was too late, but the true measure of Fulton's genius might be said to have much less to do with proving the operability of a *North River* in 1807 and much more with proving the profitability of the dozen steamboats he had in the water from 1812 to 1815. That made his achievement indelible.

❦

Nevertheless, it did not distract him from his other passion.

The coming of the War of 1812 excited Fulton to new enthusiasm for his torpedo projects, which had been abandoned after his utter (and to any other man embarrassing) failures two years before. As early as September 1812, three months after the declaration of war, he began writing to the secretary of war proposing that twelve of his weapons be used on Lake Erie—the Canadian border was the primary theater of battle for the first two years of the contest—and he arranged to have locks for them built at his own expense at the government arsenal at Harpers Ferry, Virginia: "If they do not prove the Value of Torpedoes," he vowed, "I shall be willing to give them up as bad in principle." Pressured by Fulton, an influential public figure now, Congress the following March explicitly authorized privateers to use torpedoes to attack British sailing, the bounty of a ship's assumed value to go to the attackers, and with that sanction he set out to wage his own underwater war.

First he struck a deal with one Samuel Swartwout, a young gadabout adventurer, to use two whaleboats and twenty men to plant his torpedoes on British vessels in the Delaware River, where they had been attacking settlements along the shore. Swartwout spent a month in the river searching for susceptible prey, but as soon as he prepared an attack on one likely ship, the local authorities stymied him, forbidding a raid because the vessel was carrying American prisoners—an audacity that seems to have infuriated Fulton. Next he contracted with Elijah Mix, a young sailor from Baltimore ("one of my captains," Fulton called him), who embarked with torpedoes in Chesapeake Bay in June and in July moved against a British ship of the line off Norfolk for seven consecutive nights with no more success than finally blowing up a mine fifty feet away from the target, showering it with water but leaving it otherwise undamaged, and leading it to surround itself with guard boats thereafter. Undaunted by that failure, Fulton then dispatched a colleague of Swartwout's into Long Island Sound off New London to attack a ship anchored there, but his two raids were without result; he tried to get his "captain" Mix to launch follow-up raids there as well, though if any additional attacks were made they were unnoticed. Despite this unpromising record, he next pressed the government to give him navy vessels on Lake Erie to launch floating mines against the British fleet operating there, which he asserted could be completely destroyed "with seven frigates" under his command.

And when, in 1814, the British began serious attacks on ports on the Chesapeake and its tributaries, including a devastating raid on Washington on August 24, Fulton, as if the war was now in his blood, took matters into his own hands. He rushed to the capital on September 1, rescued a cache of torpedoes he had stored at Kalorama, persuaded President Madison over dinner to let them be sent to the defense of Baltimore, and went to that city to urge them on the navy commodore there. That officer, ironically enough, turned out to be John Rodgers, who had been so scornful of Fulton's mines at the failed test years earlier, no doubt why the mines seem not to have been deployed or used against the British assault on Fort McHenry. What was used on that occasion were the new Congreve rockets that the British had developed at the same time they had experimented with Fulton's mines, and it was their trajectory that night, not torpedoes, that was made immortal.

Fulton's ardency for matters military also led him, amid all his other activity, to create still another weapon, the seventh from a mind it would seem animated by warcraft. Early in 1813 he hit upon the idea of an underwater cannon, firing regular shells but with sheaths and flaps to prevent water from entering it, something in fact closer to the modern torpedo than his floating mines; in honor of his departed friend he called this device a Columbiad. That summer he ran a series of experiments that led him to patent the device, and he then persuaded Commodore Stephen Decatur, who had become a national hero for his victories against the Barbary pirates and his recent capture of the British frigate *Macedonia,* to join him in a fifty-fifty venture to develop it and have it adopted by the navy. "If we succeed to render it of importance to our country," Fulton wrote the commodore, "there is Sufficient of fame in it to gratify the whole nation" as well as themselves, and money enough for them to be envied "for getting wealth through the medium of doing good." "We are," he concluded in this old "Riches and Fame" theme, "in disposition alike."

But torpedoes and underwater cannons were not enough. In a move as ill conceived as it was revealing, he proposed directly to President Madison in November 1814 that he be nominated to replace the retiring secretary of war, and he prevailed on Ruth Barlow, who was back in Washington, to intercede on his behalf with Dolley Madison: secretary of war–what did running a fleet of steamboats mean compared with running an army, and in time of war? Madison, predictably, was not persuaded.

The single successful project that came out of all of Fulton's martial fervency was one that at last–and it might be said inevitably–combined his expertise in steam navigation and his obsession with weaponry. This was a plan for a huge, 247-ton steam frigate, heavily planked and armored, to serve as a floating battery in New York harbor as a defense against British naval attacks. We do not know how long he had been planning such a vessel, which seemed a natural mixture of his interests, but it was in December 1813 (just before the birthday of the Prince of Peace) that he unveiled his plans before a group including Samuel Mitchill, Cadwallader Colden, and Stephen Decatur, who formed a committee in its support; thereafter he won the endorsement of Oliver Hazard Perry, the man who in September 1813 had met the British enemy on Lake Erie and made them his.

Fulton patented his frigate in March 1814–the last of his nine patents[2]–and tried to scare up private funds, but the projected sums were too much for a private subsidy and he and his allies were forced to appeal to Congress. On May 9, 1814, Washington authorized a hefty $1.5 million for one or more steam frigates, beginning with one for New York.

Fulton embarked on the project with enthusiasm, though he was still suffering from various stomach ailments, and soon the ponderous ship, which he referred to as his "steam vessel of war," began to take shape, the hull at Adam and Neal Browne's yards on the East River, the engine and machinery at his new boatyard in Jersey City. "This is a new invention *which requires all my care* to render it as complete and useful as can reasonably be expected," he wrote that fall. "*I cannot trust the construction of the machinery or the fitting out* of the vessel to be directed by *anyone but myself.*" It was a consuming labor: one workman remembered Fulton "exhausting himself night and day, in travelling from one shop to another either to alter mistakes or prevent others," and another spoke of seeing him "so constantly . . . at his occupation . . . when his labours were so severe," and added, "His habit was, cane in hand, to walk up and down for hours. I see him now in my mind's eye, with his white, loosely-tied cravat, his waistcoat unbuttoned, his ruffles waving from side to side as his movements caused their movements; he, all the while in deep thought, scarcely noticing anything passing him."

The steam frigate was built like a fortress, which in effect it was supposed to be. Its paddles were placed in the middle between two thick hulls, 167 feet long at the deck and 56 feet wide, with the engine and boiler set belowdecks so that they would be protected. The sides were built of five-foot-thick planks, to withstand any shell then known, and the gun deck had similar planking and slots for thirty thirty-two-pound cannons; to eliminate having to turn about, which would have been a bit of a trick with all this bulk, it was made double-ended, with rudders fore and aft. At a depth of twenty feet and a draft of ten, it stood well out of the water, twice the height of the other boats in the harbor, and with two stout masts and bowsprits, it was altogether an imposing sight.

When the keel of the frigate was launched at an enthusiastic ceremony on the East River on October 29, 1814, it was greeted by a cheering crowd of perhaps 20,000 and booming cannons from nearby forts. As Cadwallader Colden told it:

> *Multitudes of spectators crowded the surrounding shores, and were seen upon the hills which limited this beautiful prospect. The river and bay were filled with vessels of war, dressed in all their variety of colours, in compliment to the occasion. In the midst of these was the enormous floating mass, whose bulk, and unwieldy form, seemed to render her as unfit for motion, as the land batteries which were saluting her. Through the fleet of vessels which occupied this part of the harbour, were seen gliding in every direction, several of our large steam-boats of the burden of three and four hundred tons. These, with bands of music, and crowds of gay and joyous company, were winding through passages left by the anchored vessels, as if they were moved by enchantment.*

It was christened that day *Fulton I* (its creator referred to it as "Fulton the First"), and though the Long Island Sound steamboat had already been named the *Fulton,* it was unlikely that anyone would mistake the two.

A month later it was towed to the Jersey City works, where its 120-horsepower engine would be installed. Fulton would never see it in the water again.

In 1797, in a letter to George Washington from London, Robert Fulton proposed that a company be formed to start building a series of small canals that would run from Philadelphia to Lake Erie. It is doubtful if Washington replied, and certainly no such waterway was planned, but it was not much later that a group of prominent New Yorkers—including DeWitt Clinton, ofttimes mayor of New York, Gouverneur Morris, an architect of the Constitution, and Philip Schuyler, the Revolutionary general—began to press for such a canal to go through their state. In 1810, Clinton was named head of a Board of Canal Commissioners that examined a 360-mile route from Albany to Buffalo and concluded that a canal, possibly using inclined planes, could be constructed there for $5 million, an amount of money so vast that the commissioners declined to speculate as to how it might be raised.

In 1811, Robert Fulton was appointed to the board by the New York State legislature, and though he was an enthusiastic supporter of the project he declined to add his signature to the report issued that year, perhaps because it recommended locks instead of his beloved inclined planes to overcome the 660-foot height differential between Lake Erie and the Hudson. He continued on the board and provided Morris, who succeeded Clinton as its head, with a long, carefully argued letter showing how the canal would be "a sublime national work, which will secure wealth and happiness to millions," and published a version of his old *Treatise on the Improvement of Canal Navigation* as *Advantages of the Proposed Canal from Lake Erie to the Hudson River* to quicken public support. The war with England, however, made financing the canal difficult and construction impossible, and the board report of 1814, which Fulton did sign, said that work would be delayed until "impediments to an intercourse with Great Britain" were removed.

Immediately after the war, Clinton again led the campaign to build the canal, assuring businessmen in New

York that it would make the city "the greatest commercial emporium in the world," a prediction with more than hyperbole. Surveys and studies were authorized, costs reckoned, lenders approached, and in April 1817 the New York legislature authorized the project, the $7.6 million to be funded by the state itself, with much of the necessary land to be donated and the money to be reimbursed through tolls. Clinton, who began his first term as governor on July 1 of the same year, dug the first, symbolic spadeful three days later, and the largest public works project in the Americas since the Aztecs was begun.

Two years under schedule, the Erie Canal was finished in 1825. On October 26, Governor Clinton and assorted dignitaries in Buffalo boarded a canal boat, the *Seneca Chief,* for the inaugural voyage to New York City. On November 2, the boat descended the last lock to the Hudson, and the next day eleven boats began the journey downriver. At its head was a steamboat of majestic proportions, 157 feet long and three stories high, gleaming with golden tracery: Fulton's final boat, honoring at last the partner so important to his success, the *Chancellor Livingston.*

⚜

Steamboating was too obviously lucrative an enterprise—every one of Fulton's boats was making money, some robustly so—not to attract any craftsman or entrepreneur who could find a source of modest capital and a machine shop with a few experienced hands. By 1814 at least a dozen other men had launched vessels of their own, on waters from the Gulf of Mexico to the St. Lawrence, most of them designed along Fulton's lines, with side paddles, but with so many modifications that their owners felt no fear of a threat from Fulton's patent, which they all professed to scorn, in any case—with some confidence, in truth, because Fulton had only once challenged any of his competitors in court, and that was the suit against the Albany "pirates," settled on the strength of the monopoly, not of the patent.

It was Colonel Aaron Ogden who finally brought matters to a head, in January 1814, with a direct assault on the New York monopoly. A distinguished lawyer and former U.S. senator from New Jersey, he had been elected governor for 1812 and with his knowledge of the state legislature managed to push through a regulation in November 1813 that gave him and a partner, Daniel Dod, a monopoly right to steamboats in that state's waters. Then, since his idea was to run a steam ferry from the docks of Elizabeth, New Jersey, through Fulton's Hudson territory to Manhattan, he petitioned the New York State legislature on January 25, 1814, to repeal the Fulton–Livingston monopoly on the grounds that Livingston had not come up with a "new and advantageous" steamboat within the required year when he had first been given his exclusive right in 1798, and that the boat Fulton had eventually built to secure the monopoly had not been new, either, but merely an adaptation of the one John Fitch had patented in 1791.

The case was strong, and Fulton dispatched Thomas Emmet and Cadwallader Colden to fight for him again in Albany, but this time there was no Chancellor to pull patrician political strings and on March 18 a special Assembly committee agreed that the monopoly was "manifestly unjust." Fulton hurried to Albany to put his case before the entire Assembly, where he played the part, congenial for him, of the martyred genius, having given so much to the state of New York and reaped so little, suffering the kinds of petty attacks from avaricious interlopers like Ogden that if allowed to stand would destroy all enterprise and invention; as to the originality of his invention, he produced a couple of depositions and a copy of a letter he said he had written to Lord Stanhope from Devon twenty-one years earlier in which he reported on experiments he had made with sidewheels propelling steamboats and included a small sketch of his model. Emmet capped this with a performance of his own, full of Irish eloquence, in which he addressed Fulton directly, in words designed to play on the legislators' public spirit, rendered by Colden as:

> *Artful speculators will assuredly arise, with patriotism on their tongues, and selfishness in their hearts, who may mislead some future legislature by false and crafty declamations against the prodigality of their predecessors–who, calumniating or concealing your merits, will talk loudly of your monopoly–who will represent it as a grievous burden on the community, and not a compensation for signal benefits. . . . Such men may give your property to the winds, and your person to your creditors. . . . Yes, my friend!–my heart bleeds while I utter it; but I have fearful forebodings, that you may hereafter find in public faith a broken staff for your support, and receive from public gratitude a broken heart for your reward.*

The rhetoric and the proof of originality, along with Fulton's obvious service to the state's economy regardless of legal niceties, won the day. By a vote of fifty-one to forty-three, the Assembly denied Ogden's petition and upheld the monopoly.

In retaliation (and with no compunction about defending what he had just attacked), Ogden threatened action against the Fulton ferry, run since 1809 by John R. Livingston, which he said was violating his monopoly with its service from Manhattan up the Raritan to New Brunswick in direct competition with his ferry to Elizabeth. In a panic, Livingston filed a petition with the New Jersey legislature much like Ogden's in New York–a court case would have provided a more unbiased venue–and Ogden seized the opportunity to turn it into a wider contest about Fulton's patent that he could argue before a sympathetic crowd, even though a majority were Republicans and he a Federalist. Cunningly he sought out Nicholas Roosevelt and Benjamin Latrobe, both of whom, caught up in

164

the land speculation craze, had misused funds Fulton had sent for his Mississippi operations, incurring his wrath and threats of lawsuits, and both of whom were eager to get back at a man they felt was amassing great wealth at their expense; as Roosevelt put it, "I may therefore still come in for a share of the payments, after the loaves and fishes have so long been feasted on by Mssrs. Livingston and Fulton." Ogden also found John Delacy, who had been fired by Fulton for running up thousands of dollars in debts as his agent and simultaneously scheming in secret to set up steamboat operations in the South on his own, and Delacy was similarly willing to join the feast, acting as Roosevelt's lawyer. (One may wonder at Fulton's repeatedly bad choice of agents, or at the cupidity of the times, but a certain high-handedness in his dealings with others might also have played a part.)

When the hearings began before the legislature and a crowd of avid spectators in Trenton on January 14, 1815, Ogden's strategy was to maintain that Roosevelt had conceived the idea of side paddlewheels as early as 1781 or 1782 and had tried to persuade the Chancellor to use them on their boat in 1798, thus denying Fulton's claim to originality in his patent. Emmet, once again with Colden by his side, sought to prove that Fulton had originated the idea of sidewheels as early as 1793, producing again the contemporary copy of the letter Fulton claimed to have sent Lord Stanhope that year. Ogden examined the copy and announced to the crowd that it bore an American watermark and thus could not be contemporary and was not genuine; Fulton replied that he meant to say it was a recent copy of the original copy of the original letter, the first one having become "worn out and obscured," but the explanation was received with skepticism, underscored with bitter sarcasm by Ogden's counsel, and Fulton's case seemed to unravel.[3]

Next Ogden's lawyers produced William Thornton of the U.S. Patent Office, a longtime foe of Fulton's, who maintained that John Fitch was undoubtedly the true inventor of the steamboat, having run a successful vessel seventeen years before Fulton's, and Nathaniel Cutting, Fulton's former friend from their Paris days, who testified that Fitch's plans had been in Fulton's possession one summer in Paris and he must have borrowed from them then. The only "novel combination" that Fulton could claim, the counsel argued, was of "intrigue and powerful connections," not of levers and wheels, the proof of which was Fulton's obvious timidity in never having the validity of his patent tested in a federal court. And then, to add insult to their decisive injury, they even asserted that Fulton was not the true originator of *any* of the inventions he had patented, with Nathaniel Cutting trotted out to prove that the rope-making machine they had been partners on in Paris was a direct borrowing of Edmund Cartwright's—which Fulton embarrassedly had to admit was true, though he had never claimed otherwise.

After three days of this, Fulton was seething with such anger that he demanded that Colden immediately sue Thornton and Cutting for libel and $5,000 damages each, and he told one of Ogden's supporters that whatever the New Jersey legislature decided, he would personally seize the Ogden boat if it sailed on the Hudson and shoot its owner, too, if he had to.

The silver-tongued Emmet did what he could to rescue Fulton's esteem, calling the beleaguered inventor a modern Christopher Columbus who had accomplished great deeds only to suffer the scorn of lesser men, jealous of his feats, who tried to deny his genius. But "the outraged state of my own feelings," as he later put it, overcame his "cool reflection," and he chose to ignore the implications of what was being construed as Fulton's obvious perjury on the Stanhope letter, thus allowing the impression to remain in the public mind that Fulton was not above a bit of finagling on his own behalf.

As it turned out, it mattered little: politics trumped equity. A week later, without so much as a word of open debate, the legislature voted to repeal Ogden's monopoly and let the Livingston boat ply the Raritan; it offered no decision on the patent. One might conclude that Ogden had simply failed to justify the idea of a monopoly convincingly, however success-ful he had been at ridiculing Fulton—or that he had picked the wrong forum after all, for the vote against him went on strict party lines.

꧁꧂

Christopher Columbus was an important figure in the minds of the early citizens of the United States, seized upon by patriots as the personification of America, and hence of the republic, unmindful of the fact that he had actually come no closer to any state of the union than the Bahamas. Philip Freneau, in 1775, seems to have been the first to call English-settled America "Columbia" (on the model of "Virginia" and "Georgia"), but it was Joel Barlow who developed the figure for the new republic in his te-dious rhymed couplets, *The Vision of Columbus,* in 1787. (It was subscribed to, in the fashion of the day, by such fig-ures as Washington, DeWitt Clinton, Alexander Hamil-ton, Aaron Burr, Benjamin Franklin, Thomas Paine, and Robert Livingston.) This was the work that won Barlow early fame and of which he was so enamored that he re-worked it into ten books for the version dedicated to Ful-ton in 1807. By that time, eighteen years into the life of the nation, Columbus had given his name to the college in New York City that had previously been called King's, the capital of South Carolina, a ship and the river it discov-ered in Oregon Country, and the federal capital on the banks of the Potomac, as well as numerous clubs and so-cieties and a dozen periodicals.

It would be another twenty years before a down-at-the-heels author, working on an English translation of Columbus's first-voyage diary in Madrid, decided instead to write a full-scale biography of the explorer. (One per-haps pertinent reason for his poverty was that earlier he had invested $2,000 in a new Seine Steamboat Company, which had soon gone bankrupt.) Washington Irving's *The Life and Voyages of Columbus* was an immediate international hit, rescuing the author from penury and establishing him as America's leading literary figure, a reputation based, however, more on his fanciful novelistic exaggerations of the central character than any proximity to an accurate historical portrait. Thus propelled, Irving went on to write a series of successful books, many on Spanish subjects, until, "in the zenith of his fame," as Fulton's great-granddaughter Alice Crary Sutcliffe wrote, he "was asked by members of Fulton's family to write a biography of the inventor."

Irving had had a passing acquaintance with Fulton in the New York scene, and though he had been caustic about the torpedo "blow-up" in 1807, he turned out to be so ardent a supporter of the steamboat projects that he told a friend in 1811 he was "outraged" to see that John Stevens was running a steam ferry in opposition to Fulton's: "It grieved my very soul to see these upstart, copperhead skippers, with their opposition boat, running away with all poor Fultons well earned profits." But "after a tentative endeavor," he gave up the biography, having concluded that "Fulton's works were already immortal monuments upon the waters of the globe . . . and to write a grand eulogy or literary essay would not be a correct biography of the greatest of inventors." That timidity seems a shame, since it would have been only appropriate to have an Irvingized Fulton, along the lines of the Irvingized Columbus that Emmet evoked before the Trenton legislature.

The New Jersey hearing was a bitter experience for Fulton. He found all of his old allies ranged against him, and since they were all men to whom, as he saw it, he had gone out of his way to extend a hand of friendship—and in the case of Latrobe and Roosevelt, to finance in steamboat ventures that might have made them rich—the wound must have been deep. The suggestion that his Stanhope letter was a forgery, a blot on his oft polished scutcheon, had to have rankled, and the resurrection of the old John Fitch adventure to challenge his primacy ("Certain it is," Fulton wrote sourly right afterward, "we did not hear of it for near 20 years") hit him where, as he knew but hated to admit, he was most vulnerable. Ogden was beaten back, temporarily, but gave no sign that he actually intended to end his ferry operation.

Fulton's solace was his vessel of war. On the way back from Trenton, with Emmet and two others, he stopped for three hours at the damp and drafty boatworks in Jersey City to see how work on it had gone during the weeks he had spent at the hearings. As the little band then set out to cross the frozen Hudson on foot because no ferries were running, the portly Emmet fell through the ice, and when Fulton and his companions had pulled him from the water they were thoroughly soaked, with the inventor, his doctor later reported, "very much exhausted." Arriving home, Fulton was hoarse and "almost unable to articulate," but after several days in bed he declared he felt well enough to revisit the steam frigate, this time by coach and ferry.

It was a fatal trip. Afterward he took to his bed with signs of pneumonia, the inflammation of his lungs grew worse and spread, and he was coughing blood; within several days his neck and lower jaw were as swollen as if he had mumps, and he had developed a fever.* The doctors tried "all the usual applications," but on the night of February 22 he was hardly able to breathe and his pulse was so feeble that Hosack knew nothing could be done to save him. The next morning, February 23, 1815, Fulton died, a few months into his fiftieth year.

---

* Consumption, as at least the major part of Fulton's ailments would have been classified, was by far the largest killer in New York City at the time, claiming roughly a quarter of the 2,000 annual deaths.

Newspapers the next day carried notices of his death in heavy black borders. The legislature in session in Albany passed a resolution of regret and sorrow and called on the members of both houses to wear mourning "for some weeks" afterward—said to be the only time a private citizen never elected to office was accorded such an honor. The New York *Evening Post*'s obituary was typically lugubrious and businesslike at once: "Politicians, historians, poets etc. are found throughout the United States, and readily succeed to each other, but there is no person who will succeed to Mr. Fulton's genius as a mechanic, or be capable of prosecuting those schemes which he left in an unfinished state."

The following day, a Saturday, Robert Fulton was buried, after a funeral procession that his friend Colden said was attended "by a greater number of citizens than have been collected on any similar occasion." In the late afternoon his casket, of plain mahogany, with a metal plate bearing his name and age, was borne down the steps of his home on Marketfield Street and carried in a slow procession up Broadway to Trinity Church, with national and state officials, the city council, local magistrates, and representatives of academic and scientific societies all in attendance, accompanied by the dull sound of guns being fired from the fort at the Battery and ships in the harbor. After a brief service, Fulton's body was buried in one of the vaults owned by the Livingston family, since he had not thought to provide one for himself.

At the time of his death, not even eight years after his initial success, Fulton had thirteen steamboats of his design running on the waters of America, of the sixteen built in his lifetime: the *Car of Neptune, Paragon, Richmond,* and *Firefly* on the Hudson (the *North River* was retired in 1814, its ultimate fate unknown), the elegant *Fulton* on Long Island Sound, five ferries running from Manhattan to New Jersey and Brooklyn, the *Washington* on the Potomac, and the *Vesuvius* and *Aetna* on the Mississippi (the first *New Orleans* sank in 1814, and its replacement did not

170

run until later in the year).[4] It might be argued that Fulton might have built more boats and kept improving their design had he not put so much of his time and energy into insisting on his patent rights and defending his monopoly, letting his superior products rather than his special protections win out over competitors. But of course that does not reckon with the egoistic Fultonian personality, which regarded recognition of his accomplishment from all quarters as more significant—and more his due as the American aristocrat he felt himself to be—than seeing more of his boats on the water. And it must be said that the construction and operation of sixteen steamboats in less than eight years, all but one of which (the *New Orleans I*) ran without serious flaw or accident or loss of life, all successful, money-making, and important contributions to the nation's commercial development, is a considerable achievement, for which this one man was primarily responsible.

There were, moreover, four other steamboats that would take to the water after Fulton's death, completed at the Jersey City works in accordance with his designs, in itself a testament to his managerial skills: the grand 524-ton *Chancellor Livingston,* built for five times the cost of the *North River* ($125,000), a ferry for New Jersey, a second boat for Long Island Sound, and the steam frigate *Fulton I.* The fate of the frigate was ironic, inasmuch as the war for which it was intended had been ended by a treaty signed the previous Christmas Eve and ratified by the United States in February. It was hauled out for tests in June 1815 and proved satisfactorily to the navy that "no doubt remained that a floating battery, composed of heavy artillery, could be moved by steam," but there was not much to do with the towering fortress in peacetime, so eventually its guns and machinery were stripped and it was anchored in the Brooklyn Navy Yard to serve ignominiously as an infirmary for naval personnel. The last of Fulton's boats was his least successful and, like his other contributions to war, a disappointment.

It is somewhat difficult to measure in monetary terms the extent of Fulton's operations at his death because he chronically left his finances in disarray. The multiple operations across great distances were extremely complex at a time when banking and accountancy were in their infancy in America, and though Fulton could be precise to the penny over annual expenses and profits, he never bothered to draw the strands of his enterprise together in a regular, coherent way, and the Chancellor was even worse. What incomplete evidence we have, however, suggests that his estate would have been worth something like half a million dollars, a feat not matched by many entrepreneurs of the era.

Not that the estate, controlled by Harriet and her brother-in-law William Cutting, ever saw sums of that magnitude, much of which at any rate was tied up in the boats themselves and was not liquid. The sale of the Hudson boats in October 1815 to a syndicate headed by Cadwallader Colden allowed Harriet enough money in effect to buy out her brother's share of the Teviotdale estate, but there was not enough for her, with four small children the oldest of whom was seven, to maintain the sumptuous house on Marketfield Street, and she moved to smaller quarters on Broadway before the year was out. In November of the following year, her widow's weeds quickly put away, she married a charming Englishman, Charles Dale, and shortly after, having foisted the children on a Livingston widow at the upstate manor, they went off to England.

If Harriet's rapid remarriage suggests a certain indifference toward her husband's death, the reaction of Ruth Barlow suggests true affection. Responding to the news conveyed to her by William Cutting, she wrote, "Most feelingly my heart reciprocates every sentiment of sorrow and deep regret you express. . . . Except for the family no one can so sensibly feel this loss as myself. . . . I must dismiss this mournful subject, it affects me too much my tears blot my paper." And later, when she resettled at Kalorama, she told a friend it was there that she was able to recall the image of Fulton "that I wish to be ever present to my still bleeding heart."

Of the eulogies raised to Robert Fulton in the learned societies and banquet halls after his death we know little, but this tribute, delivered by the eminent Gouverneur Morris before the New-York Historical Society a year later may be taken as representative of the sentiment of the day:

> *Be it ours to boast that the first vessel successfully propelled by steam was launched on the bosom of Hudson's River. It was here that American genius, seizing the arm of European science, bent to the purpose of our favourite parent art the wildest and most devouring element. The patron–the inventor are no more. But the names of Livingston and of Fulton, dear to fame, shall be engraven on a monument sacred to the benefactors of mankind.*

More elegant still were the words of DeWitt Clinton before the American Academy of Arts:

> *To those who were favoured with the high communion of his superior mind, I need not expatiate on the wonderful vivacity, activity, comprehension and real clearness of his intellectual faculties: and while he was meditating plans of mighty import for his future fame and his country's good, he was cut down in the prime of his life and in the midst of his usefulness. Like the self-burning tree of Gambia, he was destroyed by the fire of his own genius and the never-ceasing activity of a vigorous mind.*

This last was a description more telling than Clinton could have known, for it was indeed that fire that fueled his unending compulsion to perfect his weapons of war, on the last of which he gave his life, that fed his prideful battles over the primacy of his patent on which he expended so much of his mental and physical well-being, and that lit the passion for wealth and fame by which he drove himself in his work his entire life, even after they were long achieved.

8.

Legacies

IT IS A MATTER of legacies.

First. To honor the dead hero, a new street connecting Robert Fulton's two ferry operations, the Paulus Hook Ferry on the Hudson and the Brooklyn Ferry on the East River, was begun a few months after his death along the old Partition and Fair streets on the west side and pushed through down to Beekman's Slip on the east, the new "great thoroughfare" inaugurated in 1816 as Fulton Street. (It was later that the street leading into Brooklyn from the ferry landing at the foot of the Brooklyn Heights bluffs was also named after the inventor.) It was a rare distinction, then as now, which Cadwallader Colden ascribed to the wisdom of "the corporation of our city, always the patrons of science and friends of its votaries."

Subsequent honors in the city whose commerce Fulton had done so much to foster were, however, meager. The Fulton Market on the East River was opened in 1822 and was used regularly by fish merchants from the start, but its name owed more to the street on which it was located than to the man in question. No lasting monuments, not even a gravestone, were erected until 1901, when the American Society of Mechanical Engineers put up a bronze plaque on a squat column along the south wall of Trinity churchyard, an approximate likeness of Fulton on one side and a plan of the *Fulton* on the other. Three years later, when the Interborough Rapid Transit company opened its subway line in lower Manhattan, it chose a tile representation of the *North River* to decorate the wall of the Fulton Street station, but no representation of the inventor. Finally, in 1906, Fulton seemed about to get his due, when a prestigious Robert Fulton Monument Association was established in New York, with Cornelius Vanderbilt (great-grandson of the millionaire) as its president and Dr. Samuel Clemens its vice president, plus an executive committee including Andrew Carnegie, Nicholas Murray Butler, and various surviving Fulton relatives. This group came up with a plan for an elaborate memorial on Riverside Drive at 110th Street, overlooking the river of Fulton's triumph, along with a landing basin, a maritime museum, and at last a tomb of his own for Fulton; but though there would appear to have been adequate wealth involved—and Vanderbilt's family money had come originally from steamboats, after all—preliminary plans and studies somehow exhausted the available funds, all attention turned to upcoming festivities in 1909 to honor Fulton and Henry Hudson together, and no great monument was ever built.

For the 1909 affair, a bust of Fulton was erected at the Hall of Fame on New York University's Bronx campus, and a full-size replica of the original *North River* (inevitably called the *Clermont* on its sternboard) was built for even less than the original price ($15,865), albeit with the dimensions of the enlarged boat of 1808 instead of the narrower 1807 model because it was decided that the earlier boat was much too unstable, as indeed it was. The celebrations went on for two weeks, the first on the lower Hudson, with two fifty-float parades in New York City, fireworks, banquets, pageants, lectures, aquatic sports, boat races, and a variety of other commemorative events (including maritime exhibitions in twenty-two museums and universities), culminating in a ceremonious procession of 1,595 vessels up the Hudson to Newburgh, led by a replica *Half Moon* and the *"Clermont"*; this was followed by a week of events in upriver towns and a final appearance of the two replica vessels in Albany. The Post Office issued a commemorative stamp—as it did again fifty-six years later for the two hundredth anniversary of Fulton's birth.

Some other honors were granted to Fulton in the century after his death, among them a statue chosen by the state of Pennsylvania in 1883 for its niche in the Statuary Hall of the U.S. Capitol, another in the Library of Congress, one (inexplicably) in Charleston, West Virginia (erected in the "early years" of the century, restored in 1883), but it was on the map that his name would be most indelible: the area in Lancaster County, Pennsylvania, where he was born was renamed Fulton Township in 1844, and towns in Missouri, New York, and Ohio were given his name, as were counties in Arkansas, Georgia, Illinois, Indiana, Kentucky, New York, Ohio, and Pennsylvania. Not negligible, but perhaps not sufficiently honorary, considering that a figure such as Christopher Columbus, who actually played no part in the nation's effulgence, has nearly one hundred place-names.

And his bones still lie, unmarked, in another man's vault.

Second. The actual legacy from the estate of Robert Fulton, deceased, was a considerable tangle, and it is difficult to determine what the assets really were and what happened to them. Fulton in 1814 had calculated the total capitalization of his boats at $340,000, not counting the steam frigate (which cost

$200,000 to build but was the property of the United States). In 1815 the estate sold its half-share in the four boats then active on the Hudson for $100,000–probably an undervaluation, inasmuch as the Hudson operations (including the monopoly) were said to be worth $620,000 in 1819 and $660,000 four years later–but retained its interest in four ferryboats (worth at least $150,000 with the monopoly) and the *Fulton* (built for $75,000), plus the Jersey City workshops, built for $25,000 and valued at $100,000 in 1820. (In addition, Fulton was supposed to have gotten half of ninety percent of the profits of the Mississippi and Potomac companies, though it is doubtful that he had received much of that at the time of his death or that any payments were made to the estate.)

That suggests an ultimate value of something approaching $400,000 in 1815, a quarter of it liquid (before the Teviotdale acquisition), a handsome heritage indeed, had it survived. It did not. There is no way of knowing from the meager records now, but by some means Harriet Fulton and William Cutting, managing the estate while the children were under age, succeeded in spending or losing it all within a decade. Harriet seems to have been in England most of that time, and Cutting died in 1821, perhaps without naming a successor, so it may be that J. Franklin Reigart in 1856 was right in asserting that "ungrateful and envious" men had robbed the estate or simply run the Fulton boats under the Fulton monopoly on their own with no payments to the nominal owners. In any case, by 1825, when Harriet returned to New York, the Fulton family was impoverished. This we know because in that year a group of New York businessmen petitioned the New York State Assembly for a banking license, sweetened by a promise to pay Harriet from a $70,000 annuity, and although the Assembly declined the deal, its report did find that the Fultons were then *"utterly destitute of support."* When Harriet died the following year, the children were still living with relatives, and when Fulton's son (who called himself Robert Jr., not Barlow as his father had called him) reached the age to inherit the bulk of his father's estate in 1829, he found there was nothing there. In a plaintive letter that year to his uncle Robert L. Livingston, half heir to the Livingston side of the steamboat properties, he pleaded for aid for his three sisters: "Money have they none, and what I can save from my small salary is by no means sufficient for even one of them. I do not wish to remind you of the manner in which they were brought up. They merely ask for necessaries, & heaven knows they are in want."

Uncle Robert was not forthcoming, for in that same year, claiming that they were "cast upon the world destitute of even the means of subsistence," the children petitioned the U.S. Congress for money they claimed was owed to their father for his work on the steam frigate and for losses from the army's misuse of the *Vesuvius* in 1815. The petition was variously bounced around committees and houses of Congress for an unconscionable length of time—sentiment being firmly in favor of the illustrious inventor's kin but strict justice finding little merit in their claims—until at last in 1842 a Senate committee approved the request and tardily in 1847 Congress voted to come through with a payment of $76,000. It was some help perhaps for his sisters, though all were comfortably married by then, but of no use to Robert, who died childless in 1841. (And with his death ended the bloodline patronym, since he was the only male child and Fulton's brother, Abraham, was also childless.)

Third. Although not one of the instruments of naval warfare that so occupied Fulton in his lifetime proved successful in his hands, it can be said that the seeds he so fervently planted did bear their strange fruit in other places at other times.

The steam frigate was never put to military use, and in 1829, after fourteen years as an infirmary for navy personnel, it was destroyed by an explosion of the two and a half barrels of gunpowder in its magazine, which killed twenty-nine men and a woman. Inevitably, though, the navy eventually turned to steam, particularly after the British navy launched steamships in the 1820s, and finally in 1837 a second steam frigate, *Fulton II*, was put in service, no longer a floating fortress but now a seagoing warship with side paddles, thinner and immensely heavier (973 tons to the *Fulton I*'s 247); its commander was Matthew Perry, brother of the Commander Perry who had supported Fulton's warship proposal in 1814, who as a young man had seen the first frigate at its initial launching. This was refitted in 1852 as the *Fulton III*, berthed in Pensacola, Florida, and destroyed ten years later, by which time steamships were a commonplace in navies in most parts of the world.

It took longer for Fulton's discarded submarine to be taken up, although several models on his general principles were used by both sides, to little effect, in the Civil War. The first really successful prototype was built by John P. Holland in 1878, incorporating much of Fulton's (and Bushnell's) design, a fact he acknowledged when he named the boat he launched in 1901 the *Fulton*. A fairly similar design by Samuel Lake was adopted by the German navy and used extensively in World War I, thus securing submarines a place in modern naval arsenals thereafter. The torpedoes in those late models were nothing like Fulton's floating "torpedoes," but they did owe something to the underwater cannon Fulton had patented, and floating "moored mines" were used by navies in both world wars.

What seems to have been the central ambition of Fulton's life, then, to use his genius to produce weapons of war—a project on which he worked for more years and often with more passion than he dedicated to his steamboats—was ultimately realized, and even his steamboats, as he found out at the end, could be transformed into military machines. This was a far cry from their leading, as he purported to believe, to the achievement of world peace and freedom of the seas, but it did prove that his ingenuity was on the right track, and, had he concerned himself more with the mechanics of his devices and less with "Riches and Fame," he might well have realized that himself during his lifetime.

Fourth. But the real legacy of Robert Fulton was to be found floating on the waters of America, principally the Hudson and the Mississippi, and then eventually on the oceans of the world, for another century and more.

The Hudson River monopoly was a boon for the Fulton–Livingston partnership, hard as it was to defend, but it was certain not to last, for too many others wanted in on the lucrative business and America at that time was a land that, despite the indefatigable pursuit of lucrative monopolies and government favoritism, was dedicated largely to the inveiglement of competition. Thomas Gibbons, an irascible man of means from Georgia—whose life a congressional committee had once described as "a scene of political corruption"—was the first to challenge the monopoly after Fulton's death, and oddly enough in competition with Aaron Ogden, who in 1815 had bought a license for his New Jersey ferry from the Hudson monopoly after failing to put it out of business. In 1818, Gibbons blithely began running a steam ferry from the Elizabeth docks to Manhattan, exactly the route Ogden had purchased for himself, and Ogden went time and again to New York courts to seek relief. Gibbons would not back down, having coffers and counselors to match his contentiousness, and at every step appealed to other and higher courts, until in 1824 the Supreme Court, Justice Marshall sitting, agreed to hear the arguments. Thomas Addis Emmet, again, defended the monopoly, along with the legal apparatus of the State of New York, but Gibbons had recruited the ever-eloquent Daniel Webster, "a man with a mouth like a mastiff," who gave one of the best performances of his career and had Marshall taking in his words, he later bragged, "as a baby takes in its mother's milk." Marshall, Federalist to the core and defensive of the centripetal governmental arrangements the Federalists had created, decreed that state privileges denying free interstate commerce were "repugnant to the Constitution and laws of the United States," and ordered the monopoly dissolved. With that prop removed, and without anyone to operate it on its merits instead of its monopoly, the North River Steamboat Company went out of business in 1826.

Once open, the Hudson welcomed anyone with the means–$20,000 to $30,000 or so–to put up a steamboat, and in 1825, according to *Niles Weekly Register,* there were no fewer than forty-three steam vessels operating out of New York, up and down the river to Albany, to ports on the Sound as far as Providence, Rhode Island, and across the ferry lanes to New Jersey, Brooklyn, and Queens. Shipbuilding operations along the East River, where the first Fulton boat had been constructed, were humming with business–James Allaire, who had bought Fulton's Jersey City works, moved them to Corlear's Hook and soon became the foremost boatbuilder in the country–and in the process a whole new manufacturing enterprise was created, with local craftsmen, engineers, designers, and owners, as the foundation of America's Industrial Revolution. By 1828 twelve steamboats a day docked at Albany and New York, a decade later more than a hundred, and at mid-century there were more than 150 steamers at work, carrying nearly 2 million passengers (995,000 on the Hudson, 840,000 to New Jersey, and 302,000 on the Sound). In terms of trips and passengers, the Hudson was the busiest waterway in the world.

And New York the busiest port. As early as 1831, Frances Trollope could observe that the city "rises, like Venice, from the sea, and like that fairest of cities in the days of her glory, receives into its lap tribute of all the riches of the earth," and by mid-century another enthralled visitor could give this account:

Huge steam ferry-boats, magnificent passenger steamers, and freight barges, ocean steamships, and every variety of sailing vessel and other water craft may be seen in the Hudson River slips, or out upon the bosom of the stream, fairly jostling each other near the wharves because of a lack of room. Upon every deck is seen busy men; and the yo-heave-o! *is heard at the capstan on all sides.*

But the most animated scene of all is the departure of steamboats for places on the Hudson, from four to six o'clock each afternoon. The piers are filled with coaches, drays, carts, barrows, every kind of vehicle for passengers and light freight. Orange-women and news-boys assail you at every step . . . whilst the hoarse voices of escaping waste-steam, and the discordant tintinnabulation of a score of bells, hurry on the laggards by warning of the near approach of the hour of departure.

Several bells suddenly cease, when from different slips, steamboats covered with passengers will shoot out like racehorses from their grooms, and turning their prows northward, begin the voyage with wonderful speed, some for the head of tide-water at Troy, others for intermediate towns, and others still for places so near that the vessels may be ranked as ferryboats.

At first the only important cargo of the Hudson steamers was people, and the goal of the owners was to attract the maximum number by offering boats of increasing comfort and ornamentation, stressing the safety of their gleaming copper boilers (and the danger of their competitors' machinery) and cutting down the hours required for their posted journeys. The leading steamboats of the 1830s—the *Constellation*, the *Constitution*, and the *Chief Justice Marshall*—were 300 tons or more but managed to trim the time of the New York–Albany run from thirty-five hours in 1825 to ten hours in 1835. They were followed by the "floating palaces" of the 1840s, 400 tons and more, equipped with huge crystal chandeliers in salons two

decks high, gleaming white columns and porticoes and bal-
conies, gingerbread decorations in pastels; they were increasingly powered by coal instead of wood, a few with the newly
invented screw propellers, and these made the Albany trip rou-
tinely in seven to eight hours.

Competition in the 1840s, chiefly between the People's
Line, owned by a native of Kingston named Isaac Newton, and
the boats of an aggressive ferry captain named Cornelius Vander Bilt, self-styled "Commodore," forced prices down from
the $7 New York–Albany fare that Fulton had established to $5
and at times to a dollar or less. At those rates upstate farmers
could afford to ship their produce and livestock to the lucrative
New York market—fruits, vegetables, grain, cattle and hogs for
slaughter, horses for the trolleys—and the amount of tonnage
that went through the Albany port increased from 400,000 in
1815 to 750,000 in 1835 to as much as 2.2 million in 1854, before railroad competition came along in earnest after the completion of the Hudson line in 1851. And with the added freight
and a full load of four or five hundred passengers, paying for
staterooms and meals as well as passage, it was said that a
steamboat from Albany in 1850 could make $1,200 a trip with
only $200 in expenses for salaries and fuel.

A journey on one of the gleaming Hudson steamboats of
the first half-century, at least in good weather, was an experience that invariably impressed foreign visitors, for whom it
was an essential part of the tour, and seldom failed to stir even
regular travelers. To the splendid luxury of the accommodations and the spectacular scenery of the Hudson's mountain-
ous banks was added the unique excitement of being aboard
the fastest conveyance on earth and at every moment appre-
hending the signs—the black smoke, the shimmering sparks,
the throbbing machinery, the churning waters—of its industrial
power. In 1832 the English actor Fanny Kemble conveyed her
sense of delight after several trips upriver in steamboats this
way: "They are admirable inventions. . . . Nothing can exceed

the comfort with which they are fitted up, the skill with which they are managed, and the order and alacrity with which passengers are taken up from, or land at, the various points along the river. . . . While despatching breakfast, the reflections of the sun's rays on the water flickered to and fro upon the cabin ceiling, and through the loophole windows we saw the bright foam around the paddles sparkling like frothed gold in the morning light.

"At every moment the scene varied; at every moment new beauty and grandeur was revealed to us; at every moment the delicious lights and shadows fell with richer depth and brightness upon higher openings into the mountains, and fairer bends of the glorious river."

It was well said, though by whom is now lost, that in the steamboat a glorious river had at last found its most consummate companion.

·❦·

It was a big, blond, blue-eyed roustabout captain named Cornelius Vander Bilt (as he wrote it), who would do anything to make a dollar, who signed on with the obstreperous Thomas Gibbons to sail his steam ferry *Mouse-of-the Mountain* on a run from Elizabeth, New Jersey, to a pier at the Battery in 1817 in open defiance of the Fulton–Livingston monopoly and Aaron Ogden's grant. Ogden, naturally, sued; Gibbons, naturally, ignored him, putting on a larger boat for a run to New Brunswick, the *Bellona* (built by James Allaire at the former Fulton boatyard), with Vander Bilt again in charge. Ogden sued again, a warrant was issued, a sheriff was dispatched, a search of the boat was made, but the captain was nowhere to be found—he had had a secret closet built in the hold—and the papers could not be served against him.

For month after month Vander Bilt evaded the constabulary, using one ruse after another and flight if need be, and the *Bellona* proved wonderfully profitable. Eventually Gibbons decided that it was he who ought to be bringing the suits, and in 1820 he hired Daniel Webster and attacked Ogden and the Fulton–Livingston monopoly in federal court. While the case was in litigation, the *Bellona* continued to run, often unloading people at the New Brunswick landing into a hotel that Vander Bilt owned with his wife, and the elusive and aggressive captain put by a tidy sum.

In 1828, after the monopoly was broken and competition filled the New York waters, Vander Bilt, then thirty-four, went into business for himself, with the *Bellona* for New Jersey and the *Citizen* for the Delaware, both so successful that the Stevens family, who had by then taken over the Hudson boats of the defunct North River Company, bought him out. Vander Bilt simply acquired two more boats for the Hudson and showed how they could be money-makers, too, until in 1834 the Stevens group bought him out again. But nothing would keep the "Commodore" out of the booming steamboat business, and he soon had the handsome 205-foot *Lexington* running on the Sound, a few New York ferries, and steamers on the Connecticut River, along the Atlantic coast from Boston to Portland, and on the Delaware and points south. By the end of the 1830s, worth more than half a million dollars, Cornelius Vanderbilt (as he was now) was one of the richest men in New York.

When Isaac Newton opened the era of high elegance on the Hudson with his "palaces" in the 1840s, Vanderbilt was quick to follow. His *Cornelius Vanderbilt*, 740 tons, was perhaps the finest steamer on the river, and he accompanied it with other grand vessels, ultimately, in 1853, with the *North Star*, an enormous 2,500-ton steam*ship*, 270 feet long, with an ornate Louis XV dining room of elaborate woodwork and a series of portraits of great Americans (including, as was the fashion, the Hispano-Italian Columbus). That ship, it was said, was Vanderbilt's claim of entry into the New York Yacht Club, which with its patrician prejudice had previously refused to admit the blunt and unlettered boat captain. The strategy worked; the club relented and voted him in.

By then, however, the Commodore, said to be worth at least $1.5 million from his various steam ventures, had found a new interest: railroads. Buying up properties and bullying smaller companies, he soon was the principal owner of a New York–Albany railroad, the mighty New York Central, and was on his way to becoming master of the Hudson by land.

⚘

But of course it was on the Mississippi, as Fulton always knew, that the greatest impact of the steamboat would be made in its first half-century. All that was needed to turn this, the most extensive waterway in the world, with more volume than all the rivers of Europe, into a powerful economic aorta was a vessel to run upstream as well as down, and Fulton had provided the first of those in 1811.

By 1815, Fulton's surrogates had turned out four boats for the Mississippi, two of them lucrative profit-makers on the New Orleans–Natchez run, and three other boats were launched by a pair of inventive mechanics, Daniel French and Henry M. Shreve, from a shop near Pittsburgh. Even with that limited beginning, the industry's potential was unmistakable: "There was never such a prospect for improvement and trade at any one time on any portion of the globe," crowed the Brownsville, Pennsylvania, *Telegraph* in 1815, "as that which is now exhibited to western America." And according to a Kentucky paper that same year, after Fulton's *Aetna* made its first trip up from New Orleans to Louisville, the feat "has opened prospects of unparalled trade and prosperity of the town of Louisville and the Western country in general."

At first the Fulton interests, led by Robert Livingston's brother Edward, chose to fight competition by enforcing their New Orleans monopoly with lawsuits against the French–Shreve interlopers, but the lower courts were not cooperative, and by 1817, with a dozen other boats rivaling them on the Mississippi, the prospect of taking case after case to the Supreme Court seemed so unappealing that they gave up the fight. In the spring of that year, moreover, Shreve's 403-ton *Washington*, with a newfangled high-pressure boiler, made the trip from New Orleans to Louisville, with a highly profitable cargo, in a record time of twenty-five days, thus convincing any who still had doubts, as one contemporary observer asserted, that "steamboat navigation would succeed on western waters." That opened the gates: twenty-five new steamboats were built in 1818, thirty-four in 1819, and by 1820 at least sixty-nine vessels, with a total tonnage of 13,890, were operating on the Mississippi and Ohio, with 198 arrivals reported at New Orleans alone that year. The steamboat was established, the rivers were conquered, and people and goods were pouring into the valleys, back and forth on the Ohio, up and down the Mississippi, into the Missouri and Tennessee and Arkansas and Red and a dozen other tributaries.

In the twenty years after the first steamboat, more people were drawn to middle America than the original colonies had attracted in two hundred years: 1.1 million people were added to the ten states of the Mississippi system between 1810 and 1820, 1.3 million more between 1820 and 1830, and in the latter year the states had a total population of 3.5 million, more than a quarter of the nation's 12.9 million people. "Nothing like it," noted the historians Charles and Mary Beard, "had yet occurred in the stirring annals of American settlement." Five new states were created by 1821 (Louisiana, Indiana, Mississippi, Illinois, and Missouri), three more before 1850 (Arkansas, Iowa, and Wisconsin). Suddenly Wheeling, Marietta, Cincinnati, and Louisville were cities, with buildings and warehouses and wharves rising along the river; Natchez, Memphis, St. Louis, and Baton Rouge were thriving ports through which millions of tons of freight passed yearly, and New Orleans was the second most important seaport of the nation, with nearly a thousand steamboat arrivals a year in the 1820s and a value of trade that had risen from less than $4 million in 1801 to $26 million in 1830.

In the next twenty years this dynamic growth continued apace, until by mid-century the Mississippi lands held thirty-six percent of the nation's people. A "mass movement of settlers from the older states, supplemented by a mounting stream of immigration from abroad," wrote historian Louis Hunter, "assumed phenomenal proportions in the second quarter of the nineteenth century" as the population of the Mississippi valleys doubled and almost doubled again, reaching 8.3 million in 1850. Manufactured goods and luxuries flooded in from Europe and the East, down from Pittsburgh and (after the Ohio Canal in 1832) Cleveland, up from New Orleans, and it was the steamboat, one writer observed, that "brings to the remotest villages of our streams, and the very doors of the cabins, a little Paris, a section of Broadway, or a slice of Philadelphia." At the same time, agricultural products, principally cotton, streamed downriver to New Orleans, and then to the markets and mills of New England and Britain—340,000 bales in 1820, 2.1 million by 1850—effectively establishing plantation production, dependent on slavery, as the basic way of life for the southern half of the region.

Regardless of the agricultural product, however, it is well to understand that the Southern plantation, like the steamboat, was an institution of the Industrial Revolution, an instrument of regulated, organized production quite similar to the European steam factories of the same time, with a similar regimented and subjugated labor force. With the steam gin to clean its produce in great bulk and the steamboat to carry it efficiently to market, the plantation implanted itself throughout the South almost everywhere below the Ohio River and from Virginia to West Texas, and became the chief system by which one-half of the nation, as the Beards put it, succumbed to "a force that was akin in spirit to the dynamic and acquisitive capitalism of the industrial world."

A Southern historian in the 1840s wrote that it was "when Fulton applied the force of steam to the navigation of the western waters" that a revolution was launched "equal to any recorded in the annals of history," which would make the Mississippi Valley the "noblest and richest country on earth." An exaggeration, to be sure, but steamboats were indeed central to the process that transformed the wilderness into manufacturers and markets, the trading posts into entrepôts and cities: 187 vessels in 1830, nearly 400 in 1836, 557 by 1840, and 740 by 1850, and these were huge structures, three and four decks tall, 200 and 300 feet long, averaging some 250 tons and some as large as four and five hundred tons. By 1850 the number of annual steamboat arrivals reached 3,653 at Cincinnati, 2,897 at St. Louis, 2,784 at New Orleans; Louisiana had more exports than any state but New York, and the South as a whole more exports than any other region. "Of all the elements of the prosperity of the West," declared a savvy James Hall of Cincinnati in 1840, "of all the causes of its rapid increase in population, its growth in wealth, resources and improvement, its immense commerce and gigantic energies, the most efficient has been the navigation by steam."

But it was not all commerce. "To improve the means of communication," wrote a Frenchman, Michel Chevalier, observing the Mississippi steamers in 1835, "is to promote a real, positive, and practical liberty. . . . It is to increase the rights and privileges of the greatest number. . . . It is to establish equality and democracy." Tocqueville in 1831 saw that "the discovery of steam has added unbelievably to the strength and prosperity of the Union, and has done so by facilitating rapid communications between the diverse parts of this vast body." Still another Frenchman in 1850 called steamboats "the salvation of the valley of the Mississippi" and "among the most essential agents of social life" and bulwark of its "rising civilization." All that meant political power, too: eight new states were added before mid-century, with as many senators as New England, New York, and Pennsylvania, and, with Kentucky and Tennessee included, the Mississippi system states had become the strongest region in the Union. Every elected president from Andrew Jackson to Zachary Taylor came from this area, with the exception of Martin Van Buren, and in the words of the great sectional historian Frederick Jackson Turner, these were the years when "the Mississippi valley became the most important influence on American politics."

A nineteenth-century champion of colonialism named MacGregor Laird made the case for steam power this way:

"We have the power in our hands, moral, physical, and mechanical, the first based on the Bible; the second upon the wonderful adaptation of the Anglo-Saxon race to all climates, situations and circumstances; . . . the third bequeathed to us by immortal Watt . . . carrying the glad tidings of 'peace and goodwill toward men' into the dark places of the earth which are now filled with cruelty."

It was the steamboat and the steamship he had in mind as the technological agents of imperialism, carrying the glad tidings of subjection and servitude to the non-industrial corners of the world, and not incidentally

191

bringing back their wealth of resources. But there was another instrument, invented at the same time the steamboat was taking its inevitable place in America's western expansion into "dark places," that would carry tidings, glad and otherwise, even faster than the steamboat: the telegraph.

Samuel Morse, like Fulton a painter who turned to tinkering, was the same age Fulton had been at the maiden voyage of the *North River* when in 1832 he began the experiments that eventually proved it was possible to send messages by electric wire—"distant words," he called it, using the Greek. He obtained a patent in 1837 and then spent six years trying to persuade Congress to lay out the $30,000 he needed to build a workable system, finally obtained in 1843. The next year he strung his wire between Washington and Baltimore, and on May 24 asked the first, and terribly apropos, question ever to be sent instantaneously over a long distance: "What hath God wrought?"

What He had wrought was, like the steamboat, a method of transcending the limits of nature, effectively removing space as a constraint on the transmission of information and for the first time allowing data to be sent and taken in without any particular local context or meaning or quality. Like the steamboat, it savored and celebrated speed, a virtue peculiar to an industrial culture ("Speed is the form of ecstasy the technological revolution has bestowed on man," is how the novelist Milan Kundera has put it) and one quite foreign to, for example, agriculture, education, writing, contemplation, dining, sexual congress, and nature. And like the steamboat, it became an essential tool of the early Industrial Age, drawing disparate sections of the country together culturally and economically, fostering commerce and creating new industries (chiefly the "penny press"), and convincing the swaggering nation by mid-century that it was destined to be the transcendent technological society of the world. As indeed it was.

❦

Of course there were costs that had to accompany the triumph of a technology as sweeping and powerful as the steamboat in middle America.

The most momentous cost was the destruction of the Indian societies east of the Mississippi. The white hordes moving into the frontier spaces steadily pushed the Indians back, aided by official and unofficial government policies, imposing the farms and plantations, the mills and mines, that brought in an industrial civilization that had no use for savages, noble or otherwise. The army led the way, often with steamboats to carry troops and supplies, establishing forts on the banks of all the larger rivers and beyond, and wherever Indian resistance was met, in at least forty major engagements between 1801 and 1845, it was crushed. Fierce or domestic, isolated or intermixed, friendly or hostile, Indians were simply hindering the surge of progress and destiny of a white society determined to have its will with the land and its resources. What came to be called the "Great Removal" began in 1828 with the election of Andrew Jackson, the first president to come from the western frontier and a man determined to advance its interests, including the forced migration of the "savage tribes" from east of the Mississippi to new homes in Oklahoma and beyond; from 1820 to 1844, some 100,000 Indians were taken by trickery, treaty, bribery, theft—and force—from their sizable ancestral lands in Georgia, Alabama, Mississippi, Ohio, Indiana, Illinois, and Wisconsin Territory, and uncounted thousands more died in resistance. It was an unrelenting process that in a few decades would succeed, as Jackson boasted to the nation in his second annual message to Congress, in placing "a dense and civilized population in large tracts of country now occupied by a few savage hunters."

Another cost was borne by the land itself, enormously transformed in less than half a century, and by the life-forms that inhabited it, many decimated or extirpated in that same period. The central ideology of western expansion was the conquest of nature: "The American people," Tocqueville said, "views its own march across these wilds, draining swamps, turning the course of rivers, peopling solitudes, and subduing nature. This magnificent image of themselves does not meet the gaze of the Americans at intervals only; it may be said to haunt every one of them in his least as well as in his most important actions and to be always flitting before his mind." The forests were the first to go, falling under the axes of farmers, builders, potash manufacturers—and steamboaters. On the Mississippi, the larger boats would regularly consume fifty to seventy-five cords a day by mid-century, and at perhaps a hundred cords per acre, that would mean the deforestation of some seventy square miles a day with all the boats in service (Ohio, for example, lost nearly half its woods by 1854); not until coal began to replace wood as the principal fuel in the 1850s did the destruction abate. Construction of the boats themselves required prodigious amounts of wood, and, since the operating principle was to build them for only a short stint on the water—Tocqueville was told that progress in boat design was so rapid they became obsolete in a few years—it is little wonder that an average of about a hundred fifty steamboats were turned out annually in the 1840s. But the real effect of steamboats was to allow a penetration into the wilderness that facilitated the wholesale hunting of its valuable birds and animals—and the convenient way of shipping out the heavy furs and hides to a newly opened Eastern market—and led to the killing of perhaps as many as 500 million creatures and the extinction (in the buffalo's case, near-extinction) of several dozen mammal and more than a hundred plant species. "It would seem," as Missouri senator Thomas Hart Benton said at the time, "that the white man alone received the divine command to subdue and replenish the earth."

One last cost bears mentioning, and, because it affected white people in large part, we know a good deal about it: steamboat accidents. As the eminent steamboat historian Louis Hunter observed, "Part of the price to be paid for the great benefits of steam navigation was a succession of disasters in kind and scale unprecedented in the peacetime experience of this region"—disasters not only sudden and ferocious and indiscriminate, and almost entirely man-made, but deadly beyond anything human enterprise in mines or mills or fields had known. Fulton's accident record was unblemished, and in fact the first accident in New York waters did not occur until 1824 (an explosion on a packet from New Jersey, which killed thirteen or fourteen people), but the condition of the western waters and particularly the cutthroat nature of competition there were conducive to far more frequent and serious accidents and far greater loss of life.

In the wide Mississippi-system rivers, snags and obstructions little encountered in the East or on the Great Lakes caused nearly sixty percent of the accidents from 1811 to 1851 and close to half of the property loss, though only about ten percent (three hundred) of the total number of lives lost; collisions, especially in the busy waters of the lower Mississippi and by boats running full-steam at night, caused less than five percent of the total number of accidents and five percent of the property loss, though with as many as six hundred human fatalities; fires and explosions, overwhelmingly the result of general indifference to human life in the drive for profit, caused not quite forty percent of the accidents but fifty-three percent of the property loss—and something like seventy-five percent of all fatalities, perhaps twenty-five hundred lives in all. Four times as many explosions occurred on western rivers as in the whole rest of the country, with four times as many casualties.

It is hard to believe that catastrophes at this scale were allowed to go on for decades without serious public outcry or at least some self-regulation by vulnerable steamboat owners. (The single most disastrous accident before the Civil War attracted almost no attention and caused no outcry, but that is because it was the sinking of the *Monmouth* in 1837, with the loss of some five hundred Creek Indians being transported to Oklahoma.) But contemporary observers tended to excuse such devastation as part of the callousness and ruthlessness of a competitive frontier life and an inevitable by-product of technology of such speed and power pressed to the limit; an English observer in 1850 saw it as the result of a culture where "business goes by steam, no time to stop and think, no! no!–'go ahead' in its full force is felt by all" and where "so long as a good percentage, or handsome dividend is the result, the loss of life and limb weighs too lightly in the opposite scale." It was not until 1852, and the loss of an additional six hundred lives, that federal regulations were passed requiring the licensing of captains and pilots and the inspection of boilers, and even then more than three hundred lives a year were lost to explosions and fires nationally in the next decade, more than eighty percent on the Mississippi system. A "go-ahead" commerce had found its necessary technology, and human lives would be an expendable side effect.

There was no place in America with river, lake, or coast that did not feel the impact of the steamboat by the middle of the nineteenth century. The first steamer on the Great Lakes, from Buffalo to Chicago, began service in 1818, and by 1831 there were eleven boats, by 1836 forty-five, and by 1847 ninety-eight; by 1825 there were a half-dozen boats on Lake Champlain and steamers on all of the New York Finger Lakes, including sixteen on Cayuga, eleven on Keuka, and ten on Seneca; by 1818 at least six boats were running on the

Delaware, and there were steam vessels on the Potomac, the James, the Savannah, and a number of other Southern rivers. A comprehensive report by the secretary of the Treasury in 1838 estimated that 1,300 steamboats had been built in the United States up to then—an average of about fifty-six every year since Fulton's death—with 260 lost by accident and 240 "worn out" but the rest still running, evenly divided between the Mississippi and Southeast rivers and the Northeast and Great Lakes systems. Later figures indicate that as many as 1,863 more boats were built from 1838 to 1850, suggesting that by the latter date there were more than 1,600 steamboats actively engaged in, and the acknowledged queens of, American waters.

By then their impact on the nation had been so powerful—transforming the commercial processes, the social customs, the patterns of migration and growth, the speed of travel and communication, for the greatest part of the country—that it was not surprising that the astute Daniel Webster could exult: "What centuries of improvement has this single agent comprised in the short space of fifty years. . . . It has essentially altered the face of affairs and no visible limit yet appears beyond which its progress is seen to be impossible."

Elsewhere in the world, too, steamboats penetrated. Canada had its first steamboat as early as 1809, operating between Quebec and Montreal, and there were eight on that run alone by 1825 and an estimated sixteen by 1848. The first British boat was on the Clyde in 1812, and steam ferries were plying between Liverpool and Glasgow and across the Irish Sea by 1819; the British navy, ahead of the American, built three steam vessels between 1820 and 1823, beginning a mastery of the seas under steam to surpass its mastery under sail. By 1820 steamboats were running in Russia, Germany, France, Spain, Austria, and India, by 1830 in Switzerland, Turkey, and China.

But by that time the steamboat had been transformed into something destined to have an even more sweeping global impact.

❦

The election of Andrew Jackson in 1828 signaled the triumph in American politics of what was known as "western"–that is to say, Mississippi Valley–power right until the Civil War.

Jackson, born in eastern South Carolina and settled in Tennessee, was a man of the frontier in every respect: without formal schooling or patrician family (the first president besides Washington with no college degree), fond of chewing tobacco and vulgar stories, a brawler and gambler, a rough soldier and plantation slave-owner, a self-made man of wealth (land speculation, mostly), and an ardent champion of frontier populism against the aristocrats of both New England and the Old South. His idea of politics was cronyism and the spoils system, which he perfected if not invented, and his idea of government was to prop up tariffs presumed to help the interior over the coast and to do away with the Eastern-tainted Bank of the United States so that the new banks that sprang up in the Mississippi region could go on a spending spree. That succeeded in producing the Panic of 1837 and the subsequent depression, but by then he was out of office–and it was the Eastern interests that were hurt most, anyway.

Succeeding presidents for the next dozen years represented "western" power, and all but two were frontiersmen. It was no accident that those years saw the annexation of Texas, the war that wrested California and the Southwest from Mexico, the treaty establishing Oregon Country, the battle cry of "manifest destiny," and the entry into the union of Arkansas, Michigan, Florida, Iowa, and Wisconsin.

It would not be correct to say that Andrew Jackson had no morality, but it could be fairly said that his was of a rough-and-ready kind peculiar to the frontier, where conquest and survival usually did not allow room for niceties, where cunning and ruthlessness were virtues, and where the business of business subsumed most ethical fastidiousness. As a commanding officer he was without mercy for "whining, complaining, seditioners and mutineers," once refusing to commute the death sentence of a nineteen-year-old in his squad who had threatened an officer with a gun, though he did have the delicacy to walk out of earshot when the firing squad performed its duty; as an Indian hunter he was pitiless and unscrupulous, razing whole villages when he deemed it proper and killing off enemy warriors without taking prisoners when he could; as a commissioner of Indian treaties from 1814 to 1824 he succeeded in depriving the Creeks of Georgia and Alabama of half their lands, then through threats, bribes, and deception managed to open additional tens of thousands of acres in the South to white settlement, bringing on the "Great Removal" he was to oversee as president; as a politician he was given to what one historian has called "campaigns of personal slander" and was not above occasional roughneck disruption of his opponents' parades and meetings; as a president he was a careful but persistent defender of the slavery status quo, a befriender of the illegal white usurpation of Creek and Cherokee lands, a friend of the "common man" who used federal troops to break a strike on the Chesapeake and Ohio canal, and a despotic and high-handed "King Andrew" who upheld those laws of the land he favored and ignored the rest.

An English visitor to the Mississippi Valley in the 1840s said that the word *morals* was "obsolete" in this territory. He was wrong; he failed to understand that a system of morals was at work there, but it was a frontier ethic, quite new in the world, and it had its own tenets and codes.

Fifth. One last legacy, deservedly Fulton's, if by indirection.

Although at one time Fulton believed that it would never be possible for a steamboat to survive in heavy ocean waters, his steam frigate, at 247 tons and 167 feet, was more of a ship than a boat and had even successfully tested the Atlantic off Sandy Hook, New Jersey; and his *Fulton,* built for the Sound, had been effectively an oceangoing vessel. And so it was inevitable that someone following his lead would gear up a paddlewheeler for true maritime travel.

The first attempt was in 1819, when the 380-ton *Savannah,* a ship built essentially along Fulton's designs except for a larger rig of sails than he had ever used on his early boats, made a journey across the Atlantic in just twenty-nine days, though in truth it did not use its paddlewheels except for eighteen hours during a mid-ocean calm and again when approaching its Liverpool dock site. It went on to St. Petersburg, Russia, mixing steam with sail, and made its way back to Georgia as the same hybrid, not exactly proving but suggesting that a steamship would eventually supplant the "canvas-back" packets on the Atlantic. Other ocean voyages were made in 1827 and 1833 by ships designed exclusively for steam, but not until 1838 did a regular service begin between England and the United States, with coal-burning steamships that regularly cut down the crossing time with each successive year, to fifteen to twenty days in the 1840s and as few as ten to twelve by 1850. At mid-century, with the eight-ship Cunard Line from Liverpool and the four-ship Collins Line from New York, the age of the steamship was truly under way, not to end for a century more.

The steamship was important also for trade along the American Atlantic coast, from Boston to Savannah, and along the Gulf of Mexico. The first coastal steamer was, appropriately, the 700-ton *Robert Fulton* in 1820, and eventually regular service was established on New York–Charleston and Baltimore–Savannah routes in the 1830s and 1840s, although several of the earlier ships were lost in the heavy seas off Cape

Hatteras before stonger-hulled coasters were put in use by 1846. At mid-century the United States had steamships of a total tonnage of 481,005 in its coastal trade, a figure whose impressiveness is conveyed by comparison with Great Britain's total mercantile steam tonnage of 187,631.

In an irony that would have been no doubt lost on Fulton, it was his steamboat, amplified into the steamship, and not his floating mines, that ultimately led the way to free trade and liberty of the seas.

It is a matter of legacies, and a man who knew a little something about steamboats from firsthand experience, and a little something about the life they created on the Mississippi, who summed up Fulton's endowment a century after his death.

"The 19th Century began the most prolific age of invention," said Mark Twain in 1907, "bringing into our daily life the convenience of machines which were recently unknown but in our dreams. At the beginning of that period of material progress stands the name of Robert Fulton.

"He made the vacant oceans and the idle rivers useful, after the unprejudiced had been wondering for years what they were for. He found these properties a liability; he left them an asset.

"By his genius Robert Fulton laid the foundation of the greatness of New York, and with his brother immortals, Watt and Stephenson, he created the stupendous prodigy, the globe's modern commerce, and with it, in vast measure, the really stupendous moral and material civilization which has resulted from it."

"By his genius"—by whose fire, in his but brief a life, he was consumed.

Epilogue

THE NEW TECHNOLOGIES that have generally succeeded in the last five hundred years are those that have enhanced the political and economic regimes in ascendance–rising, not necessarily risen–in society at the time they were introduced. They are thus regarded as the tools, the manifestations, of that society, as to some extent they are; but in a more important sense they are the shapers and determinants of the society, for they come with biases and implications built into them that are more complex, powerful, and directional than even those who benefit from them can control or mediate. From the printing press to the silicon chip, the technologies of Western society have transformed the very nature of the culture, subtly and otherwise, with psychological and social implications ultimately far more profound than mechanical or economic ones.

The steamboat in America was one such transformative technology. Of course it was a tool by which the dominant commercial interests could extend their reach and power, by which the reigning political forces could communicate and consolidate their influence, by which a restless people could penetrate new lands and develop new industries—all this, as we have seen, was clear to many at the time. What they did not know is that, necessarily if latently, it brought with it, in its engines and boilers and paddles as it were, a certain range of possibilities and demands and effects, inherent in the sort of technology it was and hence the sort of behavior it allowed and encouraged.

The steamboat first of all called forth an industrial substructure—mechanics, ironsmiths, boatwrights, boilersmiths, steamfitters, engineers, and machine shops, boatworks, rolling mills, foundries, and manufactories for them—all along the coasts and water arteries of the land, increasing in scope and complexity with each passing year. Within three years of the *New Orleans'* maiden voyage in 1811, there were at least three ironworks in and around Pittsburgh turning out steam engines, shortly afterward James Allaire was building them along the East River in New York, and by 1825, when engines were being manufactured in at least a dozen cities, no one was even thinking of Boulton and Watt: America was in the throes of its own Industrial Revolution. Within no more than a generation or two after the steamboat, industrialism was established as an American way of life.

The steamboat also permitted a nation ingrained with violence, and not especially reticent about it, to carry out its aggressive and expansive agendas, including military ones. Large, imposing, and remarkably maneuverable, unlike most previous machines, the steamboat was above all fast, and thus an ideal vessel for military use (speed being, as Sun Tzu famously noted, "the essence of warfare"). Fulton himself had come to realize this military potential, manifesting it in the steam frigate of 1814–15, but he could hardly have imagined the role steamboats were to play as an agent of war, especially for the U.S. army in its battles against the Indians and Mexicans or, after the British navy developed steamships in the 1820s, as the primary instruments of naval warfare for the next century.

The steamboat lent itself supremely well to long-distance

travel, where its efficiencies were maximized (it was used as a ferry in New York but was not especially superior to nonsteam competition), hence promoting the penetration of white people and their products farther and farther into the interior, the mingling and diffusion of local cultures into larger wholes, the extension of the nation's political and economic power, and the eventual ideology of manifest destiny. With it, too, went the pridefulness of conquest and the belief in the legitimacy, even the high moral purpose, of the perpetual march across the continent by those people intelligent and resourceful enough to devise the technologies to assist them.

The steamboat proved ideally suited for the transportation of heavy and bulky goods in large quantities, particularly for long hauls, and therefore for the development of an industrial economy. In a remarkably short time the northern Mississippi Valley was turned into a manufacturing and grain-growing section, the lower into a cotton-growing section, each with the instruments and institutions of an industrial market economy and the social and psychological habits it fosters. The range of all this, moreover, was not merely continental but intercontinental, with far-reaching implications for American politics and foreign policy.

The steamboat was a demonstration, graphic and repeated, of the triumph of human technology over nature—over time, space, geography, tide, wind, current—and over the species and systems of the natural world to which it provided access. As Cadwallader Colden saw it, in this technology "the mind of an individual has contended with nature in her grandest form, and subdued what appeared to be her irresistible opposition," the supreme demonstration that "knowledge is power." That was an abiding faith of the nineteenth-century American, and it would be well into the twentieth century before anyone would doubt the legitimacy of using for the conquest of nature any technology the nation could develop.

The steamboat, similarly, ratified the principle that in theory there were no limits to technological development, and hence to the perfectibility of human societies, or at least the rightfulness of such a quest. Fernand Braudel has pointed to the way in which the Industrial Revolution enabled Europe to transcend "the limits of the possible," and this goal was indeed a profound impetus to American technological growth throughout the nineteenth century. The effect on a society grounded in such a goal, however, which is doomed to disaster in a world where there are finite limits, is psychologically dangerous as well as practically foolish.

Finally, the steamboat, by its very success and continued improvement, served to sanction and encourage the dominance of technology itself in American society and its intimate interweaving into this country's perceived purpose of development, exploitation, expansion, and "progress." It is an indication of how deeply this resides in the American character that since its inception, and the Industrial Age it ushered in, we have tended to measure other societies and other ages by their degree of technological complexity, confident that it is an accurate gauge of basic human intellectual and cultural levels, accumulated wisdom to the contrary.

It was not the steamboat alone, of course, that created America's industrial milieu in the nineteenth century or the industrial ideology that the nation was to carry through the twentieth. But it was the first significant industrial instrument to shape that milieu and inspire that ideology, the first to embody the brash and assertive and expansionary characteristics of the peoples dominant here, the first to create that era in America, as Henry Adams had sagely noted, "which separated the colonial from the independent stage of growth." And none who ever rode its throbbing decks, or watched its majestic motility on the water, ever failed to realize that it was thus the symbol, as it was for many years the agency, of the American dream.

Acknowledgments

I would like to thank all those who have previously written (with varying levels of accuracy but none without interest) about Robert Fulton or the world of steamboats; the libraries of the Hudson Valley, particularly the Julia Butterfield Library of Cold Spring, New York, and the New York City Research Library at Forty-second Street; the New-York Historical Society and the Clermont Historical archives; and these especially helpful individuals: Ben Apfelbaum, Shirley Branchini, Brian Carey, Henry Dunow, Paul Gottlieb, Mark L. Heller, David Leshan, Anna Jardine, John Paulits, Judy Peaker, Betty Russell, Craig Siegel, Lionel Tiger, and Anthony Vaver, and my editor, Bill Rosen. I would also like to commend my daughters, Rebekah Sale and Kalista Parrish.

Notes

Complete references for sources cited in brief can be found in the list of sources on page 213.

CHAPTER 1: THE *NORTH RIVER*

1. There are many conflicting versions of the dimensions of the original steamboat, but in a deed of May 13, 1808 (Robert Livingston Papers, NYHS), Fulton says plainly that he enrolled the vessel in September 1807 in New York City with dimensions of 142 feet long, 14 feet wide, and 4 feet deep, at 79 tons. The boat was widened and lengthened considerably for its second season in the spring of 1808.
2. Some accounts have it that Andrew Brinck was the captain on this first voyage, but records in Livingston's papers showing that Davis Hunt was paid $55.60 on September 10, 1807, and Brinck $30 on September 20, suggest that Hunt was the superior employee; Philip (p. 206) also has Hunt as captain, later replaced by Brinck.
3. There is a great deal of confusion in the various accounts of this sailing about just who was on board the steamboat. Many place there Dr. Samuel Mitchill, an eminent New Yorker and former U.S. senator, and Dr. William McNiven (McNeven), dean of the cathedral of Ripon, England, although Colden carefully notes that they had been

on the boat the day before, a Sunday, when it was transferred from the East River to the Hudson dock, and says nothing about their presence on the maiden trip. We can surmise, however, from a later account probably his, that McNiven actually boarded after the steamboat put into Clermont on Wednesday morning, and it is difficult to see how (or why) he got to the Chancellor's estate so quickly if he was really on the Sunday trip. Other accounts also place Robert Livingston himself on board on Monday, but no evidence supports that, and his own account begins with the Wednesday leg from Clermont to Albany, so it was probably upstate that he joined the party. Fulton himself left no record, and there was no press coverage.

4. Confusion over an account credited to the Hudson, New York, *Bee* has led biographers to follow Colden and assert, mistakenly, that the steamboat was called the *Clermont*. The *Bee* of May 15, 1810, refers to an unusually fast journey by "the steamboat," and a later editor, compiling an *Annals of Albany* in 1854, interpolated after "steamboat" the bracketed phrase "[which has lately been known by the name of *Clermont*, that is in books]," referring perhaps to two recent biographies of Fulton. This was later read as if the *Bee* had said the boat was "lately" known as the *Clermont*—that is, in 1810—but "lately" clearly means the 1850s. Testimony that the public referred to the steamboat as the *North River* in its early years is provided by Charles Brownne, the boat's hullmaker, in a legal brief of July 23, 1811 (Fulton Papers, NYPL, Box 1). A fuller account of the error appears in *American Neptune* (Vol. 24, 1964).

CHAPTER 2: PRECURSORS

1. Legend has it that Fitch ran a steamboat on Collect Pond in lower Manhattan around 1796, but there is nothing to verify such a tale—it makes its first appearance in 1846, a report of a boyhood memory—and much to discredit it. For one thing, in all his diaries and letters, Fitch makes no mention of it, nor does Chancellor Livingston, who supposedly was on board, nor do John Stevens or Nicholas Roosevelt, who were attentive to such experiments. For another, the pond by then was a foul swamp—"a very sink and common sewer," as one description had it (see Burrows and Wallace, p. 359)—and a very unlikely place for a steamboat experiment. Besides, how could a full-

Notes

size steamboat get there, and why would one test it on a pond without current, anyway? (See Flexner, p. 238.)

2. The accounts of which steamboats operated when are generally murky, but there is good evidence for six: Samuel Morey, on the Hudson around 1796 and on the Delaware in 1797 (see William A. Duer, *A Reply to Mr. Colden's Vindication of the Steamboat Monopoly* [Albany, N.Y., 1819], pp. x–xvii); Elijah Ormsbee, in Narragansett Bay in 1792 or 1794 (see Penrose R. Hoopes, *Connecticut's Contribution to the Development of the Steamboat* [New Haven, Conn.: Yale University Press, 1936], and George H. Preble, *A Chronological History . . . of Steam Navigation* [Philadelphia, 1895]; Oliver Evans, whose 1804 boat on the Mississippi was washed inland in a flood and never tried, on the Schuylkill in 1805 (see Grenville and Dorthy Bathe, *Oliver Evans,* 1935, and Preble); and John Stevens in New York harbor in 1802 and 1804 (see Archibald D. Turnbull, *John Stevens, An American Record* [New York: Century, 1928]).

3. The only account of Morey's trip is that of the inventor himself, in a letter written in 1818 (in Duer), and it may be that he is confusing two separate events. If the trip took place in 1796, Livingston could not have offered him the "patent rights" (the Hudson monopoly), which he did not secure until 1798; the Chancellor may well have made him a later offer, since the two were in touch for several years.

CHAPTER 3: 1765–1797

1. Many accounts give 1786 as Fulton's sailing date, and Colden says he went to England in "the same year" as his stay at Bath, but a voyage in, say, May 1787, taking four to six weeks, jibes better with his statement in a 1792 letter to his mother that he had been studying "for near four years" before he got the job with Courtenay in June 1791.

2. Fulton borrowed sufficiently to have it weigh enough on his conscience that as late as June 1810 he sent money to repay old debts "at Exeter" (letter to Henry Fulton, a figure of mystery, Fulton Papers, NYPL, Box 2). A few years later he urged a friend in England to send greetings to "my amiable friends at Totness" (*sic:* Totnes is a town near Exeter) for their "many estimable good qualities and kindness which I reflect on and often with pleasure" (letter of August 8, 1813, Fulton Papers, NYPL, Box 2).

3. In his memoirs, Owen says that Fulton was welcomed into a circle of

210

Manchester friends including John Dalton, who would go on to be a distinguished scientist, Erasmus Darwin, physician and tinkerer (and grandfather of Charles), and Samuel Coleridge, though the record suggests that the poet was not in Manchester except on a speaking tour in January and February 1796 and probably not a regular of this circle, at least while Fulton was there *(Life of Robert Owen* [London, 1857], vol. 1, p. 64). It is irresistible to add that in his *Botanic Garden* (part 1, line 289) of 1789–before he would have met Fulton–Erasmus Darwin predicts: "Soon shall thy arm, unconquer'd steam! Afar / Drag the slow barge, or drive the rapid car."

CHAPTER 4: 1797–1803

1. Most biographies assert that the panorama was a scene of a Moscow fire–not the one after Napoleon's invasion of Russia, of course, but some unspecified earlier one–yet this seems an unlikely choice, and there is no way of knowing how Fulton would have been able to reproduce it accurately. Philip (p. 90), relying on an account in Germain Babst's *Essai sur l'histoire des panoramas et dioramas* (Paris, 1891), says flatly that it was a view of Paris, and this seems far more likely–and more attractive to a Parisian audience. Also, the original panorama was a scene of London, and it would have been natural to copy that idea.

2. Towing was later a feature of both Hudson and Mississippi steamboats. On the Hudson, steamers were used from the 1830s on to pull a line of boats that had made their way through the Erie Canal, and not long afterward it was common for steamboats to pull engineless floating platforms for passengers, who would be less likely to be endangered by boiler explosions or engine fires. On the Mississippi, coal and some other cargoes were pushed by steamboat tugs as early as the 1830s, but the big business of towing began after 1850 and was well established after the Civil War, again usually with cargoes such as coal, but at times with passengers.

3. A French writer in 1867 (Louis Figuier, *Les Merveilles de la science*) has the story that Napoleon complained that Fulton was just like the adventurers crowding every European capital: "They are either charlatans or impostors who have no other goal than to grab money. This American is one of that number. Do not speak to me about him again." Highly unlikely; no verification. Philip (p. 150) retails a version

that Fulton met with Napoleon and after being turned down wept in despair because Napoleon was so shortsighted. Sutcliffe (pp. 160–61) reproduces a lithograph, made in Philadelphia after 1821, of a Fulton–Napoleon meeting "in 1804," at which Fulton promises the First Consul "the largest and most powerful Navy in the World"; Napoleon, relying on his advisors' report that steam was "so feeble that a child's toy could hardly be put in motion by it," rejects Fulton's offer.

Chapter 5: 1804–1807

1. Fulton had apparently paid for a copper boiler in London, but for some reason it was not shipped to New York. In a notebook entry in March 1805, when he was still in England, he wrote only that he paid a fee for permission "to ship the Engine for America" and did not mention a boiler (Sutcliffe, p. 185). A March 16, 1807, letter to Livingston makes it clear in any case that he employed a coppersmith in New York to make a new boiler.

Chapter 6: 1807–1812

1. There is some question about who wrote this passage. Since it appeared in a British publication, the *Naval Chronicle* (vol. 19, 1808, p. 188), it might be supposed to be an account by McNiven, the dean of Ripon Cathedral. But by one report he was on the steamboat on Sunday, before it departed New York, and this writer clearly went aboard at Clermont on Wednesday morning, and it is unlikely that McNiven could have been there just two days later. Preble, in his *Chronological History . . . of Steam Navigation* (p. 44), says without being more specific that it was written by "a gentleman of South Carolina," but he is not always a trustworthy source.
2. This account, in a letter to the *American Citizen*, was dated August 20, a Thursday, but it had to have been written actually on August 21, since it refers to the arrival at New York "on Friday at 4 in the afternoon." That could be a typographical error, but seems more likely to reflect the effects of tension, and perhaps sleeplessness, on Fulton, as Charles Dyck's story also suggests.
3. The increase in width was necessary not only to support the larger machinery but also to provide a better balance for the boat than the

142-by-14-foot original, which, as later engineers discovered, was
highly unstable and easy to capsize. When a replica boat was made
for the 1909 Fulton–Hudson celebration, the committee in charge
determined that it would have to duplicate the larger 149 feet by 17
feet, 11 inches of the revised 1808 *North River.*

Chapter 7: 1813–1815

1. The launch of the *Fulton,* and its defeat of both the *Car of Neptune* and
   the *Paragon* in a race on the Hudson, revealed an important side of
   Fulton the inventor that even he might not have acknowledged. The
   design of that boat contradicted most of the arguments its builder
   had been making in favor of the originality of his steamboat proportions and systems: instead of relying on the length–breadth ratios of
   10 to 1 and 8 to 1 of the *North River* and 7 to 1 of the *Car of Neptune,*
   elongations he had insisted were essential, he now made the hull of
   the *Fulton* a little over 4½ to 1, much like a conventional sailboat, because it would have to withstand the heavier seas of the Sound; instead of the flat-bottom, straight-side shape he had maintained was
   essential to minimize water resistance and capture the full power of
   the wheels, he now used the stronger shape of a traditional oceangoing ship with a curved bottom and sloping sides. When he found that
   this curved hull did not increase the water resistance, despite his
   vaunted calculations based on Beaufoy's underwater research, he
   used it for his subsequent Eastern boats—a testament to a thoroughly
   American sense of pragmatism over theory.
2. Fulton's patents: inclined planes, once in Britain, once in France, for
   which he borrowed an ancient idea already in use in England; a rope-
   maker, admittedly modeled on Edmund Cartwright's previous design; panoramas, patented twice, copied directly from an English
   design; the steamboat, patented twice, a "new arrangement" of old
   ideas; the underwater cannon; the steam frigate. In addition, he built
   or designed a marble-cutting device, a canal-digging machine, a submarine, floating mines ("torpedoes"), an underwater cable-cutter, an
   anchored water mine, a harpoon gun, and an armor-plated torpedo
   boat, none of which he thought to patent, either because they did not
   work or were not sufficiently original.
3. There is no way to know for sure of the genuineness of the letter of
   November 4, 1793. Fulton certainly wrote to Stanhope about steam-

boats that fall, as one of Stanhope's surviving letters makes clear (Colden, pp. 114–15) and as Fulton maintained in his canal treatise published in 1796. But whether he actually proposed sidewheels at the time is unproven and made less likely by the fact that when he settled down to experiment in France in 1802 he first tried a model with rotating oval chains and it took him a year of testing to switch to fixed circular side paddles. There are peculiarities about the Fulton copied version of the letter, too, including a strange use of "in June '93 I began the experiments," when "last June" or "back in June" would have been more natural for a letter written in November. In addition, when Fulton wrote to Stanhope in April 1811 to ask him to certify to the original for the case against the Albany infringers, he received no reply.

Against all that, there is indeed a November 4, 1793, letter from Fulton in Stanhope's files, though it is marked as a copy. (The Stanhope collection is at the Centre for Kentish Studies, Kent, England, and I am grateful to Judy Peaker for her intrepid detective work there on my behalf.) If it is a copy, it is hard to know when it would have gotten there, since it appears not to be the "inclosed exact copy" Fulton sent in 1811: the writing paper is different and the folds in the letters do not match, suggesting they were not sent in the same envelope. There are no watermarks on it and the envelope was not retained, but the writing is certainly Fulton's. In addition, the tone and the careful step-by-step presentation of those purported 1793 experiments are so like the dogged and self-absorbed early Fulton that it is hard to imagine he sat down in 1811 and put himself back in that youthful mode to produce a forgery.

4. The whereabouts of the *Hope*, which Fulton had bought for $11,000 in 1812 and used for two years on the Hudson, are unknown; my hunch is that it was finally put on Lake Champlain, where Fulton seems to have had steamboat interests about which very little is known. Another boat, the *Allaire*, presumably built by and named after the James Allaire who had worked on several of Fulton's boats, was listed as part of the 1815 accounts of the Hudson boats, but the vessel is otherwise unknown.

Sources

Primary Works

The books listed below are referred to in the notes by the author's last name only; all other sources are given in full at the first instance, then by the author's last name and (sometimes shortened) title.

Burrows, Edwin G., and Mike Wallace, *Gotham: A History of New York City to 1898*. New York: Oxford University Press, 1999.

Colden, Cadwallader, *The Life of Robert Fulton*. New York: Kirk & Mercein, 1817.

Delaplaine, Joseph, *Delaplaine's Repository of the Lives and Portraits of Distinguished American Characters*, vol. 1, Philadelphia, 1816 (probably 1818).

Dickinson, H. W., *Robert Fulton, Engineer and Artist: His Life and Works*. London: John Lane, 1913.

Flexner, James Thomas, *Steamboats Come True*. Boston: Little, Brown, 1944, repr. 1978.

Hunter, Louis C., *Steamboats on Western Waters*. Cambridge, Mass.: Harvard University Press, 1948; repr. New York: Dover, 1993.

Morgan, John S., *Robert Fulton*. New York: Mason/Charter, 1977.

Parsons, William Barclay, *Robert Fulton and the Submarine*. New York: Columbia University Press, 1922.

Sources

Philip, Cynthia Owen, *Robert Fulton.* New York: Franklin Watts, 1985.

Reigart, J. Franklin, *The Life of Robert Fulton.* Philadelphia: C. G. Henderson, 1856.

Sutcliffe, Alice Crary, *Robert Fulton and the "Clermont."* New York: Century, 1909.

Todd, Charles B. *The Life and Letters of Joel Barlow.* New York: Putnam, 1886.

Collections

These are abbreviated in the notes as indicated below.

New York Public Library (NYPL): Fulton Papers

New-York Historical Society (NYHS): Randall J. LeBoeuf, Jr., Collection; Miscellaneous Fulton; Robert R. Livingston Papers

Livingston Archives, Clermont Historic Site (CHS), Germantown, New York

Kent County (England) Archives (KCA): Stanhope Collection

Source Notes

INTRODUCTION

page
3   "Like the self-burning"–Colden, p. 371.

CHAPTER 1: THE *NORTH RIVER*

5   Sources for the reconstruction of the initial part of the maiden voyage are meager and contradictory, and many are later remembrances: Colden, pp. 167–73; Sutcliffe, pp. 202–20; Joseph Story, *Life and Letters of Joseph Story,* ed. W. W. Story (Boston, 1851), vol. 2, pp. 24–25; J. M. Matthews, *Recollections of . . . New York* (New York, 1885), pp. 41–49.

6   New York torpedo experiment–RF to Thomas Jefferson, 8/28/07, Library of Congress; *Salmagundi,* 8/14/07.

8   New York City, 1807–Samuel L. Mitchill, *The Picture of New-York* (New York: I. Riley, 1807); Warren Tryon, *A Mirror for Americans* (Chicago: University of Chicago, 1952), vol. 1; *Salmagundi,* 1807; Sidney I. Pomerantz, *New York: An American City* (Port Washington, N.Y.: Friedman, 1958, repr. 1965); Burrows and Wallace.

Source Notes

8 "Nature herself intended"–James Fenimore Cooper, *Notions of the Americans* (New York: Unger, 1963), vol. 1, pp. 112, 120.

8 "All was noise"–John Lambert, *Travels Through Canada and the United States* (London: Cradock & Joy, 1813).

9 "the great mart"–Cooper, *Notions,* p. 121.

10 "As I had occasion"–Story, *Life and Letters,* p. 24.

11 "She was a queer-looking"–John Q. Wilson, in Sutcliffe, p. 247.

12 "a monster moving"–Sutcliffe, p. 208.

13 "Cousin Chancellor," "Bob has had"–Sutcliffe, pp. 209, 212.

13 "in the moments"–Story, *Life and Letters,* p. 25.

13 "she will, when"–RF to RL, 8/10/07, CHS; Sutcliffe, p. 198.

14 Letter to Boulton, Watt–Dickinson, p. 30.

14 "a passage boat"–RF–RL contract, 10/10/02, CHS; Dickinson, pp. 149–50.

14 "ingenious Steam Boat"–*American Citizen,* 8/17/07, in Sutcliffe, p. 220.

15 "In front of the house"–*Letters of Mrs. Adams* (Boston: Little, Brown, 1840), pp. 201–2.

16 Burr–Philip McFarland, *Sojourners* (New York: Atheneum, 1979); Burrows and Wallace.

17 Irving–McFarland, *Sojourners,* pp. 74–85; *Complete Works of Washington Irving,* vol. 1: *Letters* (Boston: Twayne, 1978), p. 245.

18 RF account–Story, *Life and Letters,* p. 25.

19 brief notice, "sails today"–*American Citizen,* 8/17/07, in Sutcliffe, p. 220.

20 "When the shouts"–Matthews, *Recollections,* pp. 41–49.

21 "was called the Clermont," "North River"–Colden, p. 170, after p. 274.

21 "I overtook"–Colden, p. 176; Sutcliffe, p. 234.

Chapter 2: Precursors

22 "As the component parts"–RF, *A Treatise on the Improvement of Canal Navigation,* NYPL; Philip, p. 47.

25 Fitch–Thomas Boyd, *Poor John Fitch* (New York: Putnam, 1935); Flexner.

26 "We reigned Lord"–Flexner, p. 184.

26 "THE STEAMBOAT"–*Federal Gazette,* 6/14/90, in Flexner, p. 186.

28 "A thousand special causes"–Alexis de Tocqueville, *Democracy in America* (New York: Vintage, 1954), vol. 2, bk. 1, p. 38.
29 Franklin paper–Flexner, p. 91.
30 Livingston–George Dangerfield, *Chancellor Robert R. Livingston of New York, 1746–1813* (New York: Harcourt, 1960).
31 Morey–William A. Duer, *A Reply to Mr. Colden's Vindication of the Steamboat Monopoly* (Albany, N.Y., 1819), p. xvi.
31 "perfectly new"–RL to Nicholas Roosevelt, 12/8/97, NYHS.
32 "The navigation by steam"–Dangerfield, *Chancellor,* p. 412.
32 "2 wheels"–Nicholas Roosevelt to RL, 9/6/98, NYHS.
33 "3 miles"–Roosevelt to RL, 10/21/98, NYHS; Flexner, p. 265.
35 Latrobe–*The Correspondence and Miscellaneous Papers of Benjamin Henry Latrobe,* ed. John C. Van Horne et al. (New Haven, Conn.: Yale University Press, 1984); paper, 5/20/03; Colden, pp. 134–38.
37 Stevens–Archibald D. Turnbull, *John Stevens, An American Record* (New York: Century, 1928); Stevens, *American Medical and Philosophical Register,* vol. 2 (1812).

CHAPTER 3: 1765–1797

41 Reigart, p. xxx; p. 10.
42 "Y have Nothing"–Philip, p. 4.
42 "attached no importance"–Flexner, p. 111, with no further citation of source.
42 "considered, as he"–Colden, p. 7.
44 "a neat assortment"–Delaplaine, p. 201.
44 "Fulton, Robert"–*White's Directory of the City of Philadelphia* (1785).
44 "derive emolument"–Colden, p. 8.
44 "wherein all"–François-Jean Chastellux, in Philip, p. 9.
45 "Robert Fulton, miniature"–Flexner, p. 120.
46 "some gentlemen"–Colden, p. 9.
46 "not more than"–RF to Mary Smith Fulton, 1/20/92, Dickinson, p. 17.
46 West–Dorinda Evans, *Benjamin West and His American Students* (Washington, D.C.: Smithsonian, 1980); Robert C. Alberts, *Benjamin West* (New York: Houghton Mifflin, 1978).
47 Dunlap–*History of the Arts and Design in the United States* (New York: G. P. Scott, 1834), p. 67.
47 Hunt–Flexner, p. 215.

48   "Here I had"–RF to Mary Smith Fulton, 1/20/92, Dickinson, p. 17.
48   "Recd every posable"–ibid.
49   "Last summer I"–ibid.
49   Courtenay and Beckford–James Lees-Milne, *William Beckford* (London: Compton Russel, 1976); Malcolm Jack, *William Beckford, an English Fidalgo* (New York: AMS Press, 1996); Rictor Norton, *Mother Clap's Molly House* (London: GMP, 1992); Paulina Pepys, *Powderham Castle* (Derby, England, n.d.); *Annual Register* (London, 1835), p. 222.
50   "my bachelor ideas"–RF to David Morris, 5/21/93, Morgan, p. 50.
51   "more actively"–Norton, *Mother Clap's*, p. 225.
51   "unnatural crimes" and 1811 episode–Joseph Farrington, entry of 5/17/11, *Diary* (New Haven, CT: Yale University Press, 1978), vol. 6.
51   Courtenay in New York–letter of 4/20/12, NYHS Manuscript Collection.
51   Renwick–Jared Sparks, *Lives of Eminent Individuals* (New York: Harper, 1847, repr. 1902), vol. 1, p. 163.
53   "saw the works"–RF to Mary Smith Fulton, 1/20/92, Dickinson, p. 17.
53   "He has stedily"–RF to David Morris, 5/21/93, Dickinson, p. 19.
53   "I have laid"–RF to David Morris, 9/12/96, Dickinson, p. 59.
54   "I have not"–RF to Earl of Stanhope, 11/27/93, KCA; Philip, p. 31.
54   "never made"–Earl of Stanhope to RF, 12/17/93, Philip, p. 34.
54   "I will Candidly"–RF to Earl of Stanhope, 12/22/93, KCA; Philip, p. 35.
54   "It will not be"–Earl of Stanhope to RF, 12/27/93, KCA; Philip, p. 36.
54   "to obtain practical"–RF to Gouverneur Morris, 2/22/14, Colden, pp. 275ff.
55   "a simple Machine"–Exeter *Flying Post,* 1/23/94, Philip, p. 36.
55   patent–Dickinson, pp. 28–29.
55   West–Alberts, *Benjamin West.*
57   RF letter to Stanhope–see chapter 7 (p. 163–65).
57   RF letter to Boulton, Watt–11/4/94, Dickinson, p. 30.
57   Owen–Robert Owen, *Life of Robert Owen* (London, 1857), vol. 1, pp. 64–70.

58 biographer–Philip, p. 39.
58 Fulton's *Treatise*–(London, 1796), NYPL.
59 "I am now"–RF to Earl of Stanhope, 12/28/96, Dickinson, p. 55.
59 "will soon be"–RF to Benjamin West, 2/22/97, NYHS.
60 "one fourth"–Robert Owen, 4/28/97, in Owen, *Life,* p. 70; Dickinson, pp. 59–60.
60 Church–RF to Samuel Hopkins, 5/10/08, LeBoeuf Collection, NYHS; Helene C. Phelan, *The Man Who Owned the Pistols* (Interlaken, N.Y.: Heart of the Lakes, 1951).
61 RF letter to Washington–2/5/97, Sutcliffe, p. 310.

Chapter 4: 1797–1803

63 "a curious machine"–*Memoirs of Edmund Cartwright* (London, 1843), p. 143.
63 "the liberty of"–RF to Director Paul de Barras, 10/27/98, Dickinson, p. 90.
64 "a child," "the best of"–Ruth Barlow to Joel Barlow, 1/22/97, Philip, p. 106.
64 Barlow–Todd; James Woodress, *A Yankee's Odyssey* (Philadelphia: Lippincott, 1958).
65 "commenced that strong"–Colden, p. 27.
65 *"grand garçons,"*"how happy"–Philip, p. 107.
65 "he learnt"–Colden, p. 27.
66 Bushnell–Flexner, pp. 248–53.
66 "Thoughts on Free Trade"–Seligman Papers, Columbia University Library; Philip, pp. 69–70.
66 "I turned my"–Colden, pp. 25–26.
67 "First, to navigate"–Flexner, p. 247.
67 "Nautulus" proposal–Dickinson, pp. 74–76.
68 "Friction brings"–RF to Lord Stanhope, 5/24/96, KCA.
68 "only by eliminating"–RF to Napoleon Bonaparte, 5/1/98, NYPL; Dickinson, pp. 68–70.
68 "the destruction"–RF to Directory, 7/23/98, Dickinson, p. 79.
68 Marine Ministry report–Dickinson, p. 88.
68 "Nautulus" agreement–ibid.
69 "monstrous government"–Dickinson, p. 90.
69 "A stranger greets"–Philip, p. 90.
70 "convert the overflowings"–*Memoirs of Edmund Cartwright,* p. 141.

70 "much shame"–RF to Nathaniel Cutting, 12/98, LeBoeuf Collection, NYHS.

70 "it is not"–RF to Nathaniel Cutting, 7/9/99, ibid.

71 "Poor Fulton"–RF to Nathaniel Cutting, 6/27/00, ibid.

71 "I sincerely hope"–RF to Marine Ministry, 10/6/99, Flexner, p. 260.

71 "how sincerely I"–RF to Vanstaphast, 9/29/06, LeBoeuf Collection, NYHS.

71 "furnished him"–Colden, p. 30.

72 "would annihilate"–Colden, pp. 43–44.

72 Scioto scheme–Daniel M. Friedenberg, *Life, Liberty, and the Pursuit of Land: The Plunder of Early America* (Buffalo, N.Y.: Prometheus, 1992), pp. 287–91.

74 "I have every"–RF to Marine Ministry, 4/10/00, Dickinson, p. 100.

74 "everything that could"–Pierre Forfait, Philip, p. 97.

75 "succeeded to sail"–RF to Pierre Forfait, 7/25/00, Dickinson, p. 102.

75 "all my experiments"–RF to Pierre Forfait, 8/5/00, ibid.

76 "equinoctial gales," "whether by accident," "Navigation under water"–RF to National Institute, 11/7/00, ibid., pp. 106, 108, 109.

76 "We do not"–Dickinson, p. 111.

77 "the cold and"–RF to Pierre Forfait, 12/3/00, Parsons, p. 37.

77 formal agreement–Dickinson, pp. 113–14.

78 Barlow letters–Todd, pp. 177–203; Philip, pp. 102–4, 107, 126–27, 136.

79 "an aging satyr"–Philip, p. 108.

81 "No vessel could"–RF to Napoleon's Committee, 9/9/01, Sutcliffe, p. 324.

81 "she leaked Very"–RF to Napoleon's Committee, 9/20/01; Morgan, p. 78; Philip, p. 116.

82 "accidentally met"–Flexner, p. 277.

84 "What is Fulton about?"–Thomas Paine to Joel Barlow, 5/4/07, Jack Fruchtman, *Thomas Paine: Apostle of Freedom* (New York: Harper & Row, 1994).

85 Barlow letters–Todd, pp. 177–203; Philip, pp. 102–4, 107, 126–27, 136.

86 Fulton experiments–RF to RL, 6/5, 6/13, 7/20, 9/2, all 1802, CHS.

86 "my time"–RF to RL, 6/13/02, CHS; RF manuscript "Moving Boats by Machinery," 6/5/02, NYPL.
86 "perfectly satisfied"–Joel Barlow to RF and Ruth Barlow, 7/18/02, Todd, p. 197; Philip, p. 132.
87 "desirous of bringing"–Joel Barlow to RF, 8/15/02, Todd, p. 200.
87 "I have no doubt"–RF to RL, 7/25/02, CHS; Philip, p. 134.
87 "Although the wheels"–RF to Conservatory of Arts and Trades, 1/24/03, Dickinson, p. 152.
87 Fulton's experiments–RF notes, 1/19/03, NYPL.
88 RF–RL agreement–Sutcliffe, pp. 117–22.
89 Livingston and Louisiana Purchase–Dangerfield, *Chancellor;* John Keats, *Eminent Domain: The Louisiana Purchase and the Making of America* (New York: Charterhouse, 1973).
89 "We have lived"–RL to James Monroe, 5/2/03, Keats, p. 120.
90 "My first aim"–RF to Conservatory of Arts and Trades, 1/24/03, Dickinson, p. 151.
90 "several months"–report of Aaron Vail, Flexner, p. 288.
91 "two large wheels"–*Journal des débats,* 8/9/03, Dickinson, p. 158.
91 "Oh sir, the boat"–Colden, p. 162.
92 "for an hour and a half"–*Journal des débats,* 8/9/03, Dickinson, p. 158.
93 "the project of Citizen"–Napoleon Bonaparte to Marine Ministry, 7/21/03, Dickinson, p. 156.
93 RF letter to Boulton, Watt–8/6/03, Dickinson, p. 159.

Chapter 5: 1804–1807

97 "As these inventions"–RF manuscript, "Motives for Inventing Submarine Navigation and Attack," 8/10/06, NYPL; Parsons, p. 55.
97 "utmost liberality"–ibid.
98 "exhibit the principles"–RF to William Pitt, 8/9/05, Dickinson, p. 189.
99 "some years"–RF notes, 7/20/04, NYPL; Parsons, p. 101.
99 RF agreement with Britain–Dickinson, pp. 182–84.
100 machinery costs–Sutcliffe, p. 185; and see Dickinson, pp. 168–79.
100 "my opinion is"–RF to Benjamin West, 10/4/04, NYPL; Philip, p. 163.

Source Notes

101 "fully satisfied"–RF to William Pitt, 8/9/05, Dickinson, p. 190.

101 "willing to retire"–ibid.

102 "The torpedoes"–RF to Benjamin West, 10/16/05, NYHS; Philip, p. 168.

102 "the explosion seemed"–RF, *Torpedo War and Submarine Explosions,* 1810, p. 6; Dickinson, p. 194.

102 "the most tremendous"–RF to Benjamin West, 10/16/05, NYHS.

103 "placing them is"–Sidney Smith to Castlereagh, 11/22/05, Flexner, p. 308.

103 "a mode of war"–Earl of St. Vincent, Dickinson, p. 194.

103 "of annoying the enemy"–*Correspondence . . . of Viscount Castlereagh* (London, 1851), vol. 5, p. 121.

103 "I will not disguise"–RF to William Pitt, 1/16/06, NYPL; Philip, p. 173.

104 "Let any man"–RF to Alexander Davison, 4/17/06, Philip, p. 175.

104 "two friends who," "should my Country"–RF, "Motives for Inventing."

105 RF booklet–*Letters Principally to . . . Lord Grenville on Submarine Navigation and Attack* (London, 1806), sole copy in NYPL.

105 "I consider Fulton"–John Rennie, Dickinson, p. 268.

105 £1,647–Philip, p. 176, has £1,646, 12 shillings, 6 pence; Dickinson, p. 200, has £1,653, 18 shillings, 8 pence.

105 "to burn, sink"–RF to Joel Barlow, 9/12/06, Sutcliffe, pp. 171–73; Dickinson, pp. 199–200.

107 "settle down"–RF to Vanstaphast, 9/29/06, LeBoeuf Collection, NYHS; Philip, p. 180, says the letter was to Daniel Parker, but while it has a postscript to Parker, it seems clearly addressed to Vanstaphast.

108 "my friend Fulton's"–Joel Barlow to Thomas Jefferson, 3/15/05, Philip, p. 165.

108 "very dear," "We see"–Joel Barlow to RF, 3/3/06, Sutcliffe, pp. 168–70.

109 "a certain proposition"–Joel Barlow letter, 1803, Todd, p. 203.

109 RF investment reckoning–RF to Joel Barlow, 9/12/06, Sutcliffe, p. 171; Dickinson, p. 199.

110 wardrobe–RF memorandum, 4/15/06, Misc. Fulton, NYHS.

110 RF income reckoning–RF to Joel Barlow, 9/12/06, Sutcliffe, p. 171; Dickinson, p. 199.

111 Colquhoun–see, e.g., Harold Perkin, *Origins of Modern English Society* (London: Routledge, 1972, repr. 1985), pp. 20–21.

112 "author of various"–*National Intelligencer,* 12/22/06, in Philip, pp. 183–84.

112 "I will not"–RF to Joel Barlow, spring 1807, Todd, p. 101; Flexner, p. 326.

113 "now ready"–RF to RL, 12/14/06, CHS; Philip, p. 183.

113 "not one of which"–RF to RL, 1/13/07, CHS.

113 "the boat is"–RF to RL, 3/16/07, CHS.

114 "I have now"–RF to Henry Dearborn, 3/20/07, Sutcliffe, p. 289.

114 "I have all"–RF to RL, 7/14/07, CHS.

114 "would greatly exceed"–Colden, p. 167.

115 Lewis–Richard Dillon, *Meriwether Lewis* (New York: Coward-McCann, 1965).

115 "a well spread board"–*National Intelligencer,* 1/16/07. The paper's account renders "thirst" in Fulton's toast as "thunders," which makes no sense.

118 RF in Washington–Colden, p. 72.

119 "I ran about"–RF to RL, 8/10/07, CHS; Sutcliffe, pp. 197–98.

CHAPTER 6: 1807–1812

120 "I left New York"–*American Citizen,* 8/22/07; Colden, pp. 174–75; Sutcliffe, pp. 222–23; Dickinson, p. 219.

120 "She excited"–Colden, pp. 171–73.

121 "strange dark-looking"–H. Freeland, 1/4/56, in Reigart, pp. 175–76.

121 "a backwoods saw-mill"–Helen E. Smith, *Century,* vol. 53 (12/96), p. 1.

121 Fulton descendant–Sutcliffe, p. 219.

122 "would descend"–Smith, *Century,* p. 1.

122 Harriet Livingston–Philip, pp. 216–17, 228.

122 "The excursion to Albany"–*Naval Chronicle,* vol. 19 (London, 1808), p. 188; Dickinson, pp. 220–21.

123 "At every publick"–RL, 9/2/07, NYHS; Philip, p. 202.

124 "I inquired"–Matthews, *Recollections,* pp. 41–49.

124 "so exhausted"–ibid.

124 D. E. Tyle–CHS; Sutcliffe, p. 233.

125 Pierre De Labigarre–Carl Carmer, *The Hudson* (New York: Grosset & Dunlap, 1968), pp. 147–48; Dangerfield, *Chancellor.*

Source Notes

126 "On Thursday at 9"–*American Citizen,* 8/22/07; Colden, pp. 174–75; Sutcliffe, p. 223.

126 "from every point"–Sutcliffe, pp. 231–32.

127 "We congratulate"–*American Citizen,* 8/22/07.

127 "A few whose names"–Henry Adams, *History of the United States During the Administration of Thomas Jefferson* (1889; repr. New York: Library of America, 1986), p. 1019.

128 "It will give"–RF to Joel Barlow, Todd, p. 233; Sutcliffe, p. 235.

128 "boarding all"–RF to RL, 8/28[29]/07, Sutcliffe, p. 237.

128 "THE NORTH RIVER STEAM BOAT"–New York *Evening Post,* 9/2/07; Sutcliffe, pp. 239–40.

129 Wilson–1856 (Flexner has 1855) in Sutcliffe, pp. 246–52.

131 "froze entirely across"–New York *Post,* 11/19/07; Sutcliffe, p. 257.

131 "it was soon perceived"–Colden, p. 179.

131 "our Hands are"–RF to RL, 11/2/07, CHS.

131 "after all the accidents"–RF to RL, 11/20/07, NYHS; Sutcliffe, p. 259.

132 Streets Commission–Burrows and Wallace, pp. 419–22.

133 *The Columbiad*–published by John Conrad, Philadelphia, 1807; dedication in Philip, p. 207.

134 "great satisfaction"–RF to RL, 12/1/07, CHS.

134 "the passengers will"–RF to RL, 11/21/07, CHS; Philip, p. 209.

134 "I am working"–RF to RL, 4/5/08, CHS.

134 $4,000–Sutcliffe, p. 263.

134 registration–Dickinson, p. 228.

134 *North River* description–RF to Peale, 6/11/08, and "Regulations," Sutcliffe, pp. 269, 274–77, 342–45.

135 "As the Steam Boat"–"Regulations," ibid., p. 277.

135 "her reputation"–RF to RL, 7/12/08, NYHS.

136 "Shall we unite"–RF to Joel Barlow, 6/5/08, Philip, p. 227.

136 "ideas of interior arrangement"–RF to Joel Barlow, 3/1/09, Philip, p. 235.

137 Walter Livingston–Dangerfield, *Chancellor;* Burrows and Wallace, pp. 309–10; Friedenberg, *Life, Liberty,* p. 353.

138 *Car of Neptune, Raritan* (also rendered *Rariton*)–Colden, after p. 274; Dickinson, pp. 326–27, 229–30.

138 agreement with John Livingston–8/08, NYPL.

138 *Paragon*–Colden, after p. 274; Dickinson, pp. 326–27; *Port Folio,* vol. 2, p. 264; Philip, pp. 269–70.

138 "my *Paragon* beats"–RF to Thomas Law, 4/16/12, NYPL.

139 *Jersey*–Philip, p. 277; RF, *American Medical and Philosophical Register,* vol. 3 (1813), pp. 196–203, NYPL (copy owned by Clement C. Moore).

139 *New Orleans*–Flexner, pp. 341–43, from John H. B. Latrobe, "The First Steamboat Voyage on Western Waters" (Maryland Historical Society Fund Publications, 1871); Hunter, pp. 12, 15–16.

139 "the Mississippi . . . is conquered"–RF to Joel Barlow, 4/19/12, Sutcliffe, p. 221*n*.

140 patents–Dickinson, pp. 289–325.

140 "perpetual legal"–Colden, p. 192.

140 "the whole is"–RF to RL, 11/6/07, CHS; Philip, p. 211.

141 "useful and honorable"–RF, *Torpedo War, Concluding Address of Mr. Fulton's Lecture,* 2/17/10, NYPL.

141 "coldness and procrastination"–Philip, p. 237.

142 "destroy the whole"–RF to François de Barbé-Marbois, 3/16/09, LeBoeuf Collection, NYHS.

142 "real grandeur," "The Liberty," etc.–RF, *Torpedo War.*

143 "to have originated"–John Rodgers, 3/13/10, NYHS; Philip, p. 249.

143 "beyond the limits"–Morgan, *Robert Fulton,* p. 190.

143 "every plan of booms"–*National Intelligencer,* 4/27/10, Philip, p. 251.

143 RF writing campaign–letters of 2/20, 5/4, 6/14, all 1810, LeBoeuf Collection, NYHS; letter of 4/3/10, NYPL.

144 "was taken aback"–Wallace Hutcheon, *Robert Fulton, Pioneer of Undersea Warfare* (Annapolis, Md.: Naval Institute Press, 1981).

144 William Lee–RF to Lee, 5/22/11, LeBoeuf Collection, NYHS.

145 "Freedom of the City"–Philip, p. 288.

145 RF's finances–RF to RL, 12/12/12, NYHS, for some details; related papers in Livingston Papers, NYHS.

CHAPTER 7: 1813–1815

147 "My good friends"–RF to John Livingston, 3/3/13, LeBoeuf Collection, NYHS.

147 "22 pirates"–RF to Joel Barlow, 6/18/11, Sutcliffe, pp. 286–87.

148 "Your law suit"–RL to RF, 3/24/11, LeBoeuf Collection, NYHS.

148 Stevens–Philip, pp. 232, 245; Turnbull, *John Stevens,* p. 180.

148   agreement–LeBoeuf Collection, NYHS.

148   "I am the Inventor"–RF, n.d. (1814?), NYPL; and see second steamboat patent, Dickinson, pp. 314–15, 320–23.

149   RF's health–David Hosack, Colden, pp. 264–65; RF to Robert R. Livingston, 9/24/12, RF to Robert L. Livingston, 8/12/13, Livingston Papers, NYHS.

149   "state of slavery"–RF to Robert L. Livingston, 4/6/13, NYHS.

150   RF's will–Reigart, p. 206; and see Dickinson, p. 271.

150   "Harriet has"–RF to John Livingston, 7/19/13, LeBoeuf Collection, NYHS.

150   "my lord and master"–Harriet Fulton note, 7/15/12, Livingston Papers, NYHS.

150   "very generally . . . sometimes"–Matthews, *Recollections,* pp. 41–45.

150   "at the tablecloth"–Philip, p. 323.

151   "that you should"–RL to RF, 3/24/12, Livingston Papers, NYHS; Philip, p. 279.

151   "involved in the horrible"–Harriet Fulton to RL, 7/29/12, Livingston Papers, NYPL; Philip, p. 279.

151   women's rights–Burrows and Wallace, pp. 377, 817.

152   Fulton boats–Colden, after p. 274; Dickinson, pp. 326–27.

153   cost and profit figures–RF notes 11/27/13, 6/14 (*Car of Neptune, Paragon,* "all boats"), NYPL.

153   *Nassau* figures–George H. Preble, *A Chronological History . . . of Steam Navigation* (Philadelphia, 1895), pp. 60–61.

154   "Lake Champlain to Charleston"–RF to Benjamin West, 7/12/13, NYHS.

154   *New Orleans* and Mississippi boats–Hunter, pp. 16–20.

154   *Vesuvius* in War of 1812, and suit–U.S. Senate document, 26th Congress, 2d Session, Nos. 193–94.

156   "If they do not"–RF to William Eustis, 10/24/12, NYPL.

156   privateer acts–6/26/12 and 3/3/13, Philip, p. 295.

156   torpedoes; Swartwout; Mix–twenty-one RF letters, 9/24/12–12/15/14, LeBoeuf Collection, NYHS.

156   "one of my"–RF, 8/14/13, LeBoeuf Collection, NYHS.

157   RF to Samuel Swartwout, 7/22/13, NYPL; see Philip, pp. 296–98.

157   underwater cannon–Colden, pp. 208–14.

158   "If we succeed"–RF to Stephen Decatur, 7/29/13, Princeton University Library.

158 proposal to President Madison–RF to James Madison, 11/5/14, Philip, p. 334.

158 steam frigate–Colden, pp. 221–25, 299–310; Dickinson, pp. 261–63, 326–27.

159 "This is a new invention"–RF to Jonathan Williams, 11/23/14, Dickinson, p. 263.

159 "exhausting himself"–Philip, p. 326; her citation is wrong.

159 "so constantly"–LeBoeuf Collection, NYHS; Sutcliffe, p. 217.

160 "Multitudes of spectators"–Colden, pp. 225–26.

160 RF letter to Washington–2/5/97, Sutcliffe, pp. 310–11.

161 Erie Canal–see, e.g., Burrows and Wallace, pp. 419, 429–30; Carmer, *The Hudson,* pp. 176–85.

161 RF and canal–Colden, pp. 275–87.

163 Ogden New York suit–Colden, pp. 237–46; Philip, pp. 314–17.

164 "Artful speculators will"–Colden, pp. 249–50.

164 Ogden New Jersey suit–John R. Livingston, *The Petition of John R. Livingston & Robert J. Livingston, to the Legislature of New-Jersey . . .* (New York, 1814); Lucius H. Stockton, *A History of the Steam-boat Case . . .* (Trenton, 1815); Colden, pp. 116–19.

165 "I may therefore"–Nicholas Roosevelt to Aaron Ogden, 12/15/14, NYHS.

166 RF's demand to Colden–RF notes, 1/25/15, NYPL.

166 "the outraged state"–Colden, pp. 116–19.

167 Columbus–see my *Conquest of Paradise: Christopher Columbus and the Columbian Legacy* (New York: Knopf, 1990), pp. 333–43.

168 "in the zenith"–Sutcliffe, pp. 180–81.

168 "It grieved my"–Washington Irving to James Renwick, 9/10/11, Washington Irving, *Letters,* p. 324.

168 "Fulton's works were"–Sutcliffe, pp. 180–81.

169 "Certain it is"–RF notes, 1/25/15, NYPL.

169 "very much exhausted"–David Hosack, Colden, p. 266.

170 "Politicians, historians"–New York *Evening Post,* 2/24/15, Philip, p. 1.

170 "by a greater number"–Colden, p. 254.

171 "no doubt remained"–Colden, p. 305, from *Report . . . to Navy,* 12/28/15, pp. 299–310.

172 "Most feelingly"–Ruth Barlow to William Cutting, 3/30/15, LeBoeuf Collection, NYHS.

173 "that I wish"–Ruth Barlow, Philip, p. 353.

Source Notes

173   "Be it ours"–Gouverneur Morris, Colden, p. 368.
173   "To those who"–De Witt Clinton, Colden, p. 371.

CHAPTER 8

175   Fulton Street–Colden, p. 225.
176   Monument Association–William H. Fletcher, *Extracts from the Minutes and Report of the Robert Fulton Monument Association* (New York, 1907), NYPL.
176   1909 commemoration–Hudson–Fulton Celebration Commission, *The Hudson–Fulton Celebration, 1909* (Albany: State of New York, 1910), and *Official Minutes,* 1905–11.
177   "early years"–Charleston *News and Courier,* 11/30/83, NYPL.
177   RF's estate–William Duer, in *An Examination of Cadwallader D. Colden's Book . . . by a Friend of John Fitch* ([London?], 1818 [actually 1819]), estimated $620,000; the French observer Jean-Baptiste Marestier, in *Memoir on Steamboats of the United States* (1832, repr. 1957), reckoned $660,000; John Delacy, who had an interest in exaggerating its worth, figured $689,000 in an 1823 petition (NYHS); Philip, p. 349, gives $100,000 for a capital evaluation of workshops.
178   "ungrateful and envious"–Reigart, p. 205.
178   *"utterly destitute"*–New York State Assembly Report, 2/1/25, in *Bulletin of the New York Public Library,* 1909, p. 582.
179   "Money have they none"–Robert Barlow Fulton to Robert L. Livingston, 11/19/29, Livingston Papers, NYHS; Morgan, p. 204.
179   Fulton heirs and U.S. Congress–U.S. Senate document, 26th Congress, 2d Session, Nos. 193–94; Dickinson, pp. 271–72.
179   steam frigate–Preble, *Chronological History,* pp. 86–87.
180   *Fulton II* and *III*–ibid., p. 160.
180   submarine–see Parsons, and Hutcheon, *Robert Fulton.*
181   Gibbons–see, e.g., Robert G. Albion, *The Rise of the New York Port* (New York: Scribner, 1939, repr. 1967), pp. 151–52; Carmer, *The Hudson,* pp. 160–63; George Dangerfield, *American Heritage,* October 1963.
181   "a man with," "as a baby"–Carmer, *The Hudson,* pp. 160–63.
182   Hudson steamboats–Albion, *The Rise,* chap. 8; Burrows and Wallace, pp. 433, 441–42; Preble, *Chronological History,* passim; *Niles Weekly Register,* 11/12/25.

182   Mid-century figures–Albion, *The Rise*, p. 164.

182   "rises, like Venice"–Trollope, Burrows and Wallace, p. 450.

183   "Huge steam ferry-boats"–Benson Lossing, *The Hudson, from Wilderness to the Sea* (1866; repr. [Somersworth, N.H.]: New Hampshire Paper, 1972), pp. 434–45.

183   "floating palaces"–Carmer, *The Hudson*, pp. 202–7.

184   "They are admirable"–Fanny Kemble, entry of 11/10/32, *Journal of a Residence in America*, 1832–33.

185   Cornelius Vander Bilt–see, e.g., Carl Carmer, *The Hudson*, pp. 160–61; Albion, *The Rise*, pp. 154–56; Burrows and Wallace, pp. 432–33, 541, 714; Edwin P. Hoyt, *The Vanderbilts and Their Fortunes* (New York: Doubleday, 1962); Ralph N. Hill, *Sidewheeler Saga* (New York: Rinehart, 1953).

187   Mississippi–see Hunter; Henry Sinclair Drago, *The Steamboaters* (New York: Dodd, Mead, 1967); James Hall, *The West: Its Commerce and Navigation* ([Cincinnati]: H. W. Derby, 1848); Mississippi Historical Society, "Navigation and Commerce on the Mississippi and Great Lakes to 1846" (Publication 7, 1903), p. 496.

187   "There was never"–W. H. Gephart, *Transportation and Industrial Development in the Middle West* (New York, 1909), p. 79.

188   "has opened prospects"–Hunter, p. 19.

188   "steamboat navigation"–ibid., p. 17.

188   Migration–see Peter D. McClelland, *Demographic Dimensions of the New Republic* (New York: Cambridge University Press, 1982); Page Smith, *The Shaping of America* (New York: McGraw-Hill, 1980), chap. 44.

188   "Nothing like it"–Beard and Beard, *The Rise of American Civilization* (New York: Macmillan, 1930), vol. 1, p. 525.

189   "mass movement"–Hunter, p. 29.

189   "brings to the remotest"–Frederick Jackson Turner, *The Rise of the New West, 1819–29*, vol. 14 of Albert Bushnell Hart, ed., *The American Nation* (New York: Harper, 1906), p. 104.

190   "a force that was"–Beard and Beard, *Rise of American Civilization*, vol. 1, p. 654.

190   "when Fulton applied," "Of all the"–James Hall, in Henry Nash Smith, *Virgin Land* (Cambridge, Mass.: Harvard University Press, 1950, repr. 1978), pp. 158, 159.

190   steamboat figures–Hunter, tables 2, 12.

Source Notes

190   "To improve the means"–ibid., p. 28.

191   "the discovery of steam"–Tocqueville, ibid.

191   "the salvation"–Hunter, p. 29.

191   "the Mississippi valley became"–Turner, *Rise of the New West*, p. 190.

191   "We have the power"–Laird, in Lionel Tiger, *The Manufacture of Evil* (New York: Harper & Row, 1987), p. 107.

192   "Speed is the form"–Kundera, in *Harper's*, May 1998, p. 38.

194   "The American people"–Tocqueville, *Democracy in America*, p. 74.

194   wood consumption–Hunter, pp. 113–14, 657; cords/acre figures are based on Carol L. Alerich, "1993 Forest Inventory of New York," from "Forest Statistics for New York: 1980, 1993" (USDA Forest Service, Northeastern Forest Experiment Station, Bulletin NE-132).

194   Ohio forests–Gordon G. Whitney, *From Coastal Wilderness to Fruited Plain: A History of Environmental Change in Temperate North America, 1500 to the Present* (New York: Cambridge University Press, 1994).

194   rapid progress in boat design–Tocqueville, *Democracy in America*, p. 35.

194   "It would seem"–Thomas Hart Benton, in Roy Harvey Pearce, *Savages of America* (Baltimore: Johns Hopkins University Press, 1953), p. 239–40.

195   steamboat accidents–Hunter, chap. 6, pp. 520–21, tables pp. 272, 287, 541.

195   steamboat accident figures–see Preble, *Chronological History*, passim, esp. p. 425; Hunter; Hill, *Sidewheeler Saga;* John Kennedy, *History of Steam Navigation* (Liverpool: Birchall, 1903); Treasury Secretary Report, in Preble, pp. 152–53.

196   "business goes by steam"–Hunter, p. 301.

197   Webster–in Preble, *Chronological History*, p. 161.

198   Jackson–Richard Drinnon, *Violence in the American Experience* (New York: New American Library, 1979); Michael Rogin, *Fathers and Children: Andrew Jackson and the Subjugation of the American Indian* (New York: Knopf, 1975); Howard Zinn, *A People's History of the United States* (New York: HarperPerennial, 1995): "whining, complaining," p. 126; "campaigns of personal slander," p. 212.

199   English visitor–Dorothy Dondore, *The Prairie and the Making of Middle America* (Cedar Rapids, Iowa: Torch, 1926), p. 184.

200   steamships–Preble, *Chronological History* (U.S. tonnage, p. 424); Albion, *The Rise,* esp. chap. 15; E. K. Chatterton, *Steamships and Their Story* (New York, 1910); Burrows and Wallace, pp. 649–50.

201   Twain, celebration of Fulton anniversary, Jamestown, Virginia, and Twain, letters to Cornelius Vanderbilt, 1807, and General Grant (?), n.d., in Fletcher, *Extracts from the Minutes and Report of the Robert Fulton Monument Association.*

EPILOGUE

204   "the mind of an individual"–Colden, p. 189.

205   "the limits of the possible"–Fernand Braudel, *The Perspective of the World* (New York: Harper & Row, 1979), p. 592.

205   "which separated the colonial"–Adams, *History of the United States,* p. 1019.

Index

Index

Index

Index

Hudson River, 2, 5, 8, 23, 27, 30, 37, 51, 175–77, 210*nn2, 3,* 211*n2;* canal from Lake Erie to, 161–62; commercial steamboat service on, 87, 88, 90, 112, 113, 128–31, 134–35, 138–39, 147–48, 152–53, 166, 170, 178, 181–86; maiden voyage of steamboat on, 5, 10–15, 18–21, 120–28, 192; railroads along, 184, 187; steamboat race on, 213*n1*
Humphrey, Ozias, 52
Humphreys, David, 66
Hunt, Davis, 12, 208*n2*
Hunt, Leigh, 47
Hunter, Louis, 189, 195
hunting, 194

imperialism, 191
inclined planes, 53–55, 161, 213*n2*
Indians, 15, 17, 196, 199, 203; Great Removal of, 193–94, 199
Industrial Revolution, 11, 12, 182, 189, 192, 203, 205
Interborough Rapid Transit company, 176
invention, American fascination with, 28–30
iron bridges, prefabricated, 28, 56
Irving, Washington, 6–8, 17, 168

Jackson, Andrew, 155, 191, 193–94, 198–99
Jackson, George, 12
James River, 140, 152, 197
Jefferson, Thomas, 6, 17, 18, 66, 127, 134, 135; Barlow and, 108, 136; inventions of, 28; Lewis and, 115, 116; Livingston as emissary to France of, 34–35; and Louisiana Purchase, 82, 89
Jersey (steamboat), 139, 151, 152, 153
jewelry making, 44
Jews, 126
Johnson, Caleb, 43
Jouffroy d'Abbands, Marquis Claude-François-Dorothée, 24–25, 90
Journal des débats, 91–93

Kemble, Fanny, 184–85
Kościusko, Tadeusz, 82
Kundera, Milan, 192

Labigarre, Pierre de, 125
Lady Jane Grey Before Her Execution (Fulton), 48
Lafayette, Marquis de, 82, 94
Laird, MacGregor, 191
Lake, Samuel, 180
land speculation, 16, 55–56, 155, 165; Barlow and, 64, 72–73, 137
Latrobe, Benjamin, 35–38, 92, 140, 154, 155, 164–65, 169
Lee, William, 144
L'Enfant, Pierre-Charles, 132
Leonardo da Vinci, 29
Lewis, Meriwether, 113, 115–17
Lexington (steamboat), 186
Library of Congress, 177
Life of Robert Fulton (Reigart), 41
Life and Voyages of Columbus, The (Irving), 168
Lives and Portraits of Distinguished American Characters (Delaplaine), 41
Livingston, Cornelia Schuyler, 137
Livingston, Edward, 125, 188
Livingston, Harriet, *see* Fulton, Harriet Livingston
Livingston, John (Harriet's brother), 147, 154, 155
Livingston, John R. (Chancellor's brother), 13, 135, 138, 164, 166
Livingston, Robert L., 179
Livingston, Robert R. ("Chancellor"), 13, 14, 30–33, 36, 37, 111–13, 128, 131, 137, 153, 188, 209*n1,* 212*n1;* appointed minister plenipotentiary to France, 33–35; and Barlow's *Vision of Columbus,* 167; carelessness about financial records of, 172; Clermont estate of, 20–21, 30, 45, 51; death of, 146, 147; Labigarre and, 125; and maiden voyage of *North River,* 118–23, 126; Morris's

238

Index

North River (steamboat), 20–21, 140,
147, 153, 155, 171, 209*n4*, 213*n1*;
building of, 113–14; cost of, 14,
114–15, 138; design of, 10–11,
208*n1*; initiation of commercial
voyages on, 128–30; maiden
voyage of, 5–6, 8, 10–15, 18–21,
25, 119–28, 192, 208*nn2, 3*;
patent infringement suits for
copying of, 148; refurbishing of,
133–35, 212*n3*; replica of, 176,
177, 213*n3*; retirement of, 170;
trials of, 118–19
North River Steamboat Company,
150, 153, 182, 186
North Star (steamship), 186–87

Ogden, Colonel Aaron, 163–67, 169,
181, 185, 186
Ohio Canal, 189
Ohio River, 16, 140, 188, 190
Oneida Perfectionists, 126
Ormsbee, Elijah, 210*n2*
Owen, Robert, 57–58, 60, 126, 210*n3*

Paine, Thomas, 28, 82–84, 167
paintings: acquisition of, 109–10;
miniatures, 44, 45, 150; portraits,
48, 49, 52, 53, 60, 79, 109
Panic of 1837, 198
panoramas, 69–70, 211*n1*, 213*n2*
Paragon (steamboat), 138–39, 170,
213*n1*
Patent Office, U.S., 149, 165
patents, 28, 30, 213*n2*; canal, 55, 60,
62, 63; panorama, 69, 70; rope-
making machine, 70; steam
frigate, 159; steamboat, 19, 31,
37, 38, 57, 66, 87, 140–41,
148–49, 154, 162–66, 171,
174
Peak Forest Company, 58, 59
Peale, Charles Wilson, 28, 44, 110
People's Line, 183
Périer, Jacques, 70, 71, 74, 90, 91,
94
Périer brothers, 24
Perry, Commodore Matthew, 180

Perry, Commodore Oliver Hazard,
158
Perseverance (steamboat), 147
Philadelphia Waterworks, 32, 35, 36
Phoenix (steamboat), 148
Pitt, William, 99, 101, 103–5
plantations, Southern, 189–90
portrait painting, 48–49, 52, 53, 60,
79, 109
Potomac River, 140, 152, 170, 197
power loom, 70
Puritans, 132

Quakers, 34, 43, 125, 132

railroads, 184, 187
Raritan (steamboat), 138
Raritan River, 164, 166
Reigart, J. Franklin, 41, 178
Rennie, John, 105
Renwick, James, 51–52
Republicans, 164
Revere, Paul, 138
Revolutionary War, 43, 60, 66, 83,
137, 155, 161
Richmond (steamboat), 152, 170
Rittenhouse, David, 28
Robert Fulton (steamboat), 200
Robert Fulton Monument
Association, 176
Rodgers, Commodore John, 143, 144,
157
Roosevelt, Nicholas, 31–33, 35, 37, 87,
90, 139, 154, 164–65, 169, 209*n1*
rope-making machine, 70–71, 82, 166,
213*n2*
Rumsey, James, 37, 56–57, 90
Rutherford, John, 132

Salmagundi (magazine), 6
Saône River, 24
Sargent, Nathaniel, 74
Savannah River, 197
Schuykill River, 35, 210*n2*
Schuyler, Peter, 137
Schuyler, Philip, 61, 161
Schuyler family, 61
Scioto Associates, 72–73, 137

240

Index

torpedoes (water mines), 63–64, 66, 67, 80–81, 112–13, 133, 180, 201, 213n2; Barlow's disavowal of, 108; British interest in, 96–107, 110; harpoon gun for placing, 134, 141; indifference of American government to, 141–44; New York harbor demonstration of, 6–8, 84, 118, 143–44, 168; in War of 1812, 156–58

Trafalgar, Battle of, 103

Treatise on Indulgence, A (Colquhoun), 111

Treatise on the Improvement of Canal Navigation, A (Fulton), 58, 61, 161

Trollope, Frances, 182

Trumbull, John, 55, 60

Turner, Frederick Jackson, 191

Turner, J. M. W., 52

Twain, Mark, 201

Tyle, D. E., 124

Van Buren, Martin, 191

Van Cortlandt family, 137

Vanderbilt, Commodore Cornelius, 184–87

Vanderbilt, Cornelius (great-grandson of Commodore), 176

Vanderlyn, John, 53, 79, 82

Van Rensselaer family, 137

Vanstaphast (Dutch friend of Fulton's), 71, 107

Vesuvius (steamboat), 154, 155, 170, 179

Vindication of the Rights of Women (Wollstonecraft), 151

Vision of Columbus, The (Barlow), 64, 107, 167

Volney, Count Constantin de, 82

Wadsworth, James, 56

War of 1812, 52, 107, 152, 154, 155–61, 171

warships, 66–67; attempted submarine and mine attacks on, 76, 79–81; *see also* steam frigates

Washington, George, 15, 61, 64, 115, 160–61, 167, 198

Washington (steamboat), 152, 170, 188

Watt, James, 10, 11, 18, 37, 38, 99, 191, 201, 203; *see also* Boulton, Watt & Company

wealth, distribution of, 111

weapons, 44, 173–74, 179–81; Revolutionary War, 43, 66; *see also* firearms; steam frigates; submarines; torpedoes

weaving industry, 70

Webster, Daniel, 181–82, 186, 197

Weems, Parson, 40, 41

West, Benjamin, 46–47, 52, 53, 55–56, 59, 60, 108–9, 154

West, Elizabeth, 47, 59, 108–9

West, Raphael, 55, 56

West Point, 126, 130

Western expansion, 17, 34, 115–17, 198–99; role of steamboat in, 14–15, 18, 187–95, 204

Whigs, 60

Wilson, John, 129

Wollstonecraft, Mary, 151

women's rights, 151–52

Woods, Mrs. (boardinghouse keeper), 117

World War I, 180

Wyatt, James, 50, 52, 56

Yale University, 64, 66

York (steamboat), 152, 153

242